Lecture Notes of the Institute for Computer Sciences, Social Informatics and Telecommunications Engineering 717

The LNICST series publishes ICST's conferences, symposia and workshops.

LNICST reports state-of-the-art results in areas related to the scope of the Institute.

The type of material published includes

- Proceedings (published in time for the respective event)
- Other edited monographs (such as project reports or invited volumes)

LNICST topics span the following areas:

- General Computer Science
- E-Economy
- E-Medicine
- Knowledge Management
- Multimedia
- Operations, Management and Policy
- Social Informatics
- Systems

Billy Kihei · Parth Bhavsar · Joao Carlos Ferreira
Editors

Intelligent Transport Systems

9th EAI International Conference, INTSYS 2025
Marietta, GA, USA, December 10, 2025
Proceedings

Springer

Editors
Billy Kihei
Kennesaw State University
Marietta, GA, USA

Parth Bhavsar
Kennesaw State University
Marietta, GA, USA

Joao Carlos Ferreira
Molde University College
Molde, Norway

ISSN 1867-8211 ISSN 1867-822X (electronic)
Lecture Notes of the Institute for Computer Sciences, Social Informatics
and Telecommunications Engineering
ISBN 978-3-032-38704-2 ISBN 978-3-032-38705-9 (eBook)
https://doi.org/10.1007/978-3-032-38705-9

This Springer imprint is published by the registered company Springer Nature Switzerland AG
The registered company address is: Gewerbestrasse 11, 6330 Cham, Switzerland

Preface

We are pleased to present the proceedings of the 9th EAI International Conference on Intelligent Transport Systems (INTSYS 2025). Hosted online on December 10, 2025, this year's conference brought together researchers and industry innovators to explore the rapidly evolving landscape of intelligent mobility. As cities worldwide continue to modernize, the role of Intelligent Transportation Systems (ITS) has become increasingly central to improving safety, efficiency, and sustainability across all modes of transportation.

Major cities worldwide have emerged as hubs of transportation innovation, with advancements in autonomous vehicles, smart city infrastructure, electric vehicle adoption, and next-generation communication technologies. At the same time, the deployment of ITS solutions faces persistent challenges, including high implementation costs, regulatory and policy barriers, cybersecurity risks, and the need for stronger cross-sector collaboration. INTSYS 2025 provided a timely forum to address these issues and highlight emerging technologies reshaping the future of mobility.

The technical program of INTSYS 2025 showcased a focused yet diverse set of research contributions spanning the core domains of modern Intelligent Transportation Systems. The 10 accepted full papers were selected from 24 submissions. Each submission was reviewed following a single-blind process with a minimum of 2 reviews per paper. This year's accepted papers address critical challenges in electric vehicle charging and battery resilience, V2X communication performance, in-vehicle cybersecurity, cooperative control robustness, and cross-technology data exchange. The program also highlighted emerging applications of AI and multimodal learning in mobility analytics, pedestrian safety, maritime operations, and agentic path exploration, alongside innovative work in bioinspired structural safety for electric vehicles and software-defined communication for robotic systems in smart city environments.

In addition to the technical paper sessions, the conference program included keynote presentations from distinguished leaders in transportation innovation, invited talks highlighting emerging research directions, and focused sessions addressing policy, deployment, and interdisciplinary collaboration. These sessions enriched the conference by bridging academic research, industry practice, and public-sector perspectives.

We extend our sincere appreciation to the Steering Committee for their guidance and support throughout the organization of INTSYS 2025. We are equally grateful to the Technical Program Committee and our TPC Co-Chairs for their dedication to managing the review process and shaping a strong technical program. Our thanks also go to the organizing committee, conference staff, and all the authors who contributed to this year's event, given the recent geopolitical challenges.

We believe that INTSYS 2025 continued the tradition of providing a vibrant forum for advancing intelligent transportation research and fostering collaboration across disciplines. We hope that the ideas, insights, and innovations presented in this volume will inspire continued progress toward safer, more efficient, and more sustainable mobility systems worldwide.

Billy Kihei
Parth Bhavsar
Joao Carlos Ferreira

Conference Organization

Steering Committee

Alexander Kocian	University of Pisa, Italy
Ana Lúcia Henriques Martins	Iscte – University Institute of Lisbon, Portugal
João Carlos Ferreira	Iscte – University Institute of Lisbon, Portugal

Organizing Committee

General Chair

Billy Kihei	Kennesaw State University, USA

General Co-chair

Ian Ferguson	Kennesaw State University, USA

Program Chairs

Parth Bhavsar	Kennesaw State University, USA
João Carlos Ferreira	Iscte – University Institute of Lisbon, Portugal

Web Chair

Grayson Hatcher	Kennesaw State University, USA

Posters and Demos Track Chair

Hakeem Wilson	Kennesaw State University, USA

Publicity and Social Media Chairs

Hakeem Wilson	Kennesaw State University, USA
Grayson Hatcher	Kennesaw State University, USA
Sofia Segkouli	Centre for Research and Technology Hellas, Greece

Publications Chairs

João Carlos Ferreira	Iscte – University Institute of Lisbon, Portugal
Vassilis Kilintzis	FORTH-ICS, Greece

Local Chairs

Billy Kihei	Kennesaw State University, USA
Kostas Marias	FORTH-ICS, Greece

Workshops Chair

Kostas Stefanidis	Tampere University, Finland

Technical Program Committee

Ajoy Sarkar	Kennesaw State University, USA
Ana Lucia Martins	ISCTE-IUL, Portugal
Ana Madureira	ISEP/P.PORTO, Portugal
Bruno Miguel Gonçalves Mataloto	ISCTE, Portugal
Camilla Poggianti	University of Pisa, Italy
Cris Voicu	Kennesaw State University, USA
Francesco Flammini	University of Applied Sciences and Arts of Southern Switzerland, Switzerland
Gabriel Pestana	INOV/Universidade Europeia, Portugal
Gabriele Barlacchi	ISTI-CNR, Italy
Giovanna Maria Dimitri	University of Siena, Italy
Giovanni Mauro	ISTI-CNR, Italy
Kamil Smolak	Wrocław University of Environmental and Life Sciences, Poland
Lia Oliveira	IPVC, Portugal
Luís B. Elvas	ISCTE-IUL, Portugal
Marco Cardia	University of Pisa, Italy
Marzio Di Vece	Scuola Normale Superiore, Italy
Nuno Bettencourt	Institute of Engineering of Porto – Polytechnic of Porto (ISEP/IPP), Portugal
Nuno Domingues	ISEL, Portugal
Parth Bhavsar	Kennesaw State University, USA
Razvan Voicu	Kennesaw State University, USA

Stefano Chessa	University of Pisa, Italy
Sumit Chakravarty	Kennesaw State University, USA
Tien Yee	Kennesaw State University, USA
Yaqin Shaheen	Palestine Technical University, Palestine

Contents

Electric Vehicles: Charging, Batteries, and Structural Safety

Charging Strategies, Charger Location, Battery Degradation, and RES Integration for Electric Freight Vehicles Availability: A Systematic Review 3
Ricardo Carvajal-Arango and Gilberto Osorio-Gómez

Vehicular Networking, V2X Communications, and Cooperative Control

Comparative Study of Push and Pull Communications in a Rural VANET 39
Oscar Gama, Antonio Costa, Maria Joao Nicolau, Alexandre Santos, Bruno Dias, and Bruno Ribeiro

Improving the Jamming Resilience of a Cooperative Adaptive Cruise Controller 59
Mateen Malik, Ludvig Ohlsson, Karthik Sharma, Behrooz Sangchoolie, and Johan Karlsson

Inter-technology Application Data Exchange Based on Advertisement Packets 79
Mariam Issa, Paul Couderc, and Jean-Marie Bonnin

Security, Forensics, and Trust in Connected Mobility Systems

Reflections on the Security of In-Vehicle Connectivity 103
Xiangji Chen, Jingqi Wu, Shengzhi Zhang, and Wu Zhou

A Forensic Framework for Android Emulators in macOS Environments within Ad Hoc Network Scenarios 119
Sedat Şen and Harun Artuner

AI, Multimodal Learning, and Intelligent Mobility Applications

SYNAPSE: Synthesizing Narratives from Agentic Path Spatial Exploration 143
Prateek Gupta, Daniel Antunes Pedrozo, Aleksandr Koviazin, Jorge Augusto Meira, and Antonio Ken Iannillo

Multimodal Learning for Operational Risk Detection in Delivery Route Planning 154
Prateek Gupta, Daniel Antunes Pedrozo, Jorge Augusto Meira, Antonio Ken Iannillo, and Danilo D' Aversa

AI-Based Signal Control for Balancing Pedestrian Two-Stage Crossing Safety and Traffic Flow Efficiency 166
Wei-Hsun Lee, Po-Hao Huang, and Che-Yu Chang

An Intelligent Speed Control System for Electric Bike Using Sensor Feedback and Real-Time Display 185
A. Rosi, T. Suresh, R. Porselvi, C. Nirmala, N. D. Bobby, and T. Vaishnavi

Posters and Demos

Software Defined Communication for Swarm Robotics in Smart City Search and Rescue 197
Hakeem Wilson

AI-Based Loading Conditions Automatic Generation Method for Ships 202
Young-Soo Han, Kyungho Lee, Youngsu Kim, Younwook Nam, and Soyoung Park

Author Index 207

Electric Vehicles: Charging, Batteries, and Structural Safety

Charging Strategies, Charger Location, Battery Degradation, and RES Integration for Electric Freight Vehicles Availability: A Systematic Review

Ricardo Carvajal-Arango(✉) and Gilberto Osorio-Gómez

Design Engineering Research Group (GRID), EAFIT University, Medellín, Colombia
{rcarvaj2,gosoriog}@eafit.edu.co

Abstract. The paper presents a systematic mapping review of computational models, charging strategies, charger location, battery degradation, and integration of renewable energy for electric freight vehicles (EFVs), based on 87 articles from 2015 to 2025. The study finds that mathematical modeling, especially mixed-integer linear programming, is prevalent, with growing interest in simulation and data-driven methods. Charging strategies balance cost, efficiency, and battery health, while optimizing the location of the charger considers spatial planning and network performance. Battery degradation is identified as a significant but underexplored factor in operational costs and fleet availability. The shift towards detailed techno-economic analyses in the integration of renewable energy sources (RES) highlights potential reductions in carbon emissions and grid dependency, but poses challenges in scheduling and reliability. The paper identifies research gaps, suggesting the need for integrated models that address charging logistics, battery management, and renewable variability under uncertainty. Conclusions by advocating for interdisciplinary methods, advanced analytics, and empirical data to support sustainable EFV operations and decarbonization goals.

Keywords: Optimization · Charging Strategies · Electric Freight Vehicles (EFV) · Electric Trucks · Charger Location · RES Integration Trade-offs · Battery Degradation

1 Introduction

Freight transportation is an integral part of contemporary economic systems, facilitating the distribution of goods through local, regional, and global supply networks. However, it constitutes one of the most carbon-intensive sectors, making substantial contributions to greenhouse gas (GHG) emissions, air pollution,

B. Kihei et al. (Eds.): INTSYS 2025, LNICST 717, pp. 3–35, 2027.
https://doi.org/10.1007/978-3-032-38705-9_1

and urban noise [42,99]. As climate objectives become increasingly rigorous and regulatory constraints intensify, electrification of freight transport, particularly through the adoption of electric freight vehicles (EFVs), has emerged as a crucial approach in the global transition to sustainable energy [20,43]. In addition to emissions reductions, EFVs have the potential for reduced operational costs [83], reduced noise pollution, and improved energy efficiency [16]. However, achieving these advantages on a large scale presents a considerable technical and logistical challenge [60].

The effective deployment of EFVs requires the assurance of high operational availability, which is a crucial requirement for freight operators that must adhere to stringent delivery schedules and reliability standards. The operational availability of EFVs is intrinsically related to the interaction among charging strategies, battery degradation, charger placement, and integration of renewable energy sources (RES) [105]. Although fast charging can minimize vehicle downtime, it concurrently accelerates battery degradation, resulting in increased long-term costs and reduced battery life. In contrast, the implementation of optimized charging profiles and preconditioning strategies can substantially mitigate battery degradation and extend the operational life [77,79]. The geographical placement and size of the charging stations are of paramount importance; strategically located infrastructure can significantly reduce waiting times and ensure efficient adherence of vehicles to delivery schedules, while suboptimal placement can engender bottlenecks and decrease fleet efficiency [4,104]. The integration of renewable energy sources, such as solar or wind, into the charging infrastructure can reduce operational costs and carbon emissions, but introduces variability that requires sophisticated scheduling and storage solutions to maintain reliability [18,62,74,80]. Optimization of charging schedules, service operations, and energy tariffs can alleviate infrastructure demands and operational costs while simultaneously preserving battery health. Generally speaking, maximizing the availability of EFV requires the coordination of strategies that balance the imperatives of rapid charging, battery longevity, optimal charger placement, and renewable energy usage. These efforts must be supported by advanced management systems that are skilled in accommodating the complex interdependencies among these factors. Therefore, a comprehensive analysis of these dimensions is indispensable for the development of resilient, cost-effective, and sustainable EFV systems [73].

This systematic mapping review meticulously synthesizes 87 peer-reviewed journal articles and conference proceedings published between 2015 and 2025. These studies were sourced from databases including Scopus, IEEE Xplore, and EBSCO Academic Search Complete, and were selected based on relevance, language (English and Spanish) and availability criteria. The review is structured to address five key research questions, focusing on modeling frameworks, charging strategies, charger location, battery degradation, and RES integration. Although methodologies like mixed-integer linear programming (MILP), agent-based simulation, and stochastic optimization are prevalently employed in the domain of electric mobility research, especially regarding electric buses, this review uncovers a notable scarcity of studies that explicitly focus on EFVs.

The structure of this paper is articulated as follows: Sect. 2 elucidates the methodology of the literature review, encompassing search criteria, inclusion and exclusion procedures, and methods for data extraction. Section 3 furnishes a bibliometric analysis, elucidating trends in publication volume, geographic distribution, and methodological tendencies. Section 4 comprises the systematic review analysis, synthesizing the findings concerning the five core research questions and identifying prevailing gaps and prospective directions. In conclusion, Sect. 5 delivers the closing remarks, encapsulating the principal findings and delineating a road map for future research on EFV.

2 Systematic Mapping Review Methodology

This study was designed as a systematic mapping review. While we documented methodological approaches and validation strategies, no formal risk-of-bias or quality appraisal (e.g., ROBIS [89]) was applied to the included studies. The primary objective was to map the research landscape rather than to weight findings by methodological rigor, which is more typical of full systematic reviews.

The methodology used to conduct this systematic mapping review consists of five stages [47,65,66] presented in Fig. 1.

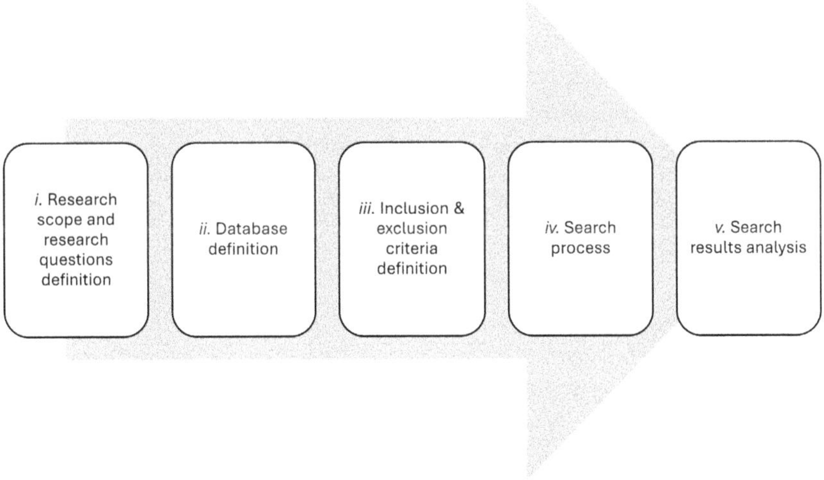

Fig. 1. Literature Review Process.

2.1 Research Scope and Research Questions Definition

The scope of this review is delineated by focusing on electric freight trucks as the primary vehicle type of interest. This emphasis underscores the increasing necessity to decarbonize freight transportation and highlights the unique operational, logistical, and technological challenges that electric freight vehicles (EFVs) present in comparison to passenger cars or buses. In contrast to passenger electric vehicles (EVs), EFVs necessitate greater energy throughput, more advanced charging coordination, and a more comprehensive understanding of the trade-offs involving battery life, operational availability, and infrastructure investments.

For a complete analysis of the literature, a single general research question has been posed along with four specific questions, presented in Table 1, have been posed. Herein, we present each research question together with its corresponding data extraction framework.

Table 1. Research Questions Overview

	General Research Question
GQ	How can computational models be formulated to quantitatively assess the interdependencies among charging strategies, battery degradation, infrastructure investments, and RES integration, with the objective of optimizing the fleet availability of electric freight vehicles?
	Focused Questions
FQ1	How do different charging strategies (including opportunity charging) affect the operational availability of electric freight vehicles?
FQ2	What is the impact of charger location on optimizing charging strategies?
FQ3	How do charging strategies (fast charging and opportunity charging) affect battery degradation in electric freight vehicles?
FQ4	How can RES be incorporated to work synergistically with the charging strategies used for electric freight vehicles?

2.2 Database Definition

The research process was carried out in three databases: *(i)* Scopus, *(ii)* IEEE Xplore and *(iii)* EBSCO Academic Search Complete, which are currently available and are renowned publishers in engineering related fields.

2.3 Inclusion and Exclusion Criteria Definition

This systematic mapping review was carried out by examining journals and conference proceedings published between 2015 and 2025. The search queries were refined according to language, title, abstract and keywords, as detailed in Table 2. Any findings not related to the field of engineering were systematically excluded.

Table 2. Search Filters by Database

Database	EBSCO Academyc Search Complete IEEE Xplore Scopus
Years	2015 - 2025
Language	English; Spanish
Document type	Journal; Proceedings
Search in:	Title, abstract & keywords
Exclude	Results not related to engineering fields Non-Available documents

2.4 Search Process Execution:

Search Query: The formulation of the search query for this systematic review was carried out using an iterative process and meticulously refined to ensure compatibility between the selected databases, as presented in Table 3. In light of the variations in query languages and functionalities, the formulation was adjusted to consistently uphold the fundamental logic and exclusion criteria.

Table 3. Search Query Logic for Database Screening

Included terms	(optim* OR minimiz* OR maximiz*) AND (charg* AND strateg*) OR (charg* AND network*) AND (electric AND (freight* OR truck))
Excluded terms	drone, fly*, v2g, vehicle-to-grid, public, aircraft, forklift, autonomous, battery management, bus, car sharing, city planning, residential, driver assignment, diesel, routing, wireless, taxi*, e-scooter, escooter, scooter, e-bike, ebike, bike, rail, train, tractor, fuel, powertrain

The query was designed to facilitate a focused retrieval of records pertaining to the optimization, encompassing both minimization and maximization, of strategies and networks for charging that are pertinent to applications involving electric freight and trucks. The terms excluded were determined through iterative pretesting to systematically eliminate literature that diverges from the scope of the review, such as works focusing on other vehicle types, non-road applications, alternative propulsion technologies, and ancillary thematic areas.

Initial Yield and Filtering Process: The comprehensive search across the three databases yielded a total of 108 documents: 38 from Scopus, 59 from EBSCO, and 11 from IEEE Xplore. An initial review process was undertaken to remove duplicate records, resulting in a curated dataset comprising 101 unique entries.

Accessibility and Scope Refinement: Subsequent screening prioritized the accessibility of documents and their relevance to the subject matter. In particular, 11 documents were omitted due to unavailability, and 3 documents were excluded as they were not pertinent to EFV, culminating in a final corpus of 87 documents suitable for analysis.

The hierarchical selection process ensures that the data set is specifically aligned with the research objective, which encompasses the assessment of charging strategies, battery degradation, charger location, and the integration of renewable energy in relation to the operational availability of EFV fleets. Each procedural step was meticulously documented to uphold reproducibility and ensure methodological transparency.

3 Bibliometric Analysis

To improve the systematic mapping review, a bibliometric analysis was performed to evaluate patterns, sources, author contributions, and global distribution within the 87 articles. Python scripts facilitated the extraction of structured metadata, including publication year, document title, document type, journal or conference name, corresponding author, DOI, and ISSN. Furthermore, the quality and impact metrics of the journal were determined by integrating this data set with the Scimago Journal Rank (SJR) indicators for 2024.

3.1 Distribution of Publications Per Year

Figure 2 illustrates the yearly publication count. A significant escalation is evident from 2023 onwards, when yearly publications within this topic grew by around 550%. By June 2025, when this review was conducted, the yearly publication count had almost reached the same publication count as in 2024, which

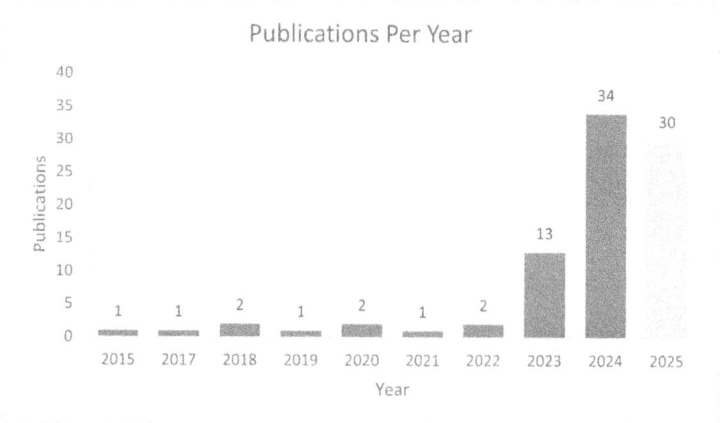

Fig. 2. Annual publication trends.

suggests that this increasing trend will continue and substantiates the hypothesis that this subject area is undergoing exponential progression.

3.2 Distribution of Document Types

The journal articles constituted the preponderance of sources, with 73 publications (approximately 84%) documented. In contrast, the conference proceedings were responsible for the remaining 14 documents (16%).

This distribution implies that the topic is progressively attracting attention within peer-reviewed journals, which means its scientific relevance and degree of advancement. The substantial volume of journal articles further enhances the consistency and caliber of the evidence evaluated in this review.

3.3 Top Journals and Source Analysis

In order to assess the quality and prestige of the publication venues addressing this subject, an analysis was undertaken utilizing four bibliometric indicators: the global Scimago Journal Rank (SJR), the SJR index, the quartile classification, and the H index. These indicators provide insights into the visibility, scientific impact, and enduring significance of the journals encompassed within the dataset.

Figure 3a depicts the global ranking of the top ten journals based on the Scimago index, a metric that evaluates both the citation count and the prestige of the journals cited. The highest-ranked journals, exemplified by *Transportation Research Part E*, *IEEE Network*, and *IEEE Transactions on Intelligent Transportation Systems*, indicate that the topic holds significant relevance within the domains of energy and transport systems while simultaneously attracting interest from prominent interdisciplinary platforms.

Figure 3b illustrates that the SJR index identifies journals such as *IEEE Transactions on Smart Grid* and *Production and Operations Management* as prominent sources. The SJR index equitably assesses the volume of citations alongside the significance of the citing sources, thereby suggesting that these journals disseminate research with substantial global relevance and impact.

The data presented in Fig. 3c illustrates that a significant portion of the selected studies (66 out of 87) were disseminated in Q1 journals. This distribution underscores the prominence of the research topic within esteemed academic venues, thereby signifying its importance, pertinence, and growing acknowledgment within the scholarly domain.

Figure 3d illustrates the leading journals as ranked by the H index, which acts as an indicator of prolonged scientific impact. Journals such as *Chemical Engineering Journal*, *Applied Energy*, and *Energy Conversion and Management* demonstrate consistently elevated H-index metrics, underscoring their enduring academic influence and pertinence in the domains of energy systems and transportation.

3.4 Top Journals by Recent Citations

The aggregate number of citations accumulated over the past three years serves as a direct measure of the influence and prominence of research disseminated through each journal. Figure 4 elucidates the top 10 journals that achieved the highest number of citations within this time frame. *Chemical Engineering Journal* and *Sustainability (Switzerland)* emerge as the most frequently cited sources, within the past three years. These findings substantiate the dominant role of journals with a focus on energy and interdisciplinary studies in the propagation of research on electric freight systems, charging strategies, and energy management. Other notable performing journals include *Energy*, *Energies*, and *Applied Energy*, which are recognized as dynamic platforms for the dissemination of research on applied energy and transport systems. Citation data underscore the importance of these journals in shaping research directions and underscore their impact on the academic landscape in this specific domain.

Table 4. Number of Publications by Country

Country	Publications
United Kingdom	37
Switzerland	20
United States	10
Other countries	20

3.5 Geographic Distribution and Collaboration

The geographic origins of the publications are presented in Table 4. In particular, the United Kingdom, Switzerland, and the United States are predominant in terms of contributions.

4 Search Results Analysis

This study seeks to delineate the evolving research landscape and integrate the modeling methodologies, optimization frameworks, assessment metrics, and empirical practices employed in the contemporary EFV literature.

Through an examination of both general and specific research questions, this section presents a methodical synthesis of the manner in which contemporary studies conceptualize the incorporation of charging strategies, charger location planning, battery degradation, and RES within the context of freight fleet operations.

The analysis is initiated with an examination of the general question (GQ), focusing on the methodologies and optimizations employed within the literature to model the EFV ecosystem. This is followed by a comprehensive analysis

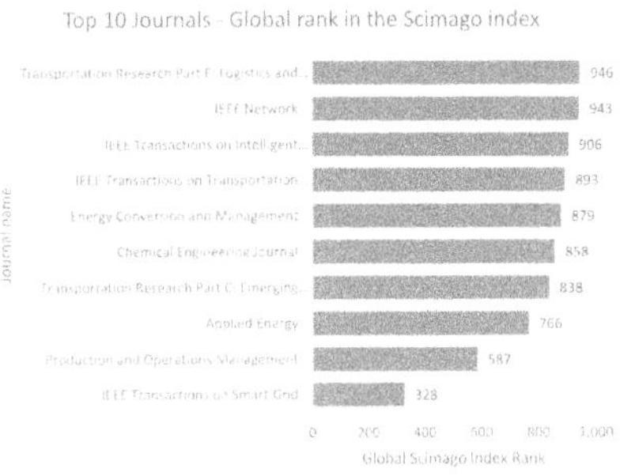

(a) Global rank in the Scimago index

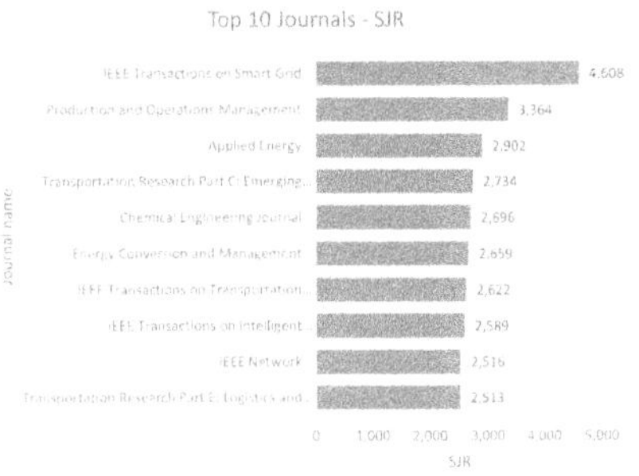

(b) Top 10 Journals – SJR Index

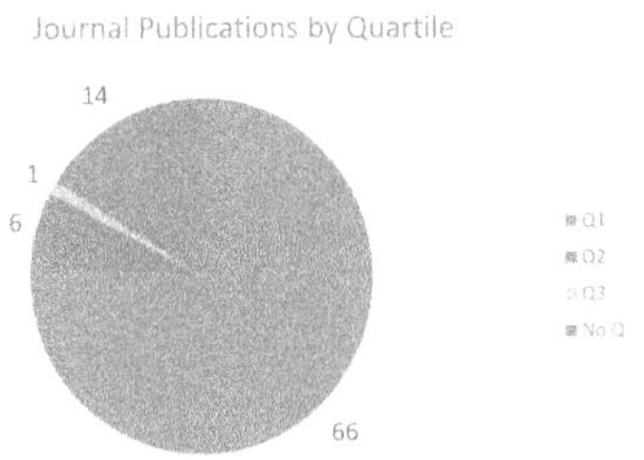

(c) Journal distribution by SJR Quartile

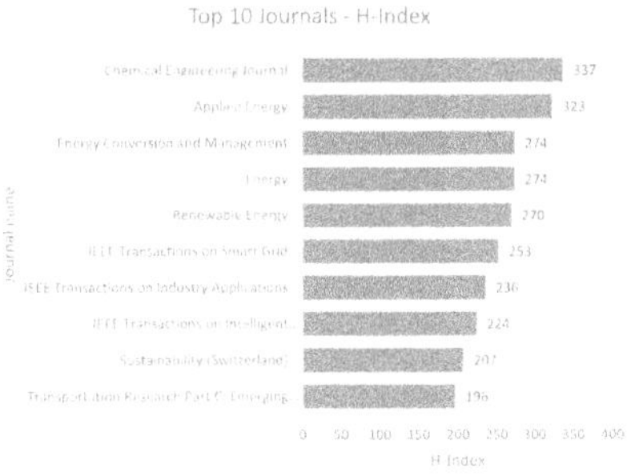

(d) Top 10 Journals – H-Index

Fig. 3. Top journal indicators for the analyzed publications.

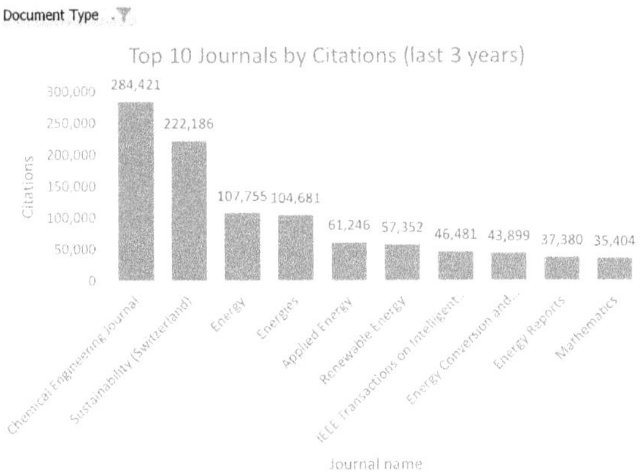

Fig. 4. Top 10 Journals by Citations (last 3 years).

of three focused questions (FQ1–FQ3), which investigate: (1) the importance of charging strategies in enhancing fleet performance; (2) the effect of charger placement on operational efficiency and cost implications; and (3) the influence of charging decisions on battery degradation. Furthermore, a fourth focused question (FQ4) evaluates the degree to which renewable energy systems are integrated into the charging infrastructures of EFV, analyzing the consequent effects on cost, resilience, and energy planning.

The findings for each research question are systematically organized in a table, where each column corresponds to a specific category of information, aiming to identify and analyze the dominant modeling paradigms, optimization frameworks, and fundamental technical challenges identified in the surveyed literature.

Table 5. Distribution of Modeling Approaches

Modeling Approach	Article Count
Mathematical Modeling	51
Simulation-Based Modeling	21
Hybrid Modeling	10
Data-driven / ML	5
Total	87

The section employs both quantitative and qualitative metrics across these dimensions to provide a comprehensive overview of current research in EFV systems. This includes assessing the prevalence of methodological strategies, the scope of trade-off analyses, and the integration of empirical validation. Through this synthesis, it identifies prevailing trends, highlights emerging research gaps, and delineates prospects for future investigation into the design of cost-effective, reliable, and sustainable electric freight operations.

4.1 GQ - General Question

This inquiry aimed to elucidate and synthesize the conceptualizations and mathematical representations of the integrated EFV ecosystem, including analyses of charging strategies, charger placement, battery degradation, and RES. The objective is to comprehend not only the existing models but also their capacity to harmonize the various trade-offs inherent in real-world implementation. The necessary information was extracted and systematically categorized as follows:

Modeling Approach: The modeling approaches adopted are presented in Table 5. Mathematical modeling dominates the literature, followed by simulation-based methods, with hybrid and data-driven approaches less common.

Exemplary instances demonstrate the methodological heterogeneity present within the scholarly discourse. Mathematical modeling, especially via mixed-integer linear programming (MILP), is extensively employed; for instance, a MILP framework was introduced in [98] to simultaneously optimize charger placement and electric truck routing under grid limitations. A comparable strategy was utilized for the coordination of charging and platooning schedules in electric freight vehicle corridors in [116]. [5] proposes bidding strategies based on stochastic optimization models.

Simulation-based modeling is prevalent in the field; agent-based simulations have been utilized to examine depot congestion and the charging dynamics of electric truck fleets [55]. In addition, national-scale agent-based models have been designed to study charger utilization and waiting times in logistics operations [45].

The adoption of hybrid methodologies is on the rise; these include frameworks that integrate MILP optimization for the strategic placement of fast-charging stations with stochastic simulations accounting for renewable variability [51], as well as the amalgamation of dynamic programming for fleet energy management with simulations of renewable profiles and dynamic port operations [10].

Data-driven methodologies and machine learning (ML) techniques, while still in their nascent stages, are increasingly gaining prominence. Notable instances include the incorporation of ML for load prediction in conjunction with scheduling optimization within the domain of mining fleet operations [109], as well as the deployment of ML-based models to anticipate depot charging requirements, thereby guiding infrastructure development [57]. Machine learning has been introduced for improved energy forecasting in heavy trucks by [30]

Overall, although mathematical optimization and simulation-based frameworks continue to predominate in the discipline, there is a discernible trend towards the adoption of hybrid and ML-driven methodologies. These approaches are considered more competent in encapsulating the uncertainties and operational complexities inherent in electric truck charging systems.

Optimization Model: The surveyed literature includes a variety of modeling strategies, which are presented concisely in Table 6. The predominance of Mixed-Integer Linear Programming (MILP) models is notable, succeeded by frameworks centered on multi-objective optimization and variants of the VRP. Conversely, methodologies such as metaheuristics, dynamic programming, and reinforcement learning are categorized as "Other models" because of their infrequent utilization.

Table 6. Distribution of Optimization Models

Optimization Model	Number of Papers
MILP	27
Multi-objective optimization	13
VRP variants	8
Other models (e.g., metaheuristics, DP, RL)	39
Total	**87**

MILP formulations have been widely used, as exemplified by [116], who utilized this approach to optimize charging and routing scheduling simultaneously. Similarly, [1] applied MILP to the joint optimization of platooning and charging strategies with the objective of minimizing system costs. Furthermore, [87] utilized MILP to determine the optimal placement and scheduling of Vehicle-to-Grid (V2G) enabled stations. [48] addressed network loses reduction based on an optimization approach.

Multi-objective models harmonized conflicting priorities. Specifically, [110] optimized both cost and battery degradation, [32] sought to minimize infrastructure investment and emissions, and [94] concurrently addressed route cost, charging time, and battery health.

Various VRP variants have addressed the incorporation of charging constraints in routing problems. Specifically, [64] formulated a time-limited electric vehicle routing problem (E-VRPTW); [82] developed a stochastic vehicle routing problem considering demand uncertainty; and [68] proposed a green vehicle routing problem that integrates considerations of routing, charging, and emissions.

The category of "Other models," encompassing 39 studies, exemplifies the field's methodological diversity and continuous experimentation. This assortment includes dynamic programming (DP) approaches [10], reinforcement learning for the deployment of portable storage systems [88], particle swarm optimization and metaheuristic scheduling methods [31,40]. [55] utilized an agent-based simulation to explore urban charging behavior and [81] used machine learning to optimize charging schedules. The prevalence of such diverse methodologies indicates that no single optimization paradigm has yet achieved predominance for EFV fleet management. Future research could benefit from comparative studies that systematically assess the computational performance, scalability, and practical applicability of these alternative modeling strategies.

Key Focus Areas: The main research themes and objectives identified in the reviewed literature are encapsulated in Table 7. This classification captures the declared primary focus of each study (e.g., the dimension explicitly placed at the center of the author's modeling or optimization framework). Under this perspective, charger location emerges as the most widely explored topic, followed by considerations of battery degradation. Charging strategies were explicitly modeled in only four studies, and no study identified renewable energy integration as its main research focus. The remaining 20 articles were classified under the "Others" category, which encompasses research on grid interaction, coordinated charging across energy systems, or overarching system-level optimization.

It is important to emphasize that Table 7 should not be interpreted as indicating the absence of RES considerations in the literature. Rather, it reflects that no study positioned RES integration as the central contribution.

Table 7. Distribution of Key Focus Areas

Key Focus Area	Article Count
Charger location	48
Battery degradation	15
Charging strategies	4
Renewable energy integration	0
Others	20
Total	**87**

The subject of charger location has been explored in 48 studies. [69] incorporated charger placement into a broader optimization framework that includes commercial buildings and grid loads. [91] co-optimized freight logistics along with charger installation in port facilities. [100] employed a set-covering model to determine optimal locations based on transport networks. [22] introduced an exact methodology to identify the optimal locations for urban freight chargers. Furthermore, [2] examined the behavioral implications of charging incentives and accessibility to facilities.

The inclusion of battery degradation as a constraint or cost factor is a prevalent theme found in 15 investigations. [25] incorporated it within the framework of a stochastic local electricity market. [56] dimensioned battery swapping stations based on constraints cognizant of degradation. [85] introduced a charge scheduling methodology that is intrinsically linked to battery health and state of charge (SoC). [24] addressed degradation in the context of portable storage dispatch on highways. Furthermore, [15] integrated considerations of battery life within a Model Predictive Control (MPC) strategy.

Various modeling approaches have been examined to explore charging strategies. A day-ahead self-dispatch system for energy control, which indirectly influences vehicle charging patterns, was proposed by [107]. A framework predicated on deep reinforcement learning to reduce overall energy costs [9,67]. The integration of dynamic programming with fleet operation scheduling was explored by [91], whereas [15] implemented the predictive control of the model to oversee megawatt charging at depots. A distributed dual-layer optimization framework was developed by [113].

A total of twenty papers explored various topics, including agent coordination, energy sharing, and comprehensive optimization frameworks. Notable examples are [107], which examines grid-level power dispatch, [9], which focuses on multi-agent learning for electric vehicle (EV) charging, and [69], which investigates collaborative energy sharing between buildings and EV stations. These studies encompass a wide array of domains and illustrate the increasing complexity and convergence observed within the field.

Key Metrics: Evaluation metrics were used in all the studies reviewed. The most widely used metric was the total reduction in emissions, which was featured in 11 studies. In contrast, three studies incorporated battery life indicators, such as degradation rates and SoH, as well as three articles on the energy cost per kilometer. Metrics related to fleet uptime or availability were the least frequently observed, used in only one study. The remaining 69 papers employed alternative or composite indicators, which were categorized under "Others".
The reduction of emissions was a significant focus in several environmental assessments. [100] explored the impact of network-scale charging policies on the adoption of electric vehicles and associated emissions. [90] investigated the integration of smart charging with renewable energy sources to mitigate the carbon footprint. [86] conducted a comparative analysis of battery swapping and fast charging with regard to emissions. The optimization of a multi-energy system that incorporates RES for the evaluation of carbon outcomes was the subject of research [115], while [37] examined the decarbonization pathways for UK freight, comparing hydrogen and electrification approaches.
The longevity of batteries was examined using metrics associated with degradation under operational conditions. [24] employed reinforcement learning to optimize portable storage solutions for highways considering battery wear. [117] introduced a life cycle framework for charging and swapping stations, which included aspects of battery degradation. Furthermore, [93] provided an extensive review of the degradation mechanisms in lithium-ion batteries when subjected to fast charging.
The determination of the energy cost per km has been examined in various studies, including [28], which optimized the charging schedules of hybrid energy storage systems to minimize economic expenditure. [78] proposed a dynamic programming strategy aimed at reducing costs in charging aggregated electric vehicle fleets.[7] assessed the influence of infrastructure on the cost efficiency of electric trucks.
The subject of fleet uptime is addressed by [69], who formulated a collaborative optimization model encompassing vehicle availability constraints for the purpose of synchronizing charging processes with the energy consumption of commercial buildings and the requirements of grid demand.

Data Source and Validation: The studies under review employed diverse sources of data inputs. A total of 33 studies used empirical data that include fleet record or quantified energy consumption. In contrast, 42 papers relied on simulated data, involving artificially constructed travel patterns and energy profiles.

A minority group, consisting of 12 studies, integrated real-world observations with scenarios generated by simulations.
The validation methodologies were diverse in all studies. For example, [15] used measured charging demand curves to substantiate their predictive control strategy. In contrast, [102] used actual infrastructure maps to assess location coverage. [25] conducted benchmarking of market results against historical pricing data. Meanwhile, [22] verified their facility placement algorithm through scenario testing and [54] performed cross-comparisons with dispatch logs and simulation outcomes.

Problem Constraints: The constraint pertaining to charge capacity was addressed in 61 studies, whereas the limitation related to battery range was examined in 37 studies. Furthermore, grid power capacity, referenced in 46 publications, and delivery time windows, cited in 30 papers, were frequently analyzed constraints within the context of electric freight applications.
Such constraints are commonly observed in multi-layered models orchestrating the coordination of fleet logistics with energy provisioning. For example, [24] integrated grid overload limitations and battery degradation trade-offs into the dispatch algorithms of mobile charging units.

Method Type: The studies encompassed a diverse range of methodological approaches. Simulation engines, encompassing discrete event simulators and multi-agent frameworks, were the most prevalent, employed in 38 papers. Reinforcement learning techniques featured in 13 investigations, whereas 14 utilized metaheuristics like genetic algorithms or PSO. A mere 3 studies employed exact mathematical programming (e.g., Gurobi, CPLEX), while 19 papers implemented various other hybrid or heuristic methods.

Through a systematic acquisition and analysis of the pertinent data, this study seeks to construct an exhaustive comparative framework delineating modeling paradigms and their aptitude in encapsulating the intricate interdependencies inherent in EFV fleet operations.

4.2 FQ1 - Focused Question 1:

This research inquiry sought to systematically delineate the ways in which charging strategies have been conceptualized, modeled, and empirically evaluated within the literature, with particular emphasis on their repercussions for fleet availability and operational efficiency. Recognizing that charging strategies constitute one of the most pivotal operational levers in the deployment of EFVs, it was imperative that this review comprehends their documented impacts and trade-offs.
The synthesis yielded insights into the strategies predominantly employed, the extent to which their advantages and limitations are quantitatively assessed, and the areas where gaps in research persist regarding their optimization.

Charging Strategies Analyzed: Various charging strategies were discerned in the reviewed literature, as outlined in Table 8. Smart or adaptive charging strategies were modeled with the highest frequency, appearing in nine studies; fast charging and battery swapping were modeled in seven and eight studies, respectively. Depot-based scheduled charging was featured in five articles, while opportunity charging was only examined in a single study. The rest of the studies either employed combination strategies, focused on higher-level system planning, or failed to provide a detailed specification of the charging protocol.

Table 8. Distribution of Charging Strategies

Charging Strategy	Number of Papers
Smart or adaptive charging	9
Fast charging	7
Battery swapping	8
Depot-based scheduled charging	5
Opportunity charging	1
Others	57
Total	**87**

Smart or adaptive charging has been explored in various studies, including [12], which coordinated electric vehicle charging with the supply of renewable energy. [90], which advanced the concept of carbon-aware smart scheduling; [39,49], which designed battery swapping infrastructure integrated with adaptive fleet management.

Fast charging featured prominently in investigations such as [63], which examined the infrastructure prerequisites for long-haul trucking; [86], which analyzed the effects on the grid in scenarios of fast charging versus battery swapping; and [21], which formulated optimization models for the charging of urban fleets.

The evaluation of battery swapping is undertaken in [107] through the application of a self-dispatch optimization framework for depots utilizing modular battery systems. Additionally, a comparative analysis of operation time and emissions is presented in [86]. Furthermore, a cost-benefit analysis focusing on trade-offs in long-distance operations is conducted in [7].

Depot-based scheduled charging has been explored in various studies, such as [17,96,97], which developed dynamic pricing strategies tailored for mobile depot fleets, and [111], which implemented multiobjective dispatch strategies in the context of electricity tariff structures. Furthermore, [70] investigated depot-centric scheduling under fluctuating grid conditions.

The concept of opportunity charging was investigated by [84], who formulated EV truck route plans under conditions characterized by stochastic charging on the road.

Impact on Fleet Efficiency or Costs: Charging strategies play a pivotal role in shaping both economic performance and operational efficiency. A total of 59 reviewed articles explicitly focused on financial implications, including aspects such as capital investment, energy expenditure, and cost-benefit analyses. Meanwhile, 46 articles concentrated on operational efficiency metrics, which include availability, routing productivity, and energy utilization. It should be noted that numerous studies concurrently addressed both dimensions, leading to an overlap in these figures.
Studies investigating the financial implications include [69], which explored the optimization of energy sharing mechanisms to mitigate peak tariff demands; [107], which assessed the financial impact of implementing modular charging units with local grid integration; and [9], which applied reinforcement learning techniques to reduce overall energy costs [67]. Furthermore, [91] integrated port scheduling with energy pricing strategies to simultaneously optimize logistics and energy consumption, whereas [15] analyzed the costs associated with peak-demand tariffs in the context of megawatt-scale charging.
The issue of operational efficiency has been examined by [102], who quantified the impact of station location on coverage of trips and productivity of fleets, as well as by [91], who introduced a methodology for dynamic re-routing contingent upon energy availability. Furthermore, additional research, including [69], has identified a correlation between energy strategies and enhancements in service lifespan and resilience of power systems.

Impact on Fleet Availability or Uptime: The subject of fleet availability and uptime was explicitly addressed in 26 of the reviewed studies. These investigations assessed the impact of charging strategies on vehicle readiness, operational windows, and downtime. Fast charging was frequently emphasized as enhancing short-term availability, although at the expense of accelerated battery degradation. Opportunity charging and coordinated depot scheduling were also identified as contributing to improved utilization.
For example, [15] implemented a model predictive control strategy geared toward the management of megawatt-scale charging, leading to improvements in the turnover of recharges and daily availability. [107] focused on self-dispatching within fleet clusters, reducing idle times through strategic scheduling. [41,100] employed location-sensitive infrastructure models to alleviate detour-related downtime and improve coverage reliability. Furthermore, [69] developed a collaborative energy sharing mechanism to maintain fleet uptime during periods of energy constraints. Lastly, [116] conducted co-optimization of platooning and charging windows, observing availability improvements of up to 17%.

Trade-Offs Between Charging Strategies, Charger Location, Battery Degradation, And/or Renewable Energies Integration: An explicit discussion of trade-off analysis was present in 78 of the 87 papers reviewed. These studies examined compromises including increased battery degradation resulting

from fast or high C rate charging, the financial burdens of infrastructure investment, and challenges associated with the stochastic characteristics of RES.
For example, [69] investigated how collaborative energy sharing contributes to minimizing infrastructure costs while maintaining operational uptime. [107], introduced strategies for self-dispatch to reduce expenses and address load variability caused by renewable energy sources. [9] examined the application of reinforcement learning-based approaches to optimize charging solutions in the context of conflicting costs and costs. In the context of port logistics, [91] achieved joint optimization of terminal scheduling alongside charging placement to ensure a balance between power reliability and operational needs. Furthermore, [15] explored the degradation and charge cost as competing objectives within the framework of predictive control of the model. Further analyses, such as those in [103], explored the trade-offs between location and energy in electric truck corridors, while [114] implemented distributed optimization techniques to balance charging logistics with battery degradation considerations.

4.3 FQ2 - Focused Question 2

The objective of this research inquiry is to determine the implications of charger location decisions on the design and efficacy of charging strategies within EFV systems. Given that charging infrastructure constitutes one of the most capital intensive and operationally crucial components of EFV deployment, a comprehensive understanding of its impact is vital for both fleet operators and policymakers.
To methodically address this inquiry, pertinent details were meticulously extracted from each paper, following the four dimensions delineated below. Furthermore, this inquiry facilitated a thorough evaluation of the interplay between charger location optimization and the design of the charging strategy, vehicle uptime, and cost efficiency.

Impact of Charger Location on Charging Strategies: Among the 87 articles reviewed, 41 explicitly addressed the impact of charger location on the selection and efficacy of charging strategies.
Numerous studies have scrutinized the impact of the spatial configuration of charging stations on the facilitation or limitation of specific strategic approaches. For example, [69] investigated the influence of the co-location of chargers with commercial buildings on the scheduling of shared infrastructure. [91] demonstrated that the integrated optimization of port timetables and charger locations can effectively mitigate routing detours. Within the realm of logistics, [103] used a network-based model that harmonizes the coverage of the fleet route with the strategic positioning of energy-constrained chargers. In addition, [22,27] formulated an exact model aimed at minimizing total deviations from optimal transport routes based on charger locations. Furthermore, [2] proposed incentives-driven charger seating schemes that dynamically modify the placement to shape the user charging behavior.

Methodologies Used to Optimize Charger Location: A diverse array of methodological approaches was utilized to ascertain the optimal location for the charger, with mathematical optimization prevailing as the predominant method. Table 9 presents a comprehensive breakdown of the techniques employed.

Table 9. Methodologies for Charger Location Optimization

Method Type	Number of Papers
Mathematical optimization (e.g., MILP, FLP)	13
Simulation-based approaches	3
Multi-objective location-routing optimization	1
Geospatial or real-demand-based analysis	4
Total (non-exclusive)	—

Mathematical formulations were prevalent, exemplified by [22], which employed an exact mixed-integer linear programming (MILP) model for determining the optimal location of freight depots, and by [103], where a set-covering location problem was modified to incorporate logistics-energy constraints. Simulation-based methodologies were explored in studies such as [11,53], utilizing agent-based modeling to examine spatial deployment under conditions of demand uncertainty. Although less frequently encountered, geospatial methodologies were utilized by [61], who utilized actual geographic information on fleets and demand. Hybrid strategies, as demonstrated in [6,34,38], integrated routing-aware optimization with infrastructure sizing considerations. Lastly, [2] introduced incentive-based algorithms aimed at adaptive charger configuration in response to user behavior.

Influence of Charger Location on Vehicle Availability or Uptime: The placement of chargers was explicitly associated with vehicle availability or operational uptime in 17 of the studies reviewed.

Strategically situated charging stations have consistently been evidenced to decrease downtime and enhance vehicle availability. For instance, [69] developed a co-optimization model wherein the siting of chargers minimized detours and optimized the utilization of infrastructure. Furthermore, [103] employed a set-covering optimization framework to ensure accessibility along truck corridors, thereby directly affecting vehicle readiness. In addition, [2] proposed adaptive location incentives that enhanced service rates in zones with high usage. Meanwhile, [101] conducted an assessment of an industry-driven corridor electrification strategy, demonstrating availability improvements of up to 15%. Lastly, [3] showed that distributed location-aware charging coordination augments the effective usage of charging windows while reducing idle fleet time.

Influence of Charger Location on Energy Cost: In 10 out of the 87 reviewed studies, the decisions regarding charger locations were specifically associated with implications for energy costs. These works assessed the impact of spatial deployment on grid tariffs, necessary infrastructure upgrades, and operational expenditures.
For example, [61] investigated photovoltaic-powered corridors and demonstrated the influence of location-specific solar potential on the costs associated with charging energy. [95] assessed the cost-optimal scheduling for fleet charging, taking into account the location of the depot and the corresponding grid tariffs. [24] introduced a deep reinforcement learning model that incorporates location-based marginal price signals into the charging process. [4] developed a model for long-haul electric freight operations that considers dynamic grid tariffs connected to location based on routes. Finally, [71,72] investigated the impact of electricity price zoning on the planning of charging infrastructure and OPEX.

4.4 FQ3 - Focused Question 3

This research question sought to investigate the impact of various charging strategies on battery degradation mechanisms, which are crucial determinants of the long-term cost and operational efficacy of EFVs. Given that battery replacements constitute a substantial portion of the overall cost of ownership, comprehending these effects is critical to formulating sustainable charging policies.
Through a systematic categorization of the subsequent data, this inquiry elucidated the trade-offs embedded within charging policy design, thereby demonstrating how operational decisions influence battery health trajectories and affect the long-term economic viability.

Trade-Offs Between Charging Strategies and Battery Degradation: Of the total of 87 reviewed articles, 19 made an explicit connection between charging strategies, specifically fast charging and opportunity charging, and battery degradation indicators, including capacity loss, SoH, and reduction in cycle life. Charging profiles characterized by high C-rates have frequently been linked to accelerated battery degradation. For example, [15] designed a model predictive control strategy that explicitly integrates capacity fade models. In the study conducted by [25], stochastic game theory methods were used to harmonize the convenience of rapid charging with the penalties associated with long-term SoH. A capacity configuration strategy for battery swapping systems was introduced by [56], with a focus on modeling degradation per cycle. Furthermore, [85] utilized comprehensive optimization models to evaluate charging routes for heavy duty trucks, considering the implications of battery aging. Similarly, [23] employed deep reinforcement learning to improve charging behavior by applying degradation-aware policies.

Impact of Battery Degradation on Charging Times and Fleet Uptime: The impact of battery degradation on operational performance was identified in

4 of the 87 reviewed studies. These studies examined how the reduction in battery capacity resulting from aging influences the duration of charge, the usable range, and vehicle availability.
In [85], battery degradation models have been incorporated into the planning of charging routes, demonstrating that aging exacerbates the required dwell time and limits the coverage of the daily distance. [35] refined a swapping-based battery scheduling framework aimed at minimizing SoH deterioration to improve system uptime. In the context of multistage scheduling, [106] illustrated that elevated degradation levels diminish battery availability for dynamic day-ahead planning. Furthermore, [46] examined the decrease in charging efficiency attributed to the advanced age of batteries in urban delivery fleets.

Key Factors Increasing Battery Degradation: Numerous studies have identified both operational and environmental factors as significant contributors to battery aging.
For example, [59] formulated a one-dimensional electrothermal battery model to assess the influence of temperature and current loads on cell aging. In addition, [46] incorporated SoH aware scheduling within a multi-depot delivery fleet model to mitigate the aging effects associated with frequent cycling. Furthermore, [92] conducted an extensive review of the impacts of fast charging, emphasizing the significance of high C-rate and temperature spikes. Currently, [36] examined microgrid-integrated fleets, highlighting the depth of discharge as a key degradation factor in economic dispatch routines.

Charging Strategies Designed to Balance Battery Longevity and Operational Efficiency: Among the 87 studies reviewed, eight outlined strategies that concurrently address the extension of battery lifespan and operational requirements.
Multi-objective and degradation-sensitive optimization frameworks are prevalent among the studies. For example, [25] utilized a stochastic game-theoretic model to concurrently optimize both the cost and battery aging under conditions of rapid charging. [24] implemented deep reinforcement learning methodologies to adaptively regulate charging schedules based on real-time SoH. [33] introduced a day-ahead optimization strategy that incorporates thermal and longevity constraints to safeguard battery integrity. Moreover, [35] designed a strategy to synchronize battery swapping with preservation of cycle life, while [106] introduced a multistage charging system capable of adjusting the intensity of charge in response to degradation levels.

4.5 FQ4 - Focused Question 4:

This research inquiry aims to elucidate the mechanisms by which RES are integrated into EFV charging systems and to analyze their impacts on energy expenditures, grid reliance, and operational resilience. As noted earlier in the discussion of Table 7, no study explicitly framed RES integration as its primary focus, which explains its absence in that classification. Nevertheless, a substantial number of papers incorporated RES as a secondary or supporting element (for example, when modeling hybrid depots, analyzing grid dependency, or integrating photovoltaic availability into charging schedules). FQ4 therefore complements Table 7 by examining these cross-cutting contributions in greater detail.

Incorporation of RES is progressively recognized as a strategy to enhance the sustainability and economic efficiency of fleet electrification [58]. However, the technical and economic ramifications of such integrations continue to represent a dynamic field of scholarly inquiry. To systematically examine this topic, the review extracted the following information from each study.

Energy Source Types Considered: Out of the 87 articles examined, 77 specifically address the energy sources utilized for charging electric trucks, incorporating various combinations of renewable and grid-based energy resources.
Instances encompass research that jointly optimized photovoltaic and grid supply systems for drayage trucks [91], simulated corridor hubs incorporating solar and wind energy [61], or conducted comparative analysis of emissions under scenarios of renewable-powered charging [69].

Analysis of Electric Energy Generation or Self-Generation Technologies: A total of 36 scholarly articles were examined to explore on-site or hybrid electric generation technologies, predominantly through solar photovoltaic systems, microgrids, or configurations integrating hybrid renewable and grid technologies.
As an illustration, the study conducted by [13] resulted in the development of a techno-economic model tailored for the deployment of extensive solar power facilities, while [112] managed the integration of distributed energy resources for corridor charging initiatives. [8,26,44,52] examine grid integration with flexibility trading and local market mechanisms.

Use of Energy Supply Simulation Models: Eleven studies used energy simulation models to examine grid-renewable interactions, optimize dispatch, or assess power flow reliability.
Illustrative cases encompass the alignment of supply and demand in photovoltaic-integrated systems [19], as well as the lifecycle energy assessment for charging and storage infrastructures [117].

Analysis of Grid Dependency: The dependency on the grid was systematically analyzed in 54 studies, with a primary focus on examining resilience and cost implications during outages or periods of peak demand.
For instance, the study conducted in [15] assessed various strategies to enhance the resilience of microgrids, while the research presented in [108] examined the impact of photovoltaic storage combinations on reducing peak electricity dependency.

Presentation of Energy Cost Analysis (RES Vs. Grid Supplied): Nineteen studies revealed comparative cost analyzes, which generally indicates potential savings of 20–35% through RES integration.
Research works, as exemplified by [90] and [61], have conducted assessments of the lifecycle costs associated with solar-powered charging in comparison to reliance on the conventional electrical grid. [14,50] covers the importance of IoT flexibility & multi-energy synergy, as well as local flexibility for energy markets.

Impact of Integrating Renewable Energy Into Charging Strategies: An analysis of 26 research papers demonstrates that RES impacts not only the cost structure but also the form and scheduling of the charging processes.
As exemplified in the literature, [69] introduced charging windows that are in accordance with photovoltaic (PV) availability, while [112] implemented a dual-layer renewable energy source (RES)-aware scheduling framework. [29,75] analyzed hybrid energy storage and PV utilization in charging station operations.

Analysis of Renewable Energy Integration on Charging Costs: A total of 23 academic publications conducted detailed calculations or simulations to assess the impacts of renewable energy sources on the charging costs per session and the overall cost of ownership.
Illustrative examples encompass simulations aimed at minimizing cost per session in hybrid depots [76], along with strategies for mitigating battery wear expenses through the integration of photovoltaic systems, as discussed in [33].

5 Conclusions

This systematic review presents an exhaustive synthesis of recent advancements, challenges, and research trajectories within the domain of electric vehicle (EFV) charging systems. Through the examination of 87 peer-reviewed articles published over the past decade, the review elucidates a field that has rapidly developed in both methodological sophistication and thematic diversity. The predominant modeling frameworks are anchored in mathematical optimization, particularly mixed-integer linear programming. However, simulation-based approaches, hybrid methods, and, more recently, data-driven and machine learning techniques have been increasingly utilized to tackle the intricate, dynamic, and interdisciplinary aspects of EFV operations.

The analysis identified four main technical focus areas: charging strategies, charger location optimization, battery degradation, and the integration of renewable energy. Charging strategies remain pivotal, and the literature highlights the operational, economic, and technical trade-offs inherent in the selection among fast charging, depot charging, opportunity charging, and battery swapping. The impact of charger location on operational efficiency, vehicle uptime, and infras tructure cost emerged as a recurring theme, emphasizing the criticality of spatial planning and the application of robust optimization methodologies for station location. Battery degradation, though relatively underexplored compared to infrastructure or scheduling, is increasingly recognized as a crucial determinant of total ownership cost and operational reliability, thus encouraging the development of charging protocols and multi-objective optimization approaches that explicitly prioritize battery health. The integration of renewable energy sources, such as photovoltaic and wind power, has evolved from conceptual frameworks to more detailed techno-economic analyses, with an expanding body of evidence endorsing their efficacy in diminishing grid dependency and operational emissions, notwithstanding the introduction of new complexities in scheduling and system resilience. It should be reiterated that while renewable energy integration appeared with zero studies in Table 7 due to the absence of works identifying it as their primary focus, the focused analysis of FQ4 demonstrated that RES was frequently incorporated as a secondary or cross-cutting element, underscoring its growing relevance for EFV system design.

Notwithstanding these advances, the review highlighted several persistent research gaps and avenues for future research. There exists a significant need for computational models and digital twins capable of comprehensively capturing the interdependencies among charging strategies, infrastructure deployment, battery health trajectories, and the integration of renewable energy within the context of real-world operational uncertainties. Empirical validation remains inadequately utilized, necessitating further endeavors to bridge the divide between theoretical modeling and field data obtained from varied freight fleets. The advancement of adaptive, data-driven energy and fleet management systems, which can co-optimize vehicle routing, charging behavior, and energy procurement in response to real-time conditions, represents a particularly promising frontier. Furthermore, increased attention is warranted towards the equity and economic viability of large-scale EFV charging networks, encompassing the impact of evolving energy markets, regulatory measures, and regional grid capacities.

A limitation of this study is that, as a systematic mapping review, no formal risk-of-bias or quality appraisal (e.g., ROBIS) was applied to the included studies. While methodological approaches and validation strategies were documented, the review was designed to map the research landscape rather than to weight findings by methodological rigor.

In summary, the transition towards decarbonization in freight transport via EFVs requires concerted advancements in modeling, system design, and practical implementation. Future scholarly efforts should prioritize the creation of integrated multiscale optimization frameworks, underpinned by empirical data and sophisticated analytics, to enable scalable, resilient, and sustainable EFV operations. Only through such interdisciplinary and comprehensive approaches can the operational, economic, and environmental advantages envisioned by the electrification of freight transport be fully realized.

References

1. Alam, M.R., Guo, Z.: Co-optimization of charging scheduling and platooning for long-haul electric freight vehicles. Transp. Res. Part C Emerg. Tech. **147**, 104009 (2023)
2. Azin, B., Yang, X.T., Marković, N., Xiong, C.: An incentivized scheme for electric vehicle charging demand management. Transp. Res. Part C (2023). https://doi.org/10.1016/j.trc.2023.104288
3. Bai, T., Li, Y., Malikopoulos, A.A., Sun, L.: Distributed charging coordination for electric truck fleets considering infrastructure accessibility. IEEE Trans. Intell. Transp. Syst. (2024)
4. Barba, L., Ahmed, S., Alamaniotis, M., Gatsis, N.: Dynamic modeling and optimization of long-haul EV charging networks. In: 2025 IEEE Texas Power and Energy Conference (TPEC). pp. 01–06. IEEE (2025)
5. Baringo, L., Amaro, R.S.: A stochastic robust optimization approach for the bidding strategy of an electric vehicle aggregator. Electr. Power Syst. Res. **146**, 362–370 (2017) https://doi.org/10.1016/j.epsr.2017.02.004, https://research-ebsco-com.ezproxy.eafit.edu.co/linkprocessor/plink?id=b4ecff66-b9dd-33ae-b700-c6e6bf138284
6. Bertucci, J.P., Salazar, M., Hofman, T.: Battery electric truck infrastructure co-design for corridor logistics: A multi-level optimization framework. Transp. Res. Part C (2025)
7. Bharti, A., Chauhan, R.K.: Impact of charging infrastructure on cost-benefit analysis of electric truck fleets. In: 2025 International Conference on Cognitive Computing in Engineering, Communications, Sciences and Biomedical Health Informatics (IC3ECSBHI) (2025)
8. Chemudupaty, R., Hornek, T., Pavić, I., Menci, S.P.: Optimizing trading of electric vehicle charging flexibility in the continuous intraday market under user and market uncertainties. Appl. Energy, **381** (2025) https://doi.org/10.1016/j.apenergy.2024.125103, https://research-ebsco-com.ezproxy.eafit.edu.co/linkprocessor/plink?id=e145e52c-e154-35b9-8805-2736a7e4a285
9. Chen, G., Yang, L., Cao, X.: A deep reinforcement learning-based charging scheduling approach with augmented Lagrangian for electric vehicles. Appl. Energy (2025). https://doi.org/10.1016/j.apenergy.2024.124706
10. Chen, L., Xu, T.: A dynamic programming model for joint optimization of electric drayage truck operations and charging stations planning at ports. Transp. Res. Part E (2020)
11. Cui, J., Cao, Y., Wang, B., Wu, J.: Multi-stage adaptive expansion of EV charging stations considering impacts from the transportation network and power grid. Applied Energy **386** (2025).https://doi.org/10.1016/j.apenergy.2025.125544, https://research-ebsco-com.ezproxy.eafit.edu.co/linkprocessor/plink?id=9af4b0a5-6a54-34fa-93df-db98fce881fe
12. Dai, S., Mansouri, S.A., Huang, S.: A multi-stage techno-economic model for harnessing PV and smart charging in depot-based EV operations. Renew. Energy (2023). https://doi.org/10.1016/j.renene.2023.121473
13. Dai, S., Mansouri, S.A., Huang, S.: A multi-stage techno-economic model for harnessing renewable charging for logistics fleets. Energy Convers. Manage. (2023)
14. Dai, S., Mansouri, S.A., Huang, S., Alharthi, Y.Z., Wu, Y., Bagherzadeh, L.: A multi-stage techno-economic model for harnessing flexibility from IOT-enabled appliances and smart charging systems: developing a competitive local flexibility

market using Stackelberg game theory. Appl. Energy **373** (2024) https://doi.org/10.1016/j.apenergy.2024.123868, https://research-ebsco-com.ezproxy.eafit.edu.co/linkprocessor/plink?id=761d010b-acbe-31a2-abb5-6d4b8eb8865a
15. Dalir, A., Jaman, S., Geury, T., Hegazy, O.: A high-level optimal charging management strategy using model predictive control for megawatt charging station. In: 2024 International Symposium on Power Electronics, Electrical Drives, Automation and Motion (2024)
16. Dallepiane, P.G., Rangel, C.S., Mallmann, L., Dallepiane, F.G., Neves, L.S.: Optimized support system for mobility in the logistics processes of routes with electric trucks. Sustainability (Switzerland) **17** (2025).https://doi.org/10.3390/su17104607, https://www.scopus.com/inward/record.uri?eid=2-s2.0-105006522053&doi=10.3390%2fsu17104607&partnerID=40&md5=3c941708da5f69ed3ce5b142a233c0d4
17. Decher, S., Schäfers, H.: Assessing flexibility in battery electric truck charging depots considering grid impact. In: 8th E-Mobility Power System Integration Symposium (EMOB 2024). vol. 2024, pp. 270–276 (2024).https://doi.org/10.1049/icp.2024.3761
18. Decher, S., Schäfers, H.: Assessing flexibility in battery electric truck charging depots considering grid impact. In: IET Conference Proceedings, pp. 270–276. IET (2024)
19. Decher, S., Schäfers, H.: Assessing flexibility in battery electric truck charging via supply-demand simulation. J. Energy Storage (2023)
20. Díaz-Ramírez, J., Zazueta-Nassif, S., Galarza-Tamez, R., Prato-Sánchez, D., Huertas, J.I.: Characterization of urban distribution networks with light electric freight vehicles. Transp. Res. Part D Transp. Environ. **119**, 103719 (2023)
21. Dimatulac, T., Maoh, H., Carriveau, R.: Development and application of an optimization-based framework for EV fast-charging in mid-sized cities. Energy Rep. (2025)
22. Dimitriou, P., Nikolopoulou, A., Gkiotsalitis, K.: An exact approach for the charging station location selection problem in urban freight transport. In: Operational Research (2025). https://doi.org/10.1007/s12351-025-00900-w
23. Ding, Y., Qu, G., Chen, X., Wang, J., Song, J., He, G.: Deep reinforcement learning-based spatiotemporal decision of utility-scale highway portable energy storage systems. IEEE Trans. Ind. Appl. **60**(1), 966–975 (2023)
24. Ding, Y., Qu, G., Chen, X., Wang, J., Song, J., He, G.: Deep reinforcement learning-based spatiotemporal decision of utility-scale highway portable energy storage systems. IEEE Trans. Ind. Appl. (2024). https://doi.org/10.1109/TIA.2023.3274729
25. Dolatabadi, S.H.H., Bhuiyan, T.H., Chen, Y., Morales, J.L.: A stochastic game-theoretic optimization approach for managing local electricity markets with electric vehicles and renewable sources. Appl. Energy (2024). https://doi.org/10.1016/j.apenergy.2024.123518
26. Dolatabadi, S.H.H., Bhuiyan, T.H., Chen, Y., Morales, J.L.: A stochastic game-theoretic optimization approach for managing local electricity markets with electric vehicles and renewable sources. Appl. Energy **368** (2024) https://doi.org/10.1016/j.apenergy.2024.123518, https://research-ebsco-com.ezproxy.eafit.edu.co/linkprocessor/plink?id=e5cf3425-25ac-3398-8ca0-c258639b7801
27. Du, Z., Zheng, L., Lin, B.: Influence of charging stations accessibility on charging stations utilization. Energy, **298** (2024).https://doi.org/10.1016/j.energy.2024.131374, https://research-ebsco-com.ezproxy.eafit.edu.co/linkprocessor/plink?id=fc1e4143-a067-39e6-93c3-c7fdd9baafa5

28. Erdogan, G., Hassen, W.F.: Charging scheduling of hybrid energy storage systems for EV charging stations. Energies (2023). https://doi.org/10.3390/en16186656
29. Erdogan, G., Hassen, W.F.: Charging scheduling of hybrid energy storage systems for EV charging stations. Energies (19961073) **16**, pp. 6656 (2023).https://doi.org/10.3390/en16186656, https://research-ebsco-com.ezproxy.eafit.edu.co/linkprocessor/plink?id=7f5df929-0f18-30a2-8c1d-771f020b0a45
30. Fan, Y., Nowaczyk, S., Wang, Z., Pashami, S.: Evaluating multi-task curriculum learning for forecasting energy consumption in electric heavy-duty vehicles. In: Nowaczyk, S., Spiliopoulou, M., Ragni, M., Fink, O. (eds.) CEUR Workshop Proceedings. vol. 3765. CEUR-WS (2024), https://www.scopus.com/inward/record.uri?eid=2-s2.0-85206261149&partnerID=40&md5=d3a682f810f5ec23db9e2bdb95831501
31. Fernandez, G.S., Krishnasamy, V., Kuppusamy, S., Ali, J.S., Ali, Z.M., El-Shahat, A., Aleem, S.H.E.A.: Optimal dynamic scheduling of electric vehicles in a parking lot using particle swarm optimization and shuffled frog leaping algorithm. Energies (19961073) **13**, pp. 6384 (2020).https://doi.org/10.3390/en13236384, https://research-ebsco-com.ezproxy.eafit.edu.co/linkprocessor/plink?id=3e60cfac-9505-330f-8bfa-8fbb33580c98
32. Gao, F., Chen, Y.: Bi-objective optimization of charging infrastructure deployment and emission reduction for electric freight transport. J. Clean. Prod. (2022)
33. Gao, P., Deng, Z., Qi, X., Yu, G., Ni, M.: Multi-objective day-ahead optimization of distributed electric truck charging under battery aging constraints. Energy Rep. (2025)
34. Guler, N.: Smart allocation and sizing of fast charging stations: a metaheuristic solution. Int. J. Sustainable Energy **43**, pp. 1–15 (2024) https://doi.org/10.1080/14786451.2024.2350970, https://research-ebsco-com.ezproxy.eafit.edu.co/linkprocessor/plink?id=fad49ef5-9a38-3e76-b402-080277f1816b
35. Gull, M.S., Khalid, M., Ahmad, N., Ahmad, S.: Multi-objective optimization of battery swapping operations considering battery aging and fleet availability. J. Energy Storage (2024)
36. Guo, S., He, J., Ma, K., Yang, J., Chen, Y.: Robust economic dispatch for microgrid-connected electric truck fleets considering battery aging. Energy (2025)
37. Haugen, M.J., Flynn, D., Greening, P., Tichler, J., Blythe, P., Boies, A.M.: Electrification versus hydrogen for UK road freight: conclusions from a systems analysis of transport energy transitions. Energy Sustain. Dev. (2022). https://doi.org/10.1016/j.esd.2022.03.011
38. He, K., et al.: Leasing business model for trunk mobile charging stations: from the view of operators. IEEE Tran. Transport. Electr. (2025). https://doi.org/10.1109/TTE.2025.3557026
39. Hu, X., Yang, Z., Sun, J., Zhang, Y.: Optimal pricing strategy for electric vehicle battery swapping: Pay-per-swap or subscription? Transportation Research Part E: logistics & Transportation Review **171** (2023) https://doi.org/10.1016/j.tre.2023.103030, https://research-ebsco-com.ezproxy.eafit.edu.co/linkprocessor/plink?id=b4468d34-5aa5-38a3-a554-ec2c6ef8b81f
40. Huang, Z., Lin, J.: An exact approach for the charging station location selection problem in urban freight transport. Eur. J. Oper. Res. (2018)
41. Husinec, M., Strielkowski, W., Vacek, T., Vondracek, M.: "optimizing electric vehicles charging for enhancing environmental sustainability and reducing carbon emissions of freight transport: case of czech republic". Environ. Econ. **15**, 16–31 (2024).https://doi.org/10.21511/ee.15(1).2024.02, https://www.scopus.com/

inward/record.uri?eid=2-s2.0-85184618604&doi=10.21511%2fee.15%281%29.2024.02&partnerID=40&md5=b8b36362fcf161fe5fb33a587005ba0c
42. Inkinen, T., Hämäläinen, E.: Reviewing truck logistics: solutions for achieving low emission road freight transport. Sustainability **12**(17), 6714 (2020)
43. Iwan, S., Nürnberg, M., Jedliński, M., Kijewska, K.: Efficiency of light electric vehicles in last mile deliveries-Szczecin case study. Sustain. Cities Soc. **74**, 103167 (2021)
44. Khwanrit, R., Javaid, S., Lim, Y., Charoenlarpnopparut, C., Tan, Y.: Hierarchical multi-communities energy sharing management with electric vehicle integration. Energies (19961073) **18**, pp. 393 (2025).https://doi.org/10.3390/en18020393, https://research-ebsco-com.ezproxy.eafit.edu.co/linkprocessor/plink?id=2256f920-9f1b-3e6c-83e7-bd5f41eed3ac
45. Kiba, M., Chen, D.: Battery electric truck charging infrastructure simulation in large-scale freight networks. In: Simulation Modelling Practice and Theory (2021)
46. Kim, H., Lee, J., Lee, S.: Optimizing day-ahead scheduling of urban electric delivery fleets under battery aging constraints. Transp. Res. Part D (2025)
47. Kitchenham, B., Brereton, P.: A systematic review of systematic review process research in software engineering. Inf. Softw. Technol. **55**(12), 2049–2075 (2013)
48. Kwon, S.Y., Park, J.Y., Kim, Y.J.: Optimal operation of mobile energy storage devices to minimize energy loss in a distribution system. In: 2018 IEEE International Conference on Environment and Electrical Engineering and 2018 IEEE Industrial and Commercial Power Systems Europe (EEEIC / I&CPS Europe). pp. 1–6 (2018) https://doi.org/10.1109/EEEIC.2018.8494447
49. Li, B., et al.: Centralized charging station planning for battery electric trucks considering the impacts on electricity distribution systems. Energy Rep. **9**, 346–357 (2023)
50. Li, J., Yang, M., Zhang, Y., Li, J., Lu, J.: Micro-grid day-ahead stochastic optimal dispatch considering multiple demand response and electric vehicles. Energies (19961073) **16**, PP. 3356 (2023) https://doi.org/10.3390/en16083356, https://research-ebsco-com.ezproxy.eafit.edu.co/linkprocessor/plink?id=11669272-60a3-3c2f-87de-abd64364e3a3
51. Li, W., Chen, X.: A data-driven integrated framework for fast-charging facility planning using multi-period bi-objective optimization. Energy (2020)
52. Lin, F.J., Lu, S.Y., Hu, M.C., Chen, Y.H.: Stochastic optimal strategies and management of electric vehicles and microgrids. Energies (19961073) **17**, PP. 3726 (2024) https://doi.org/10.3390/en17153726, https://research-ebsco-com.ezproxy.eafit.edu.co/linkprocessor/plink?id=f06078d3-54d7-3590-aeee-8f739a00ab85
53. Liu, H., Xing, Z., Zhao, Q., Liu, Y.: An orderly charging and discharging strategy of electric freight vehicles considering charging infrastructure deployment. Sustain. Cities Soc. (2024)
54. Liu, H., Xing, Z., Zhao, Q., Liu, Y., Wang, J.: An orderly charging and discharging strategy of electric truck clusters considering grid constraints and fleet scheduling. IEEE Access (2024). https://doi.org/10.1109/ACCESS.2024.3337151
55. Liu, Y., Wang, X.: Agent-based simulation of electric truck charging behaviors in urban logistics. J. Clean. Prod. (2020)
56. Lu, Y., et al.: Capacity configuration approach for battery swapping station: a staged programming model via double-end non-segmented-driven strategy. Renewable Energy (2025). https://doi.org/10.1016/j.renene.2025.122747
57. Ma, H., Li, Z.: Data-driven charging demand prediction for electric freight vehicles. Energy (2021)

58. Ma, W., Ma, Y., Deng, F.: Two-stage scheduling optimization of grid-connected hybrid energy microgrid considering the integration of electric vehicles. IAENG Int. J. Appl. Math. **55**, PP. 378–390 (2025), https://research-ebsco-com.ezproxy.eafit.edu.co/linkprocessor/plink?id=d0760831-1132-3829-9bdb-c1e336bbf7e8
59. Maciocha, M., Short, T., Thorat, U., McDonagh, M.: One-dimensional electro-thermal modelling of battery aging in heavy electric freight vehicles. Appl. Therm. Eng. (2024)
60. Melander, L., Nyquist-Magnusson, C., Wallström, H.: Drivers for and barriers to electric freight vehicle adoption in Stockholm. Transp. Res. Part D Transp. Environ. **108**, pp. 103317 (2022)
61. Mourad, A., Hennebel, M., Amrani, A., Ben Hamida, A.: Analyzing the fast-charging potential for electric vehicles with local photovoltaic power production in French suburban highway network. Energies **14**(9), 2428 (2021). https://doi.org/10.3390/en14092428
62. Mourad, A., Hennebel, M., Amrani, A., Hamida, A.B.: Analyzing the fast-charging potential for electric vehicles with local photovoltaic power production in French suburban highway network. Energies **14**(9), 2428 (2021)
63. Mourad, A., Hennebel, M., Amrani, A., Touati, A.: Analyzing the fast-charging potential for electric trucks in urban networks. IEEE Trans. Transp. Electr. (2023). https://doi.org/10.1109/TTE.2023.3299183
64. Peng, Z., Huang, Q.: Capacitated electric vehicle routing problem with time windows for urban freight distribution. Comput. Oper. Res. (2021)
65. Petersen, K., Feldt, R., Mujtaba, S., Mattsson, M.: Systematic mapping studies in software engineering. In: 12th International Conference on Evaluation and Assessment in Software Engineering (EASE). BCS Learning and Development (2008)
66. Petersen, K., Vakkalanka, S., Kuzniarz, L.: Guidelines for conducting systematic mapping studies in software engineering: an update. Inf. Softw. Technol. **64**, 1–18 (2015)
67. Qian, Q., Gan, M., Yang, X.: Empirical analysis of intelligent charging decisions: Boosting efficiency for electric trucks. Transp. Res. Part D Trans. Environ. **139** (2025).https://doi.org/10.1016/j.trd.2024.104572, https://www.scopus.com/inward/record.uri?eid=2-s2.0-85214237749&doi=10.1016%2fj.trd.2024.104572&partnerID=40&md5=2bfb1bc5f0f23f7cc30d963fb7c5b11b
68. Qin, Y., Wu, D.: Green electric vehicle routing and charging problem considering carbon emissions. Appl. Energy (2021)
69. Quddus, M.A., Shahvari, O., Marufuzzaman, M., Usher, J.M., Jaradat, R.: A collaborative energy sharing optimization model among electric vehicle charging stations, commercial buildings, and power grid. Appl. Energy (2018). https://doi.org/10.1016/j.apenergy.2018.08.018
70. Rostami, A., Verbas, O., Ghafarnejad, B.: Exploring impacts of electricity tariff on charging station choice of electric commercial fleets. Energy Policy (2023). https://doi.org/10.1016/j.enpol.2023.113501
71. Rostami, A., Verbas, O., Ghafarnejad, B.: Exploring impacts of electricity tariff on charging infrastructure and operational cost of electric trucks. Transp. Res. Part D (2024)
72. Rostami, A., Verbas, O., Ghafarnezhad, B., Soltanpour, A., Ghamami, M., Zockaie, A.: Exploring impacts of electricity tariff on charging infrastructure planning: an activity-based approach. Transp. Res. Part D Trans. amp Environ. **136** (2024).https://doi.org/10.1016/j.trd.2024.104451, https://research-ebsco-

com.ezproxy.eafit.edu.co/linkprocessor/plink?id=b53a64e6-3af1-3ce4-9282-c8832d02f44d
73. Saha, A., Simic, V., Dabic-Miletic, S., Senapati, T., Yager, R.R., Deveci, M.: Evaluation of propulsion technologies for sustainable road freight distribution using a dual probabilistic linguistic group decision-making approach. IEEE Trans. Eng. Manage. **71**, 7227–7241 (2024). https://doi.org/10.1109/TEM.2023.3253300
74. Shern, S.J., Sarker, M.T., Haram, M.H.S.M., Ramasamy, G., Thiagarajah, S.P., Al Farid, F.: Artificial intelligence optimization for user prediction and efficient energy distribution in electric vehicle smart charging systems. Energies **17**(22), pp. 5772 (2024)
75. Shern, S.J., Sarker, M.T., Haram, M.H.S.M., Ramasamy, G., Thiagarajah, S.P., Farid, F.A.: Artificial intelligence optimization for user prediction and efficient energy distribution in electric vehicle smart charging systems. Energies (19961073) **17**, pp. 5772 (2024) https://doi.org/10.3390/en17225772, https://research-ebsco-com.ezproxy.eafit.edu.co/linkprocessor/plink?id=ade6b7c2-ad40-3510-aab3-83382ce83cfc
76. Shern, S.J., Sarker, M.T., Husaain, M., Ahmed, S.: Artificial intelligence optimization for user-oriented cost-efficient charging in renewable-powered stations. Energy AI (2024)
77. Shi, J., Zeng, T., Moura, S.: Electric fleet charging management considering battery degradation and nonlinear charging profile. Energy **283**, 129094 (2023)
78. Skugor, B., Deur, J.: Dynamic programming-based optimisation of charging an electric vehicle fleet system represented by an aggregate battery model. Energy (Elsevier) (2015). https://doi.org/10.1016/j.energy.2015.03.057
79. Soni, A., Oh, J., Noras, M., Smith, M., Williams, W.: Solar PV augmented battery electric vehicle state of charge and temperature analysis in Simscape. In: Conference Proceedings - IEEE SOUTHEASTCON. pp. 837–843. Institute of Electrical and Electronics Engineers Inc. (2025).https://doi.org/10.1109/SoutheastCon56624.2025.10971500, https://www.scopus.com/inward/record.uri?eid=2-s2.0-105004577390&doi=10.1109%2fSoutheastCon56624.2025.10971500&partnerID=40&md5=6919f6e52e462bdd7b82f0086aed824c
80. Su, J., Lin, Q., Chen, M.: Follow the sun and go with the wind: Carbon footprint optimized timely e-truck transportation. In: e-Energy 2023 - Proceedings of the 2023 14th ACM International Conference on Future Energy Systems. pp. 159–171. Association for Computing Machinery, Inc (2023).https://doi.org/10.1145/3575813.3595193, https://www.scopus.com/inward/record.uri?eid=2-s2.0-85163748637&doi=10.1145%2f3575813.3595193&partnerID=40&md5=90b8e327c66ccbaaa15be14fc16c8376
81. Sun, Q., Wu, J.: Machine learning assisted optimization of charging schedules for urban electric truck fleets. Appl. Energy (2021)
82. Tan, J., Liu, S.: Stochastic vehicle routing and charging problem for electric freight vehicles with uncertain demand. Transp. Res. Part E (2020)
83. Teoh, T., Kunze, O., Teo, C.C., Wong, Y.D.: Decarbonisation of urban freight transport using electric vehicles and opportunity charging. Sustainability **10**(9), 3258 (2018)
84. Wan, Y., He, Z., Gao, Y., Xue, Y.: Long-haul truck charging planning problem considering opportunity charging under uncertainty. Transp. Res. Part D (2023). https://doi.org/10.1016/j.trd.2023.103682
85. Wang, F.Y., Chen, Z., Hu, Z.: Comprehensive optimization of electrical heavy-duty truck battery swap stations with a soc-dependent charge scheduling method. Energy (Elsevier) (2024). https://doi.org/10.1016/j.energy.2024.132773

86. Wang, R., et al.: Electrifying heavy-duty trucks: Battery-swapping vs fast charging. IEEE Trans. Smart Grid (2025). https://doi.org/10.1109/TSG.2025.3571819
87. Wang, Y., Zhou, L.: Optimal siting and scheduling of vehicle-to-grid enabled charging stations for electric freight trucks. Appl. Energy (2020)
88. Wei, Q., Sun, H.: Deep reinforcement learning-based spatiotemporal decision of utility-scale highway portable energy storage systems. IEEE Trans. Smart Grid (2022)
89. Whiting, P., Savović, J., Higgins, J.P., Caldwell, D.M., Reeves, B.C., Shea, B., Davies, P., Kleijnen, J., Churchill, R.: Robis: A new tool to assess risk of bias in systematic reviews was developed. J. Clin. Epidemiol. **69**, 225–234 (2016)
90. Will, C., Zimmermann, F., Ensslen, A., Fraunholz, C., Jochem, P., Keles, D.: Can electric vehicle charging be carbon neutral? uniting smart charging and renewables. Appl. Energy (2024). https://doi.org/10.1016/j.apenergy.2024.123549
91. Wu, X., Zhang, Y., Chen, Y.: A dynamic programming model for joint optimization of electric drayage truck operations and charging stations planning at ports. IEEE Trans. Intell. Transp. Syst. (2023). https://doi.org/10.1109/TITS.2023.3285668
92. Xiao, H., Zhao, J., Gao, Q., Zhang, W.: Recent advances in fast-charging lithium-ion batteries: Mechanisms, degradation, and mitigation strategies. J. Power Sources (2023)
93. Xiao, H., et al.: Recent advances in fast-charging lithium-ion batteries: mechanism, materials, and future opportunities. Chem. Eng. J. (2025). https://doi.org/10.1016/j.cej.2025.159927
94. Xu, H., Zhao, T.: Multi-objective optimization of routing and charging strategy for electric freight vehicles. Transp. Res. Part C (2020)
95. Yang, H., Xue, Y., Zhou, Z., Ge, H., Pan, Z., Sun, H.: Collaborative optimization scheduling of coupled power-traffic system in mining areas considering time-of-use price. In: 2022 IEEE 6th Conference on Energy Internet and Energy System Integration (EI2), pp. 2660–2665. IEEE (2022)
96. Yang, J., He, F., Shen, Z.J., Lin, X.: Dynamic pricing and service fulfillment of mobile charging systems with stochastic demands. Prod. Oper. Manag. (2025). https://doi.org/10.1177/10591478241310212
97. Yang, J., He, F., Shen, Z.J.M., Lin, X.: Dynamic pricing and service fulfillment of mobile depot fleets for electric commercial vehicles. Transp. Res. Part B: Methodol. (2020). https://doi.org/10.1016/j.trb.2020.05.006
98. Yang, X., Li, J., Zhao, Y.: Battery electric truck infrastructure co-design via joint optimization and agent-based simulation. Transp. Res. Part C (2021)
99. Ye, Z., Yu, N., Wei, R.: Joint planning of charging stations and power systems for heavy-duty drayage trucks. Transp. Res. Part D Trans. Environ. **134** (2024) https://doi.org/10.1016/j.trd.2024.104320, https://www.scopus.com/inward/record.uri?eid=2-s2.0-85199000098&doi=10.1016%2fj.trd.2024.104320&partnerID=40&md5=0152ed5c465e882e8af5a710320cbcad, export Date: 18 June 2025; Cited By: 2; Correspondence Address: N. Yu; Department of Electrical and Computer Engineering, University of California, Riverside, United States; email: nyu@ece.ucr.edu; CODEN: TRDTF
100. Yu, H., Sun, X., Thordarson, D.S., Solbakken, K., Solvang, W.D.: A network-based set covering model for charging station location problem: A case study in norway. In: Wang, Y., Yu, T., Wang, K. (eds.) Lecture Notes in Electrical Engineering. vol. 1154 LNEE, pp. 204–211. Springer Science and Business Media Deutschland GmbH (2024) https://doi.org/10.1007/

978-981-97-0665-5_26, https://www.scopus.com/inward/record.uri?eid=2-s2.0-85187782328&doi=10.1007%2f978-981-97-0665-5_26&partnerID=40&md5=af2680d65b8967802c11765f25c75f22
101. Yu, H., Sun, X.: Can an industry-led infrastructure development accelerate electric truck adoption? a quantitative evaluation in freight corridors. Transp. Res. Part D (2024)
102. Yu, H., Sun, X.: Can an industry-led infrastructure development strategy facilitate electric truck adoption? Transp. Res. Part D: Transp. Environ. (2024). https://doi.org/10.1016/j.trd.2024.104356
103. Yu, H., Sun, X., Thordarson, D.S., Guldbrandt, K., Zhang, Z.: A network-based set covering model for charging infrastructure planning of electric trucks considering logistics and energy constraints. Transp. Res. Part C (2024). https://doi.org/10.1016/j.trc.2024.104281
104. Yu, H., Sun, X., Thordarson, D.S., Solbakken, K., Solvang, W.D.: A network-based set covering model for charging station location problem: a case study in Norway. In: Wang, Y., Yu, T., Wang, K. (eds) Advanced Manufacturing and Automation XIII. IWAMA 2023. Lecture Notes in Electrical Engineering, vol. 1154, pp. 204–211. Springer, Singapore (2023). https://doi.org/10.1007/978-981-97-0665-5_26
105. Yv, H., Han, W.: Multi-stage battery charging scheduling optimization at battery swapping stations. In: 2024 IEEE PES 16th Asia-Pacific Power and Energy Engineering Conference (APPEEC), pp. 1–5. IEEE (2024)
106. Yv, H., Han, W.: Multi-stage battery charging scheduling optimization considering battery health for electric truck fleets. Energy Rep. (2025)
107. Zhang, M., Li, W., Yu, S.S., Li, H., Lv, Y., Shen, J.: A day-ahead self-dispatch optimization framework for load-side virtual control units participating in active power regulation of power grids. Energy (Elsevier) (2025). https://doi.org/10.1016/j.energy.2025.134791
108. Zhang, M., Li, W., Yu, S.S., Zhang, H., Zhang, P.: A day-ahead self-dispatch optimization framework for renewable-powered electric truck charging. Energy (Elsevier) (2025)
109. Zhang, Y., Gao, S.: Collaborative optimization scheduling of coupled power-traffic system in mining areas considering time-of-use price. IEEE Trans. Intell. Transp. Syst. (2021)
110. Zhao, B., Li, C.: Multi-objective optimization of charging scheduling for electric freight vehicle fleets considering battery degradation. Energy (2021)
111. Zhao, S., Ma, C., Cao, Z.: Improved multi-objective strategy diversity charging for EV fleets. Appl. Energy (2024). https://doi.org/10.1016/j.apenergy.2024.121102
112. Zhou, B., Zhang, Z., Xi, C., Liu, B.: A novel two-stage, dual-layer distributed optimization framework for hybrid energy charging. Mathematics. (2023)
113. Zhou, B., Zhang, Z., Xi, C., Liu, B.: A novel two-stage, dual-layer distributed optimization operational approach for microgrids with electric vehicles. Mathematics (2023). https://doi.org/10.3390/math11214563
114. Zhou, B., Zhang, Z., Xi, C., Liu, B.: A novel two-stage, dual-layer distributed optimization model for coordinated charging and dispatching of electric truck fleets. Appl. Energy (2025). https://doi.org/10.1016/j.apenergy.2025.125376
115. Zhou, J., Liu, D., Yang, C., Wang, Y., Yang, S., Wu, Y.: Coupling geospatial suitability simulation and life cycle carbon emissions towards uncertain optimization planning for wind-photovoltaic-hydrogen multi-energy complementary system. Energy Convers. Manage. (2024). https://doi.org/10.1016/j.enconman.2024.119103

116. Zhou, K., Wang, M., Chen, P.: Co-optimization of charging scheduling and platooning for long-haul electric freight vehicles. Appl. Energy (2022)
117. Zhu, F., Li, Y., Lu, L., Wang, H., Li, L., Li, K., Ouyang, M.: Lifecycle optimization framework of charging–swapping integrated energy supply systems for multi-type vehicles. Appl. Energy (2023). https://doi.org/10.1016/j.apenergy.2023.121759

Vehicular Networking, V2X Communications, and Cooperative Control

Comparative Study of Push and Pull Communications in a Rural VANET

Oscar Gama(✉), Antonio Costa, Maria Joao Nicolau, Alexandre Santos, Bruno Dias, and Bruno Ribeiro

Centro Algoritmi, Universidade do Minho, Braga, Portugal
{b2583,b7214}@algoritmi.uminho.pt, {costa,alex,bad}@di.uminho.pt, joao@dsi.uminho.pt

Abstract. Vehicle-to-everything (V2X) communications are expected to become increasingly common on roadways in the near future. This advancement will support the development of safety applications that significantly improve the protection of vulnerable road users (VRUs). Pedestrians are particularly exposed to accidents in rural areas, where dedicated walkways are frequently absent. This work evaluates two distinct communication paradigms - pull and push models - each implemented in both centralized and decentralized architectures, using a safety monitoring system developed for a simulated rural vehicular network. The pull model is implemented using Named Data Networking (NDN) paradigm, which inherently supports a pull-based communication approach where consumers actively request data from providers. In contrast, the push model follows a publish-subscribe scheme, where consumers subscribe previously to specific information and producers proactively deliver data to subscribers. The simulation results show that the push-based model is more efficient than pull-based model in reducing network congestion and packet loss, despite the latter's enhanced coordination capabilities. In terms of time responsiveness, both communication models performed similarly within the developed VRU safety application.

Keywords: Vehicular ad-hoc network · Named Data Networking · Vulnerable road user · Road traffic · Safety application · Simulation

1 Introduction

Many civil parishes have roads lacking sidewalks or dedicated pedestrian walking spaces. As a result, pedestrians are forced to share the roads with motor

This work is supported by national funds, through the Operational Competitiveness and Internationalization Programme (COMPETE 2020) [Project nº 179491; Funding Reference: SIFN-01-9999-FN-179491].

B. Kihei et al. (Eds.): INTSYS 2025, LNICST 717, pp. 39–58, 2027.
https://doi.org/10.1007/978-3-032-38705-9_2

vehicles, putting these vulnerable road users (VRUs) at risk. To mitigate the collision risk between vehicles and pedestrians, it is essential that both drivers and pedestrians are made aware of each other's presence. This mutual awareness enables proactive measures to be taken by both road agents, enhancing overall safety in shared road environments. With this objective, the authors are developing a monitoring system for roads in civil parishes that lack sidewalks, whereby a red alert is wirelessly transmitted when a vehicle and a pedestrian approach each other. In this safety system, communication plays a key role, as both vehicles and pedestrians wirelessly interact with Roadside Units (RSUs). To determine a suitable communication model for the system, two distinct communication paradigms were considered and evaluated in this study: the pull-based, and push-based communication models.

The pull-based communication model was implemented using the Named Data Networking (NDN) paradigm [11], which is receiver-driven and relies on the exchange of Interest and Data packets. A consumer initiates communication by sending an Interest packet that specifies the name of the desired content. A Data packet, containing the requested content, is then returned by a provider. So, NDN inherently supports a pull-based paradigm, where data is retrieved only in response to explicit requests. Each NDN node maintains three key data structures: the Content Store (CS), the Pending Interest Table (PIT), and the Forwarding Information Base (FIB). The CS serves as a temporary cache for Data packets, enabling future Interests to be satisfied locally. The PIT records Interests that have been forwarded but not yet satisfied, ensuring that returning Data packets are forwarded to the appropriate consumers. The FIB holds forwarding rules that associate name prefixes with outgoing interfaces, guiding the forwarding of Interest packets. In vehicular ad-hoc networks (VANETs), the FIB usually plays no role, as road users generally operate with a single communication interface, and packets are typically flooded [2].

The push-based communication follows a different model. Consumers (e.g., road users) subscribe to content in advance, while producers (e.g., RSUs) actively distribute information, either periodically or in response to events such as safety alerts, to subscribed consumers within their coverage areas.

The pull model offers several advantages over the push model, particularly in terms of bandwidth management and transmission control. For instance, in a network of closely spaced RSUs, Interest packets can be coordinated so that only one RSU transmits at a time. This coordination reduces channel contention and helps minimize packet collisions, resulting in a more efficient use of the wireless medium. Additionally, the pull model enables RSUs to request information from specific data providers, such as pedestrians. As this model can reduce significantly the amount of useless data transmissions to nonexistent receivers, NDN seems an appropriate model for environments with reduced number of road users, as it happens in rural environments. Moreover, NDN natively ensures data confidentiality, integrity, and authenticity, features that are essential for securing communications in VANET environments. However, the pull model presents certain limitations. As data is only sent after an Interest is received, pedestrian devices must wait for a request before transmitting, which may introduce additional delay and affect the performance of time-sensitive applications. The push model avoids this issue by allowing asynchronous transmissions.

This work aims to evaluate and compare experimentally the performance of both communication models using the safety monitoring system developed for a simulated rural vehicular network. Additionally, two system architectures were implemented: *i)* decentralized, where decisions of the alert signals for road users are made locally at the RSUs, and *ii)* centralized, where information is forwarded from the RSUs to a Fog Node for processing and decision. A centralized architecture offers advantages in some scenarios, such as, when: *i)* roads are too long for a single RSU to manage effectively the entire road; and *ii)* vehicles transitioning to another road could pose a risk to a vulnerable road user (VRU) near the intersection or crossing. In such situations, having a global view of the roads set, rather than relying only on local information, becomes essential for ensuring timely and coordinated safety decisions.

After presenting related work, the paper proceeds with the implementation description of the communication paradigms under evaluation, the setup of the test scenario, the analysis of the results, and the final conclusions.

2 Related Work

Diverse studies and projects have addressed VRU safety in VANETs by integrating communication, sensing, and data processing technologies [7], including approaches based on vehicular NDNs [3]. For example, Teixeira *et al.* [9] proposes a multi-sensing and communication approach to prevent potential accidents between vehicles and VRUs. The system uses communication based on ITS-G5 and cellular technologies, aggregated data fusion from sensors, and collision detection algorithms. Safety systems have been also developed using Vehicle-to-Pedestrian (V2P) communications, where vehicles and VRUs exchange periodically messages containing real-time status and position-related data. The communication channel could be implemented through direct ad-hoc technologies, such as IEEE 802.11p, or infrastructure-based communication, such as cellular technology. For example, Rabieh *et al.* [5] presents a two stages solution to detect a potential collision between VRUs and vehicles based on radio signal strength, and locations of vehicle and VRU exchanged within a V2P communication. Hybrid communication technologies have been used in VRU safety projects, including 5G architectures to support low-latency, high-reliability communication, as required by V2X safety applications [12].

Although many projects explored different architectures and technologies to enhance VRU protection [1,6], the comparative performance of communication paradigms - namely, push *versus* pull models - in rural environments has not been yet studied, to the best of our knowledge. This work seeks to bridge this gap by experimentally comparing both communication models in a simulated rural VANET.

3 Implementation Details

The implementation of pull- and push-based communication modes in both decentralized and centralized architecture is discussed next.

3.1 Decentralized Architecture

Push-Based Communication Mode. Let us consider multiple vehicles and pedestrians on a road monitored by an RSU. Both vehicles and pedestrians periodically transmit data packets containing their geographic positions, speeds, and timestamps, as shown in Fig. 1. The RSU receives this data and stores it in a table with the following fields: id, roadId, ruType, coordX, coordY, speed, time. Here, "id" is the identification of the vehicle or pedestrian, "roadId" identifies the road where the vehicle or pedestrian is located, "ruType" indicates whether the road user is a vehicle or a pedestrian, "coordX" and "coordY" represent the position coordinates of the road user, "speed" refers to that of the road user, and "time" is the timestamp associated with the received information. This table containing the latest data is named *CurrentDataTable*. Likewise, the RSU periodically broadcasts data packets with a table containing the state of the alert signal, and other information, of each vehicle and pedestrian on the road. Each road user must extract from the received RSU table only the information relevant to their own situation. Messages sent by road users and RSUs are completely asynchronous.

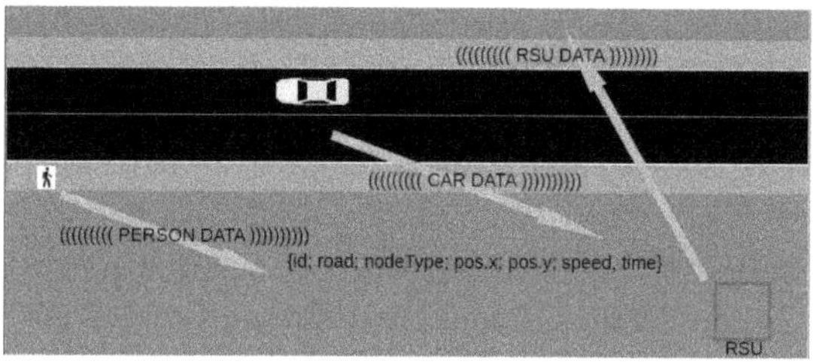

Fig. 1. Illustration of the push-based communication mode.

Any vehicle-pedestrian pair approaching each other receives a red alert. The state of this signal is determined by the RSU, based on the data received from vehicles and pedestrians on the road. In the event of an alert, the data packets also include the distance and the estimated meeting time between the approaching vehicle and pedestrian. This process is applied to all vehicle-pedestrian pairs on the road. By receiving these data packets from the RSU, the vehicles and pedestrians can take the appropriate actions based on the received alert signals.

To determine the state of the alert signal, the RSU maintains another table, named *PreviousDataTable*, to store previous data. The *CurrentDataTable* stores the most recent data received from vehicles and pedestrians, while the *PreviousDataTable* retains the second-last received data. Whenever an entry in the *CurrentDataTable* is updated, only the previous version of that entry is moved to the *PreviousDataTable*. By comparing both tables, the RSU can identify vehicle-pedestrian pairs that are approaching each other and determine the alert signals, which are stored in a table called Content Store (CS), a term borrowed from NDN. An illustrative example of this process is shown in Fig. 2. Note that the RSU can determine a road user's speed by comparing position coordinates and timestamps from both tables.

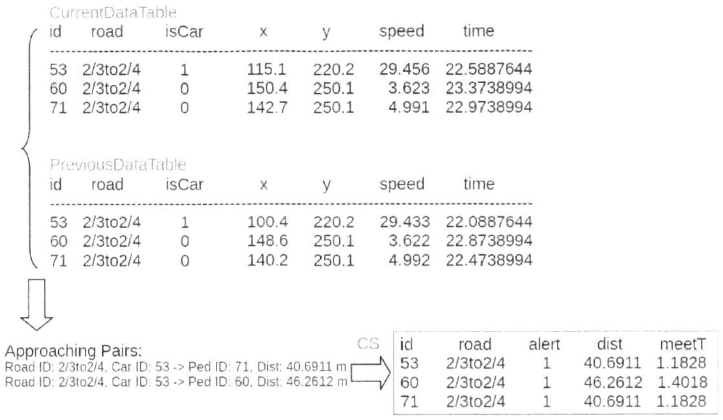

Fig. 2. An example of the CS determination process. By comparing both tables, the approaching pairs are identified, and subsequently used to construct the CS table.

Pull-Based Communication Mode. After receiving an Interest from the RSU, the roadId is checked by the road user. Only the pedestrians and vehicles in the road identified as roadId reply to the Interest, sending a Data packet with the same name of the Interest, along with the following information: nodeType, posX, posY, speed, and timestamp (Fig. 3). The meaning of these parameters were already discussed previously. As the road users are configured for not caching the content of any other node, the pedestrian's CS only holds the own road user's content. If the reply of a road user is lost because of a communication problem in the wireless channel, a more updated data packet can be sent in response to the next Interest broadcast by the RSU. The name of the Interests sent by vehicles and pedestrians has the format: /alertId/RSU/roadId/nodeType/ posX/posY/speed/time, where /alertId is the identification of the domain name of the alert service, and "RSU/roadId" is the content's directory path. The nonce and the hop limit are also sent within the Interest packet [4]. The hop limit is set to one for the vehicles not forwarding any received Interest. The RSU that should reply to the Interest can be decided from the component roadId. After receiving an Interest from a road user, the roadId is checked by the RSU. Only the RSU in the road identified as roadId replies to the Interest, sending a data packet to the road user with the same name of the Interest, along with the following information: road user identification, road identification, alert, distance, meeting time, timestamp. The meaning of these parameters were discussed previously.

The method by which the RSU determines the alert signal is the same as that described in push mode.

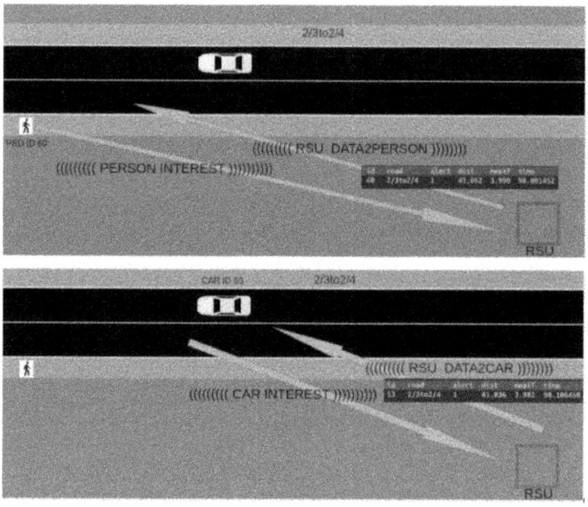

Fig. 3. Illustration of the pull-based communication mode, showing the case of a vehicle (bottom) and a pedestrian (top) communicating with an RSU.

3.2 Centralized Architecture

The push- and pull based communication modes in the centralized architecture follow similar approaches to their respective counterparts in the decentralized architecture, with one key difference: the determination of the CS content takes place at a Fog Node rather than at the RSUs. Like the RSUs in the decentralized architecture, the Fog Node also maintains a new data table (*CurrentDataTable*) and an old data table (*PreviousDataTable*). All data received by the RSUs from vehicles and pedestrians is periodically collected by the Fog Node and stored in its *CurrentDataTable*. Similarly, the *PreviousDataTable* retains the second-last received data, that is to say, whenever an entry in the *CurrentDataTable* is updated, the previous entry is moved to the *PreviousDataTable*. By comparing both tables, the Fog Node identifies vehicle-pedestrian pairs approaching each other on the same road and determines the corresponding alert signals, which are stored in a global CS table, as shown in Fig. 4.

Then, the Fog Node distributes the relevant entries of the global CS table to each RSU based on its specific area, identified by the road identification. In the case of the push-based communication mode, each RSU subsequently broadcasts the received CS table content, allowing vehicles and pedestrians to filter and extract the data relevant to them, including the state of the alert signal. In the pull-based communication mode, each RSU transmits only the information relevant to the requesting vehicle or pedestrian upon receiving the corresponding Interest packet. Consequently, in both push and pull modes, communications within the VANET work as described in their respective decentralized cases.

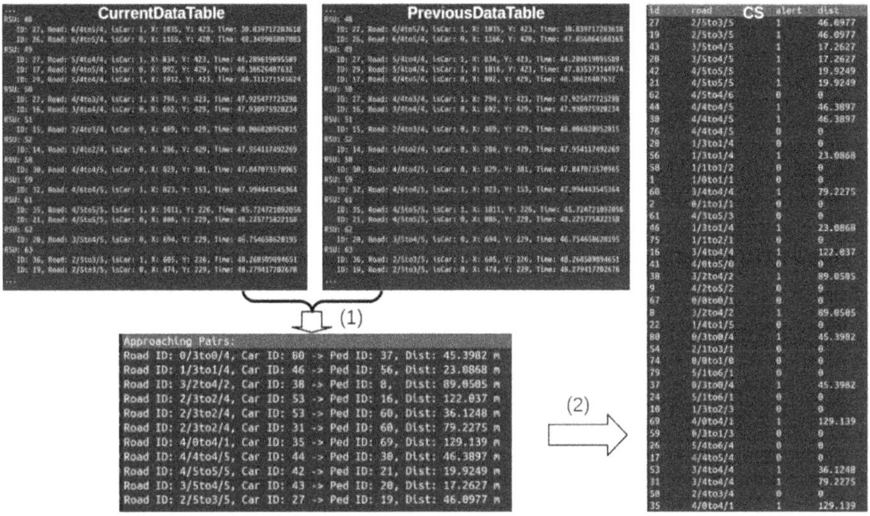

Fig. 4. Steps for CS determination. By comparing the CurrentDataTable with the PreviousDataTable, approaching pairs are identified (1) and subsequently used to construct the global CS table (2). (The displayed CS table is cropped of the "meeting time" and "timestamp" columns).

The communication between RSUs and the Fog Node can employ a technology other than IEEE 802.11p, operating over the backbone infrastructure. These communications must be fast enough to maintain the system's real-time performance. The implementation of backbone communications in the simulation scenario is detailed in the next section.

4 Test Environment

This section provides an overview of the scenario, wireless communication methods, setup parameters, and types of runs applied in the simulation tests.

4.1 Test Scenario Description

Veins-5.0 [10] was employed to implement the rural VANET environment. Veins is a vehicular network simulation framework that couples the traffic simulator SUMO (Simulation of Urban Mobility) [8] with a wireless network simulator built on the discrete event simulator OMNeT++. Veins uses the IEEE 802.11p communication standard and was extended by the authors to support pedestrian communications, as well as concurrent transmissions on multiple channel bands.

A set of contiguous horizontal segments within a grid road layout was used to evaluate both the pull-based and push-based communication modes. Eight distinct configurations were considered, each consisting of X pedestrians and X vehicles per road segment, with X ranging from 1 to 8. Figure 5 illustrates the scenario for X=2 and X=5. Values up to X=8 were used to assess the scalability of the communication system, even though some road user densities (particularly at higher X values) may exceed those typically observed in rural environments.

Each road has an RSU positioned at its midpoint. To simulate an RSU with two antennas operating on different frequencies, two RSUs - each configured with a distinct frequency - were placed side by side at the midpoint of each road. Both RSUs communicate directly with each other using internal simulator messages, not via wireless links. From an external perspective, the RSUs work effectively as a single entity with two antennas. The RSU on the leftmost road remained turned off and had no pedestrians during the simulations, as shown in Fig. 5. This was done to prevent the possibility of having X+1 vehicles on that road. So, the VANET scenario included five active RSUs.

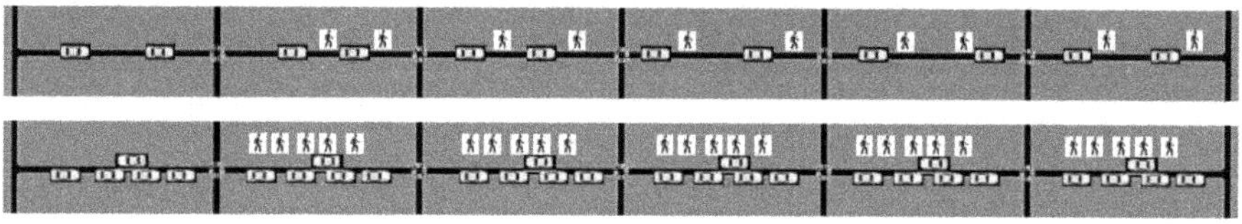

Fig. 5. The simulation scenario for X=2 (top) and X=5 (bottom). When $X \geq 5$, vehicles are present in both lanes of the road. RSUs are present at the roads midpoints.

4.2 Backbone Communications

Since the backbone infrastructure consists of fixed nodes (RSUs and the Fog Node), it is typically not a primary focus in VANET studies, more concerned with the challenges posed by dynamic and rapidly changing network conditions. However, the backbone infrastructure plays naturally a crucial role in data aggregation, coordination, and global network efficiency, in terms of latency, reliability, and scalability of a real-world deployment. Given that backbone networks are typically fast and controlled, it is reasonable to assume they can provide efficient communication between the nodes of a rural VANET and a Fog Node. Without delving into the analysis of which network technology would be most suitable for the backbone of the alert system under study, we abstract away from the specifics of the network technology. Instead, in the test scenario, backbone communications were modeled as one-hop transmissions between each RSU and the Fog Node, operating on a separate channel from the VANET. The backbone communications followed a polling mechanism, where the Fog Node sequentially queried each node for new data. Interest packets were used by the Fog Node to retrieve data from the RSUs, and likewise, RSUs used Interests to receive data from the Fog Node. This approach was also implemented in the backbone infrastructure of the push-based centralized architecture.

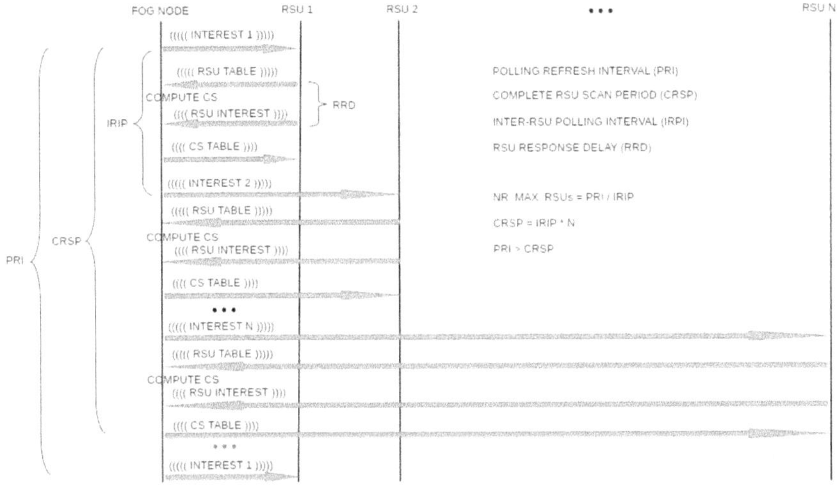

Fig. 6. Communication process between the Fog Node and the RSUs, along with the involved parameters.

Figure 6 illustrates the communication process between the Fog Node and the RSUs. The Fog Node initiates communication by sending an Interest packet to the first RSU, which responds with a data packet containing its *CurrentDataTable*. The Fog Node then updates the global CS with the received information. Following this, after a "RSU Response Delay" (RRD) to allow the Fog Node to process the data, the first RSU sends an Interest packet requesting its respective CS. In response, the Fog Node transmits a Data packet containing only the portion of the global CS relevant to that RSU. After the "Inter-RSU Polling Interval" (IRPI), measured from the moment the first Interest packet is sent, the Fog Node proceeds to communicate with the second RSU, repeating the process. This sequence continues iteratively for each RSU until the last one is reached. The total time required for the Fog Node to collect information from all RSUs is defined as the "Complete RSU Scan Period" (CRSP), which is calculated as $CRSP = IRPI \cdot N$, where N is the number of RSUs in the VANET, and IRPI is the time elapsed between two consecutive Interest packets sent by the Fog Node to the RSUs. Once the CRSP has elapsed, the process resets after a "Polling Refresh Interval" (PRI), during which the Fog Node sends a new Interest packet to the first RSU, restarting the cycle. To ensure proper operation, PRI must be greater than CRSP. Furthermore, the maximum number of RSUs supported in the VANET is determined by the unrounded integer part of $\frac{PRI}{IRPI}$. These transmissions took place on channel 11 (5.91 GHz) of the IEEE 802.11p frequency band, with a transmission rate of 24 Mbps, and a transmission power of 1 W to ensure one-hop communications.

4.3 Simulation Setup Parameters

The parameter settings used in the simulations are listed in Table 1. While some parameter names are self-explanatory, some require further clarification, as detailed next. The "maximum interference distance" defines the maximum range at which a node's transmission can cause interference to other nodes (i.e., pedestrian, vehicle, RSU), regardless of whether those nodes are within the communication range of the transmitting node, addressing the hidden node problem. The "noise floor" is the baseline level of noise that is present in the environment, even when no communication signals are being transmitted. It represents the minimum signal strength (receiver's radio sensitivity) that a node can effectively detect and process a communication packet. The "minimum power level" defines the lowest transmission power that a node can use when sending packets. The "alpha" parameter is the path loss exponent used in the radio propagation model. It determines the rate at which the signal power decays with distance from the transmitter.

In the pull-based mode (NDN), when a vehicle arrives to a road, it starts sending Interests to the RSU with a periodicity of "car interest transmission period" seconds, in order to get the alert signal and, if the alert is set up, the distance to each pedestrian in the road, as well as the time predicted for the vehicle to reach the pedestrian. In the same way, when a pedestrian arrives to a road, it starts sending Interests to the RSU with a periodicity of "person interest transmission period" seconds, in order to get the alert signal too. The RSU broadcasts Interests every "RSU interest transmission period" seconds to pedestrians and vehicles on the road it controls, allowing it to determine which users are currently present.

In the push-based mode, when a pedestrian or vehicle arrives to a road, the mobile agent starts sending data packets to the RSU with a periodicity equal to those of the Interests in pull-mode. The RSU announces the state of the alert to the cars and pedestrians with a periodicity of "RSU interest transmission period" seconds too. All packets in the VANET are affected by a "send delay limit", which represents the maximum wait time before packet transmission. The parameters "polling refresh interval", "inter-RSU polling interval", and "RSU response delay" were discussed in the previous section.

Based on the parameters in Table 1, in push mode each pedestrian and vehicle sends a data message to the RSU every 500 ms, and the RSU likewise broadcasts its alert states to all road users at the same interval. In pull mode, both RSUs and road users send Interest packets every 500 ms.

Table 1. Parameter settings used in the simulated scenario.

maximum simulation time	500 s
max. interference distance	1000 m
noise floor	-98dBm
alpha	2
radio carrier frequency	5.89, 5.91 GHz
radio transmission power	30, 300 mW
radio transmission bit rate	6, 24 Mbps
radio minimum power level	-85dBm
propagation delay	used
service channel (SCH)	not used
road length	200 m
car speed	20, 40, 60 km/h
pedestrian speed	4.7 km/h
RSU interest transmission period	0.5 s
polling refresh interval	0.05 s
inter-RSU polling interval	0.0015 s
RSU response delay	0.0005 s
car interest transmission period	0.5 s
person interest transmission period	0.5 s
send delay limit	0.050 s
wireless communication protocol	WSMP/IEEE 802.11p

4.4 Simulation Runs

To evaluate the communication performance of the push- and pull-based modes in the VANET, simulations were conducted for 500 s for each mode within the test scenario. Tests were done for both the centralized and decentralized architectures. Eight different sets of "X pedestrians + X vehicles" were considered, where X goes from 1 to 8. Tests were conducted at different vehicle speeds, transmission bit rates and power levels to evaluate their impact on communication performance. To ensure that all RSUs were properly initialized, data collection began after the first five seconds of simulation.

The following results represent the average values obtained from N simulation runs for each push- and pull based communication mode. The sample size N is indicated in the title of each graph.

5 Results Analysis

This section presents the results obtained for the following communication metrics: sent packets, received packets, packet loss, backoff overhead and message delay. Packet-related metrics are analyzed at the physical/MAC layers, while message delay is assessed at the application layer. The evaluation considers both RSUs and road users (i.e., vehicles and pedestrians), excluding the RSUs of the backbone and the Fog Node from the statistics.

Results were obtained using vehicles traveling at maximum speeds of 20 km/h and 60 km/h. After normalization, the graphs for all metrics exhibited similar patterns across both vehicle speeds, with only minor variations. This consistency is due to the number of cars and pedestrians on each road remaining fixed at X cars and X pedestrians, regardless of the vehicle speed. As soon as a vehicle or pedestrian leaves a road, a new one enters to maintain the X value constant. The only notable difference is that as vehicle speed increases, the total number of nodes participating in the VANET also increases, while the number of sent and received packets per node decreases. Nevertheless, the overall normalized average values of the metrics remained nearly unchanged. Therefore, this section presents only the graphs corresponding to the maximum vehicle speed of 60 km/h and highlights the differences observed at 20 km/h.

5.1 Communication Metrics

To assess the impact of different transmission bit rates and power levels, tests were done using 6 Mbps and 24 Mbps in combination with 30 mW and 300 mW. The results of the considered communication metrics are presented and discussed next. The graphs of sent packets and received packets are normalized to 100%, representing the values shown in the title of each graph. The dataset size (N) used to compute the average for each metric is indicated in the title of the corresponding figure ($N \geq 10$). This number is sufficient to capture the overall trend of the curves, as increasing N primarily serves to smooth the curves rather than alter their general behavior.

From a communication perspective within the VANET formed by road users and RSUs, there is no significant difference between the centralized and decentralized architectures. Indeed, both architectures exhibit similar performance across the evaluated metrics, as reflected by the overlapping curves observed in the results. For this reason, the subsequent communication-related graphs do not differentiate between the two architectures. In the graph legends, "PULL" represents the pull-based communication mode, whereas "PUSH" denotes the push-based mode.

Sent Packets. The analysis of the number of sent packets in the VANET scenario provides an important reference for assessing the impact of the two communication modes on the wireless channel occupancy. Figure 7 presents the average number of packets sent by the RSUs (right graph) and road users (left graph), using a transmission power of 30 mW and a transmission bit rate of 6 Mbps, with a vehicle speed of 60 km/h.

From the RSU graph, it is evident that the push-based communication mode result in significantly fewer packets compared to the pull-based mode. With push-based mode, the average number of sent packets per RSU remains constant as X varies (around 942 packets). In contrast, with pull-based mode, it increases linearly with X. This behavior is attributed to the increase in the number of Interests received by the RSUs, driven by the growing number of road users (pedestrians and vehicles), as both generate Interests periodically.

On the road users' side, the number of sent packets per node remains nearly constant as X varies: about 380 packets for pull-based, and 210 for push-based communication mode - approximately 1.8 times lower than in the pull-based mode. This difference occurs because road users must reply to the Interests sent by the RSUs, which is not required in the push-based mode.

As expected, increasing the transmission power or transmission bit rate has not a significant effect on the total number of packets sent. This was verified through tests conducted with 300 mW and 24 Mbps. Specifically, for RSUs, when using a transmission power of 300 mW with a bit rate of 6 Mbps, 100% corresponds to 15663 packets, which is close to the 15692 packets recorded at 30 mW. Likewise, with a transmission bit rate of 24 Mbps and a power of 30 mW, 100% corresponds to 15418 packets.

For road users, a similar trend is observed as with the graph obtained at a transmission power of 30 mW and a bit rate of 6 Mbps. In fact, using a transmission power of 300 mW at the same bit rate of 6 Mbps also results in 100% corresponding to 381 packets, which is almost identical to the outcome at 30 mW. Likewise, with a transmission bit rate of 24 Mbps and a power of 30 mW, the graph of total number of sent packets remains nearly unchanged, with 100% corresponding to 379 packets.

The presented values are the average number of packets sent per road user, considering both pedestrians and vehicles collectively. However, there is a significant difference in the total number of packets sent in average by each, as illustrated in the left graph of Fig. 7. This compares the average number of packets transmitted by pedestrians and vehicles, highlighting the disparity. For example, under the pull mode with X=8, each pedestrian sends an average of 1123 packets, while each vehicle sends only 242 packets. This difference arises because pedestrians move at a much lower speed than vehicles, causing them to remain in the simulation for a longer duration. Consequently, pedestrians have more opportunities to send messages to the RSUs compared to vehicles.

Received Packets. Figure 8 presents the results for the packets successfully received by both RSUs and road users, using a transmission power of 30 mW and a transmission bit rate of 6 Mbps, with a vehicle speed of 60 km/h. The average number of received packets is naturally higher in pull mode than in push mode, as a direct result of the greater number of transmitted packets.

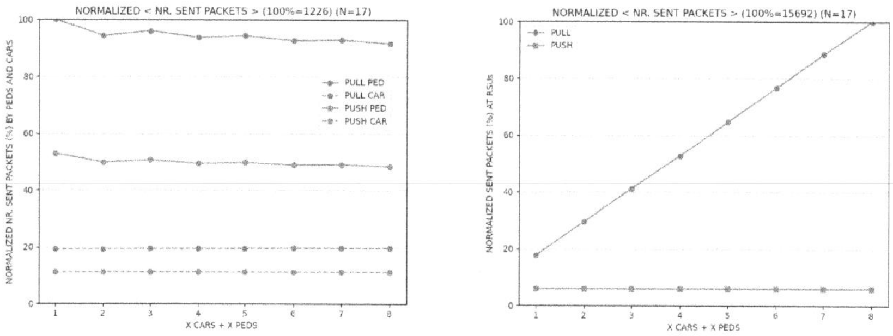

Fig. 7. Average number of packets sent partially by pedestrians and cars (left), and per RSU (right). Graphs normalized to the reference values indicated at the titles.

For RSUs, when using a transmission power of 300 mW with a transmission bit rate of 6 Mbps, the graph maintains the same shape as that observed at 30 mW. However, 100% now corresponds to 220933 packets, which nearly doubles the value observed at 30 mW, where 100% corresponds to 102486 packets. Similarly, with a transmission bit rate of 24 Mbps and a transmission power of 30 mW, the graph shape remains unchanged, but with 100% corresponding now to 37750 packets, which is almost one third of the value obtained at 6 Mbps with 30 mW.

For road users, the trend is the same. With a transmission power of 300 mW and a transmission bit rate of 6 Mbps, the graph maintains the same shape as with 30 mW, with 100% corresponding to 51582 packets (24016 packets at 30 mW). Likewise, when using a transmission bit rate of 24 Mbps with a transmission power of 30 mW, the graph shape remains unchanged, but with 100% corresponding to 10855 packets.

Thus, the number of received packets increases with higher transmission power, as the signal reaches a larger area and more nodes can receive the transmission. Conversely, it decreases with higher transmission bit rates, because the transmission range is lower.

The shape of the graphs corresponding to vehicle speed of 20 km/h exhibits minimal variation compared to those obtained at 60 km/h. In the road users graph, 100% corresponds to 43744 packets, indicating that the number of received packets increased by a factor of almost 1.8 when the speed was reduced by a factor of 3. Conversely, in the RSUs graph, 100% corresponds to 97327 packets, indicating that the number of received packets remained largely unchanged under the same speed reduction.

Packet Loss. This is a key metric in network communications, used to assess transmission reliability and quality. It also serves as an indirect indicator of wireless channel occupancy, as higher packet loss suggests increased channel congestion due to competing transmissions.

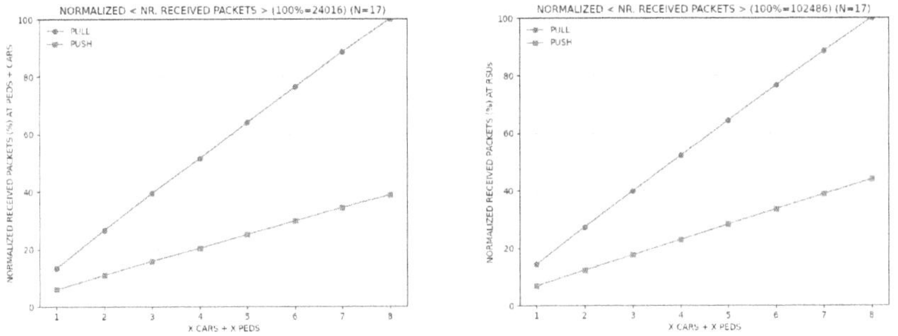

Fig. 8. Average number of packets received per road user (left), and per RSU (right).

Packet loss can occur due to various reasons, namely Signal-to-Noise and Interference Ratio (SNIR) issues and Transmission-Reception (TxRx) failures. The SNIR lost packets represent packets lost due to bit errors caused by collisions or interferences at the receiver. The TxRx lost packets occur when a packet arrives at a wireless interface precisely when another packet is being transmitted, preventing both from being successfully processed. The total packet loss at a node is the sum of SNIR lost packets and TxRx lost packets.

It is usually more convenient to express packet loss as a Packet Loss Ratio (PLR), in percentage. The PLR can be calculated using the following expression:

$$PLR = \frac{\text{LostPkt}_{\text{SNIR}} + \text{LostPkt}_{\text{TxRx}}}{\text{LostPkt}_{\text{SNIR}} + \text{LostPkt}_{\text{TxRx}} + \text{RecvdPkt}} \times 100\%$$

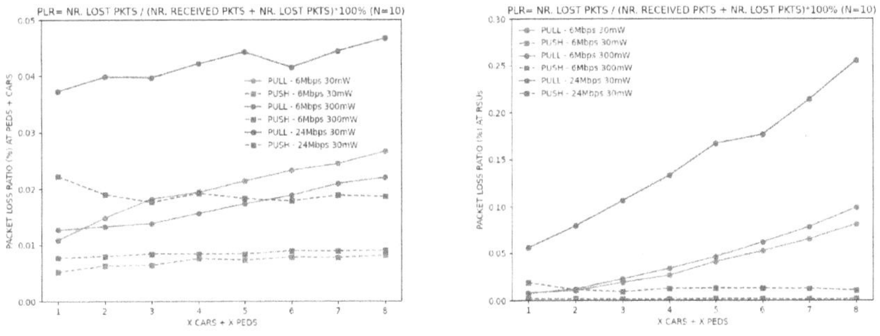

Fig. 9. Packet loss ratio for road users (left) and RSUs (right).

where $LostPkt_{SNIR}$ is the number of packets lost due to SNIR-related errors, $LostPkt_{TxRx}$ is the number of packets lost due to simultaneous transmission and reception conflicts, and *RecvdPkt* is the number of successfully received packets. This method is particularly well-suited for broadcast environments, such as

VANETs, as opposed to the traditional unicast formula: $PLR = \frac{\text{LostPkt}}{\text{SentPkt}} \times 100\%$ This traditional approach is less effective in VANETs because the sender lacks direct knowledge of how many packets were lost at each receiver. Instead, measuring packet loss from the receiver's perspective is more appropriate, allowing each node to compute its own loss based on the packets it should have received. In all performed tests, packet loss due to collisions was consistently zero across all communication modes, meaning that the SNIR component was null. So, the packet losses were all caused by TxRx problems.

Figure 9 presents the graphs obtained under three different configurations: 30 mW with 6 Mbps, 300 mW with 6 Mbps, and 30 mW with 24 Mbps. In all scenarios, the pull-based communication mode consistently presents higher packet loss ratios than the push-based mode, for both RSUs and road users. Among the road users, the PLR is on average 2.3 times higher, while for RSUs, it can exceed ten times (even 20 times in some cases) the value observed with push-based communication. The highest PLR values were observed under the 30 mW with 24 Mbps configuration. Nevertheless, the PLR remains below 0.05% for road users and below 0.3% for RSUs. It is observed that in push mode, the PLR remains relatively unaffected by variations in X, whereas in pull mode, the PLR increases with X.

At a vehicle speed of 20 km/h, the shape of the PLR graphs for both road users and RSUs remains largely unchanged compared to the corresponding graphs obtained at 60 km/h.

Backoff Overhead. This metric measures the backoffs due to busy channel. It represents the percentage of additional backoff instances relative to the number of successfully sent packets, indicating how often a node experiences contention before successfully transmitting. Since the protocol always performs a backoff before sending, even when the channel is idle, some backoff events are not due to channel contention but just part of the normal procedure, as IEEE 802.11p adopts the IEEE 1609.4 Enhanced Distributed Channel Access (EDCA) behavior. Thus, the difference TimesIntoBackoff - SentPackets represents the cases where a node attempted to send but had to backoff due to the channel being busy. Consequently, the backoff overhead (BO) is given by:

$$BO = \frac{\text{TimesIntoBackoff} - \text{SentPackets}}{\text{SentPackets}} \times 100\%$$

which expresses the percentage of retransmission backoff ratio. This metric is important in vehicular networks, particularly those using IEEE 802.11p, because the backoff process directly impacts network performance (e.g., latency) and reflects the level of the communication channel occupancy.

Figure 10 presents the results for different transmission powers (30 mW and 300 mW) and transmission bit rates (6 Mbps and 24 Mbps). As expected, the backoff overhead increases with higher transmission power since a sent packet can be listened by nodes at greater distances, leading to more frequent backoffs. Conversely, the backoff overhead decreases with higher transmission bit rates, as packets occupy the channel for shorter durations, reducing the probability of contention. Additionally, in pull mode, it is observed that RSUs experience lower backoff overhead compared to road users.

At a vehicle speed of 20 km/h, the shape of the backoff graphs for both road users and RSUs remains essentially the same as those observed at 60 km/h.

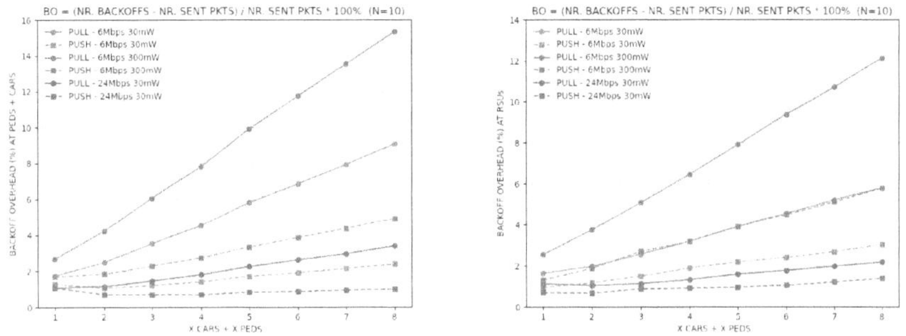

Fig. 10. Backoff overheads for road users (left), and RSUs (right).

Message Delay. The transmission delay of application-layer messages from road users to RSUs was also measured. Results showed a nearly constant average delay of approximately 25 ms, regardless of the value of X or the communication mode employed. This consistency arises from the fact that all packets are transmitted with a uniformly distributed random delay within the range [0, 50] miliseconds. Consequently, the expected average delay, derived from the mean of this uniform distribution, is 25 ms. As the dataset sizes for each communication mode is very large ($N > 500000$), the computed average delay closely aligns with the expected statistical value.

When the "send delay limit" parameter is set to zero, the average delay is approximately 0.30 ms. However, due to the high packet loss ratio observed with this setting, its use was excluded from the simulation tests.

5.2 Alert (De)activation Delay

To evaluate the time required for a vehicle to activate the alert signal indicating the presence of a pedestrian on the road, a vehicle enters the road with the alert signal unset. A pedestrian is already present in the road. The test measures the time elapsed from the vehicle's entry into the road until it receives the red alert signal from the RSU, as shown in Fig. 11 (left). The alert activation distance is calculated by simply multiplying the time delay by the vehicle's speed, which can be 20, 40 or 60 km/h.

Conversely, to evaluate the time it takes for a vehicle to deactivate the red alert signal after reaching a pedestrian, a vehicle approaches the pedestrian with the red alert active. Upon reaching safely the pedestrian, the time elapsed until the vehicle receives the green alert signal from the RSU is measured, as shown in Fig. 11 (right).

The left graph of Fig. 12 presents the results for the pull and push communication modes, showing the average delays based on a dataset of red alert activation samples (N = 315). The distance traveled by the vehicle before receiving the red alert signal is indicated on the right y-axis of the graph. For speeds of 20 km/h, 40 km/h and 60 km/h, the values read from this axis must be multiplied by one, two and three, respectively. The results, obtained using the centralized architecture, indicate no significant differences in the average red alert activation delay among the communication modes, with values ranging from 1.12 to 1.23 s. Similarly, no significant differences were observed in the decentralized architecture. Here, for instance, the push mode showed an average alert activation delay of approximately 1.1 s across the three speeds.

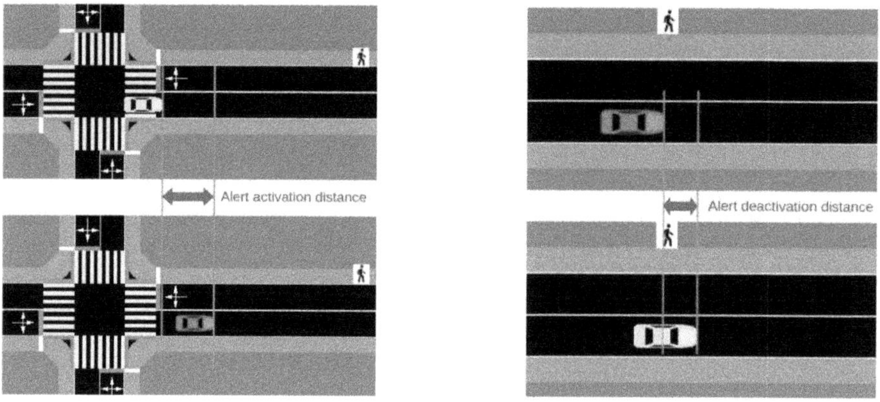

Fig. 11. Red alert activation distance (left), and red alert deactivation distance (right). (Color figure online)

The right graph of Fig. 12 presents the results for both communication modes, showing the average delays based on a dataset of red alert deactivation samples (N=150). It is noticed that, on average, deactivation is approximately 1.5 times faster than activation. This trend was also observed in the decentralized architecture.

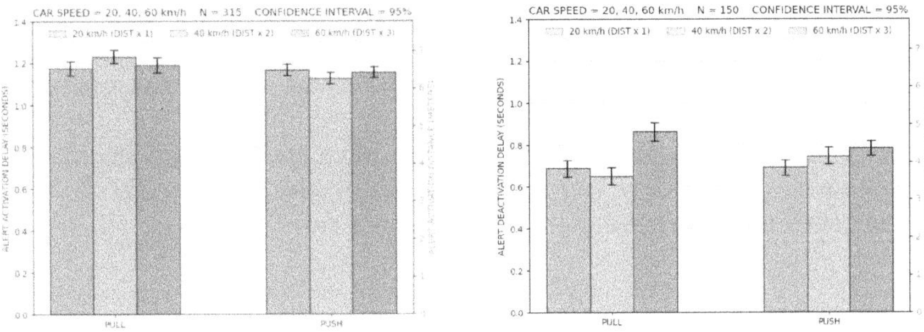

Fig. 12. Alert activation (left), and alert deactivation (right) delay or distance, for the pull and push communication modes in the centralized architecture.

The results indicate that the pull-based communication mode within a centralized architecture does not impact significantly the time responsiveness of the implemented VRU safety application when compared to the push-based mode within a decentralized architecture - which, *a priori*, is expected to offer the best responsiveness.

6 Conclusions

This work evaluated the performance of two communication modes: push and pull. The push mode adopts a publishsubscribe model, in which producers proactively transmit data to subscribed consumers. The pull mode is implemented using the NDN paradigm, which natively supports consumer-driven communication. Both push and pull modes were implemented under centralized and decentralized architectures within a simulated rural environment. Various performance metrics were analyzed, including packet transmission volume, packet reception, packet loss, backoff overhead, and message delay, under different configurations of transmission power, transmission bit rate, vehicle speed, and number of road users.

No significant differences were observed between the centralized and decentralized architectures in terms of communication performance within the VANET formed by road users and RSUs. However, the communication mode had a notable impact. The pull-based (NDN) approach introduced substantial overhead due to Interest-Data exchanges, leading to higher channel usage, packet loss, and backoff contention, especially as the number of road users increased. Conversely, the push-based model demonstrated greater efficiency, generating fewer packets, maintaining lower packet loss ratios, and exhibiting more stable backoff performance across different network loads.

Transmission power and bit rate had predictable effects, as increasing power improved reception rates and increased backoff overhead, while higher bit rates reduced contention due to decreased transmission range.

Regarding the time responsiveness of the VRU safety application, results show that the pull-based mode in a centralized architecture performs comparably to the push-based mode in a decentralized setup, despite the latter being expected to offer superior performance.

In summary, although pull-based models offer greater flexibility in terms of communication coordination, the push-based model proves more effective in reducing network congestion and packet loss in a rural VANET.

References

1. El Hamdani, S., Benamar, N., Younis, M.: Pedestrian support in intelligent transportation systems: challenges, solutions and open issues. Transp. Res. Part C: Emerging Technol. **121**, 102856 (2020)
2. Grassi, G., Pesavento, D., Pau, G., Vuyyuru, R., Wakikawa, R., Zhang, L.: Vanet via named data networking. In: 2014 IEEE Conference on Computer Communications Workshops (INFOCOM WKSHPS), pp. 410–415. IEEE (2014)
3. Khelifi, H., Luo, S., Nour, B., Moungla, H., Faheem, Y., Hussain, R., Ksentini, A.: Named data networking in vehicular ad hoc networks: State-of-the-art and challenges. IEEE Commun. Surv. Tutorials **22**(1), 320–351 (2020)
4. Project, N.D.N.: Interest packet—NDN packet format specification version 0.3 (2025) https://named-data.net/doc/NDN-packet-spec/current/interest.html
5. Rabieh, K., Aydogan, A.F., Azer, M.A.: Towards safer roads: An efficient VANET-based pedestrian protection scheme. In: 2021 International Conference on Communications, Computing, Cybersecurity, and Informatics (CCCI), pp. 1–6 (2021)
6. Sewalkar, P., Seitz, J.: Vehicle-to-pedestrian communication for vulnerable road users: Survey, design considerations, and challenges. Sensors, **19**(2), (2019)
7. Silva, R.M., et al.: Vulnerable road user detection and safety enhancement: a comprehensive survey. Expert Syst. Appl. **292**, 128529 (2025)
8. SUMO: Simulation of urban mobility (2025), https://eclipse.dev/sumo
9. Teixeira, P., Sargento, S., Rito, P., Luís, M., Castro, F.: A sensing, communication and computing approach for vulnerable road users safety. IEEE Access **11**, 4914–4930 (2023)
10. Veins: Vehicles in network simulation - the open source vehicular network simulation framework (2025), https://veins.car2x.org
11. Zhang, L., Afanasyev, A., Burke, J., Jacobson, V., claffy, k., Crowley, P., Papadopoulos, C., Wang, L., Zhang, B.: Named data networking. SIGCOMM Comput. Commun. Rev. **44**(3), 66–73 (2014)
12. Zoghlami, C., Kacimi, R., Dhaou, R.: 5g-enabled v2x communications for vulnerable road users safety applications: a review. Wireless Netw. **29**(3), 1237–1267 (2022)

Improving the Jamming Resilience of a Cooperative Adaptive Cruise Controller

Mateen Malik[1,2](✉), Ludvig Ohlsson[2], Karthik Sharma[2], Behrooz Sangchoolie[1], and Johan Karlsson[2]

[1] Dependable Transport Systems, RISE Research Institutes of Sweden, Stockholm, Sweden
{mateen.malik,behrooz.sangchoolie}@ri.se

[2] Chalmers University of Technology, Gothenburg, Sweden
{mateenma,ludohl,ravika,johan}@chalmers.se

Abstract. This paper presents the results of extensive simulations to assess the resilience of several Cooperative Adaptive Cruise Control (CACC) algorithms against barrage jamming. CACC is an extension of ACC that utilizes V2V communication to maintain string stability and appropriate inter-vehicle spacing in automotive platooning systems. We conduct simulations using four existing CACC algorithms: two employ a Constant Time Headway (CTH) policy, and two employ a Constant Vehicle Spacing (CVS) policy. CACC algorithms based on the CTH policy primarily rely on local sensor data, whereas those following the CVS policy depend mainly on information received from other vehicles via wireless communication. Our simulations show that CTH-based algorithms are resilient to barrage jamming attacks. In contrast, CVS-based algorithms are highly vulnerable due to the lack of fallback mechanisms for handling communication failures, such as the use of local sensors. However, since CVS enables higher traffic density and flow, we investigate whether a CVS-based algorithm can achieve jamming resilience comparable to that of CTH-based algorithms. To this end, we propose two extensions to one of the CVS-based CACC algorithms to improve its jamming resilience. Our results demonstrate that both extensions significantly reduce the number of collisions compared to the original CVS implementation. Notably, one of the extensions enables the CVS-based CACC algorithm to achieve the same level of jamming resilience as the tested CTH algorithms.

Keywords: Simulation-based testing · Jamming attacks · Jamming resilience · Cooperative Adaptive Cruise Control (CACC) · Platooning applications

B. Kihei et al. (Eds.): INTSYS 2025, LNICST 717, pp. 59–78, 2027.
https://doi.org/10.1007/978-3-032-38705-9_3

1 Introduction

In an era of rapid advancements in vehicular technology, Cooperative Driving Automation (CDA) has gained significant attention as a transformative approach to modern transportation. CDA relies on Vehicle-to-Vehicle (V2V) communication to coordinate the movement of vehicles, increasing traffic density and minimizing the risk of accidents. To this end, CDA relies on vehicles to exchange information about their acceleration, speed, location, direction, and other relevant information. While this exchange of data can enhance the performance of autonomous or semi-autonomous driver support systems, it also makes such systems potentially vulnerable to communication failures and jamming attacks.

This paper presents the results of extensive simulations conducted to investigate the impact of jamming attacks on several Cooperative Adaptive Cruise Control (CACC) algorithms, which provide longitudinal control of vehicles in platooning applications. Their objective is thus to maintain safe inter-vehicle distances among the vehicles in a platoon, while enforcing string stability. The string stability implies that changes in the speed of the platoon leader should not result in unbounded variations in the inter-vehicle distances as such speed changes propagate towards the end of the platoon [1,2].

The **first goal** of this paper is to evaluate and compare four previously published CACC algorithms with respect to their resilience to barrage jamming attacks. Among the four algorithms considered, Ploeg [3] and Consensus [4] implement a Constant Time Headway (CTH) control policy, whereas Plexe 1 (P1)[1] and Flatbed [6] adopt a Constant Vehicle Spacing (CVS) strategy.

The **second goal** of this paper is to present and evaluate two extensions of P1 aimed at improving the algorithm's resilience to communication failures. Thus, we want to investigate whether it is possible to achieve the same level of jamming resilience for an extended version of P1 as that achieved for Ploeg and Consensus. This investigation is partly motivated by the fact that CVS (used by P1) has an advantage over CTH (used by Ploeg and Consensus) in that it can potentially support higher traffic flows.

To conduct the simulations, we utilized a simulation engine known as ComFASE [7] [2], which models and automates barrage jamming attacks using the Veins simulation framework [9]. Barrage jamming attacks introduce high-powered noise-like energy across the entire frequency spectrum used by the target signals for V2V communication. Lichtman et al. [10] therefore classify them as non-protocol aware and non-time correlated attacks in their jamming taxonomy. Barrage jamming is of particular interest because it is relatively easy to implement and can significantly affect the target system's safety. This type of jamming does not require physical access to the target vehicle and can be executed without detailed knowledge of the message content or communication protocol.

[1] We refer to this algorithm as **P1** (Plexe 1) since it is the first CACC algorithm implemented in Plexe by Segata et al. [5]

[2] ComFASE is developed within our research group and is available for download at [8].

The remainder of the paper is organized as follows. Section 2 presents the background. Section 3 describes the P1 algorithm and its extensions: P1A and P1B. Section 4 presents the experimental setup. Section 5 presents the experimental results. Finally, Sect. 6 provides a summary of the paper and presents some future directions.

2 Background

2.1 CACC Algorithms

In this section, we present four cooperative adaptive cruise control algorithms that we investigate in this paper: P1, Flatbed, Ploeg, and consensus. These algorithms are available in the Plexe simulation framework.

The **P1 algorithm** is developed by Segata et al. [5]. P1 has a *platoon leader following* information flow topology [2]. It is designed to maintain a constant inter-vehicle distance by employing a Constant Vehicle Spacing (CVS) policy [11]. The CVS policy does not rely on the speed of the other vehicles in a platoon. Instead, it always aims to maintain a fixed distance between vehicles. To achieve this, each vehicle requires information, such as speed and acceleration, from other vehicles in order to calculate its speed and acceleration and maintain the desired spacing. P1 relies on data received from inter-vehicle communication to ensure string stability and safety of the platoon. It uses speed and acceleration data from the preceding and the leader vehicles to calculate the appropriate speed and acceleration for the following vehicle. The CVS policy does not rely on the speed of the other vehicles in a platoon. Instead, it always aims to maintain a fixed distance between vehicles. To achieve this, each vehicle requires relevant information, such as speed and acceleration from other vehicles, to calculate its speed and acceleration and maintain the desired spacing.

The **Flatbed algorithm** has a *platoon leader following* information flow topology [2]. It models the platoon as if all vehicles are virtually connected to a moving platform (the "flatbed"). Each vehicle's control decision is based on its relative motion with respect to this virtual flatbed rather than relying solely on the motion of the preceding vehicle. This model is inspired by a spring-damper system, where springs model the distance control and dampers model speed synchronization. The virtual vehicle (the flatbed) moves at a reference speed V shared across the platoon. The Flatbed uses both local sensor data and limited V2V communication. Limited V2V means that Flatbed does not require frequent data exchange from every platooning vehicle. It may only need the virtual flatbed's common reference speed V. The algorithm is primarily driven by onboard sensors and uses V2V data to enhance performance.

The **Ploeg algorithm** [12] uses a Constant Time Headway (CTH) control policy and has a *predecessor vehicle following* topology [2]. In the CTH spacing policy, the gap between vehicles depends on their speed. As vehicles move faster, the gap between them increases to maintain string stability and ensure safety. The key concept in CTH is the headway, which refers to the time it takes for the front bumper of a following vehicle to reach the same point on the road

Table 1. Comparison of CACC control algorithms.

Control algorithm	Spacing policy	Data source - Predecessor vehicle			Data source - Leader vehicle		
		Distance	*Speed*	*Acceleration*	*Position*	*Speed*	*Acceleration*
ACC	CTH*	Radar	Radar				
CACC (P1)	CVS*	Radar	Wireless	Wireless		Wireless	Wireless
Flatbed	CVS	Radar	Wireless/Radar			Wireless	
Ploeg	CTH	Radar	Radar	Wireless			
Consensus	CTH	Radar			Wireless	Wireless	

**CTH = Constant Time Headway; *CVS = Constant Vehicle Spacing.*

that the rear bumper of the preceding vehicle has just passed [11]. Algorithms that use CTH policy have the drawback of reduced traffic density as vehicles rely on their onboard sensors to maintain larger gaps between each other. The Ploeg only accepts beacons from the preceding vehicle. It ensures string stability while incorporating a fallback mechanism in case of communication losses. The Ploeg CACC enables vehicles to switch between CACC and ACC using a custom hardware gateway called MOVE.

The **Consensus algorithm** [13] also employs the CTH control policy and has a *platoon leader following* topology [2]. Consensus uses data from all vehicles to determine its desired acceleration. Consensus verifies the received information before it is used. It maintains string stability by combining information from onboard radar sensors and wireless beacons shared among vehicles. While the consensus-based model is inherently resilient to many types of communication failures, the authors note that its reliability declines significantly when the Packet Error Rate (PER) exceeds 60%. Beyond this threshold, the available information becomes insufficient for the consensus mechanism to operate effectively, leading to unreliable or potentially unsafe control outcomes. Moreover, this model does not support complex maneuvers such as overtaking, merging, and splitting (Table 1). A summary of all the above CACC algorithms is presented in Table 2.

2.2 Jamming Techniques

Previous research has investigated various jamming techniques that can interfere with wireless communication by partially degrading signals or completely blocking transmission. Lichtman et al. [14] categorize jamming attacks based on the jammer's capabilities, which include protocol awareness, time correlation, learning ability, and signal spoofing. Protocol awareness refers to the jammer's knowledge of the communication protocol. Time correlation indicates how well the attacker's signals are synchronized with legitimate signals. Learning ability allows a jammer to adapt by analyzing communication patterns over time. Lastly, signal spoofing involves faking or altering legitimate signals to mislead receivers. Different types of jamming attacks that Lichtman et al. studied in their work are summarized in Table 2.

Table 2. Summary of jamming attack types and their properties.

Jamming Type	**Description**	*Correlated in time*	*Non-correlated in time*	*Protocol aware*	*Non-protocol aware*
Barrage Jamming	Noise energy across the entire spectrum		x		x
Partial band jamming	Jamming a fraction of the entire signal		x	x	
Automatic Gain Control (AGC) Jamming	Jamming attack targeting AGC with high instantaneous power		x	x	
Equalization Jamming	Jamming any mechanisms related to equalization that compensate for distortions	x	x	x	
Synchronization Jamming	Jamming one or more synchronization signals	x		x	
Nulling	Transmitting a structured waveform so the targetâĂŹs received energy is driven as close to zero as possible	x		x	
Repeater Jamming	Barrage jamming only when there is energy on the channel	x			x

Barrage jamming is the simplest form of jamming attacks that is usually defined as the jammer continuously transmitting noise energy across the entire portion of the frequency spectrum [10] used by the IEEE 802.11p communication protocol [15]. Barrage jamming is non-protocol-aware and not time-correlated. In contrast, pilot jamming and nulling precisely target synchronization of attacker's and legitimate signals in wireless networks, which makes them more efficient while requiring knowledge of the protocols involved. Repeater jamming is time-correlated, where the jammer listens to the target's signal and transmits a modified version to disrupt the communication.

Moser et al. [16] developed a jamming method to simulate the effects of interference and signal nulling on the Cyclic Prefix (CP), a technique used to enhance signal integrity by duplicating the end portion of a signal at its beginning. These attacks aim to weaken or eliminate legitimate signals, effectively causing a denial of service.

2.3 Related Work

Part of our study is closely related to the work by Van der Heijden et al. [17] regarding the test setup for target CACC algorithms. In their work, they evaluated the jamming resilience of three CACC algorithms (P1, Consensus, and Ploeg) implemented in Plexe. Their analysis focused on denial-of-service (DoS) attacks and compared algorithms using collisions and spacing errors as primary classification metrics. Their results show that P1 is highly susceptible to jamming, with most attacks ending in collisions. In contrast, Consensus caused no collisions, while Ploeg caused only a few, reflecting greater robustness due to its reliance on local sensing. This weak performance of P1 is expected, since its implementation lacks mechanisms to handle communication failures.

Alipour-Fanid et al. [18] also examined a CACC algorithm similar to the P1. They introduced a destructive interference attack [19] on a platoon of four vehicles to assess string stability. According to their findings, attacker placement is critical, with positions near the lead vehicle resulting in the most collisions. This vulnerability increases when the leader is decelerating. Broader security issues in connected and cooperative systems are also discussed in [20].

In contrast to prior studies, our work explicitly introduces jamming resilience into a CACC algorithm operating under a CVS policy, a mode vulnerable to jamming attacks. We introduce an attack-aware communication-to-control interface that adapts the algorithm's behavior based on the quality of V2V data, specifically regarding packet loss.

3 Extentions of the P1 Control Algorithm

This section provides a detailed description of the extensions of the P1 algorithm. We selected P1 as our baseline CACC algorithm because it relies exclusively on wirelessly communicated data and lacks any fallback mechanism. Our goal is to investigate whether an algorithm based solely on a Constant Vehicle Spacing (CVS) policy can be enhanced to improve its resilience against jamming attacks. To this end, we propose two extensions of P1: P1A and P1B. We present the P1 algorithm in Sect. 3.1 before going into the details of these extensions in Sects. 3.2 and 3.3.

3.1 P1 Control Algorithm

P1 has a CVS policy to maintain a fixed distance between vehicles. In the Plexe simulations, the desired spacing of CVS can be configured, allowing flexibility in different testing scenarios. The P1 algorithm consists of an upper-level controller and a lower-level controller. The upper-level controller calculates the desired acceleration for each vehicle to maintain the predefined spacing. The lower-level controller converts this acceleration into throttle and brake commands.

Each vehicle's upper-level controller receives real-time data from the lead and preceding vehicles. This data includes the controller's desired acceleration (m/s^2), the vehicle's actual acceleration (m/s^2), speed (m/s), position (m), and the timestamp (s) indicating when the measurements were taken. The controller processes this information to compute the desired acceleration for each vehicle using Eq. 1 [5].

$$\ddot{x}_{i\_des} = \alpha_1 \ddot{x}_{i-1} + \alpha_2 \ddot{x}_0 + \alpha_3 \dot{\varepsilon}_i + \alpha_4 (\dot{x}_i - \dot{x}_0) + \alpha_5 \varepsilon_i \tag{1}$$

where,

$$\dot{\varepsilon}_i = \dot{x}_i - \dot{x}_{i-1}$$

$$\varepsilon_i = x_i - x_{i-1} + l_{i-1} + \mathrm{gap}_{\mathrm{des}}$$

In this equation, $\ddot{x}_{i\_des}$ is the desired acceleration. $\ddot{x}_0$ and $\dot{x}_0$ are the acceleration and speed of the leader, respectively, while $\ddot{x}_{i-1}$ is the acceleration of the preceding vehicle. The distance error ε_i is based on a constant desired distance [5], while $\mathrm{gap}_{\mathrm{des}}$ is the desired spacing gap between the vehicles. The length of the preceding vehicle is denoted by l_{i-1}, x_i is the position of the ith vehicle, and finally, x_{i-1} is the position of the preceding vehicle. The alpha terms in Eq. 1 are defined in Eq. 2 [5].

$$\alpha_1 = 1 - C_1, \alpha_2 = C_1, \alpha_5 = -\omega_n^2$$

$$\alpha_3 = -(2\xi - C_1(\xi + \sqrt{\xi^2 - 1}))\omega_n$$

$$\alpha_4 = -C_1(\xi + \sqrt{\xi^2 - 1})\omega_n \tag{2}$$

In Eq. 2, C_1 is a weight factor between the accelerations of the leader and the preceding vehicles (default set to 0.5), ξ is the damping ratio (default set to 1), and ω_n is the bandwidth of the controller (default set to 0.2 Hz). Except from the constant alpha factors, the first four variables in Eq. 1, $\ddot{x}_{i-1}$, $\ddot{x}_0$, $\dot{\varepsilon}_i$ and $(\dot{x}_i - \dot{x}_0)$ mainly depend on the information received from the V2V communication.

The gap error ϵ_i in Eq. 1 relies mostly on sensor data obtained from each vehicle's onboard radar, making it resilient to communication losses. In P1, the radar is primarily used to maintain a constant spacing between vehicles (`gap2pred`) that is based on the 'position of the ith vehicle and preceding vehicle' and the desired spacing ($\mathrm{gap}_{\mathrm{des}}$) as shown in Eq. 1. The radar also calculates the preceding vehicle's speed (`predSpeed`). However, unlike standard ACC systems, P1 takes the speed value from the communication network and does not utilize the radar speed for collision avoidance. This design choice of P1 allows us to assess the impact of communication failures on string stability without interference from collision avoidance mechanisms.

3.2 P1A Control Algorithm

In the P1A algorithm, the controller switches to a degraded mode of operation (degCACC) when a communication failure is detected. In degCACC mode, when a vehicle loses communication, it relies on its radar to estimate and regulate the inter-vehicle distance, instead of using data transmitted by the lead and preceding vehicles over the wireless channel.

We have developed two versions of the P1A control algorithm: P1A_a and P1A_b. In P1A_a, the fallback mechanism is activated in the case of complete communication loss, where the target vehicle receives no transmitted messages from a leader or preceding vehicles in a given time. In P1A_b, the fallback mechanism is activated on partial communication loss, when only one message, either by the preceding or the lead vehicle, is received. Note that the P1A_b control algorithm can handle partial and complete communication losses.

$P1A_a$ Control Algorithm. In the event of complete communication loss, detection is based on the calculated time difference between the current time and the time when the latest message was received. For every vehicle in the platoon, P1A_a operates by regularly comparing the current time with the timestamp of the most recently received network packet. If the time difference is smaller than 100 ms, representing the beaconing interval at which the leader vehicle transmits information, the vehicle assumes that the communication link to other vehicles is still up and continues to use the P1 algorithm. However, if the time difference is larger than or equal to 100 ms, signaling a communication loss, the vehicle switches to a fallback mechanism.

$P1A_b$ Control Algorithm. To detect partial communication loss, P1A_b checks every 100 ms if a message has been received from the preceding or the leader vehicle within that time frame. The fallback mechanism activates if either of the messages is lost. In both P1A_a and P1A_b algorithms, the transition occurs only for vehicles that experience communication failures while the rest of the platoon continues to operate under the P1 algorithm. When a message loss is detected, the system transitions[1] to retrieving the value of `predSpeed` from onboard radar instead of relying on external sensor data received from wireless communication. Additionally, the desired inter-vehicle spacing, gap_des, is increased tenfold. These modifications significantly improve the algorithm's ability to maintain string stability despite communication failures.

In summary, the fallback mechanism, *degCACC*, of the P1A algorithm is triggered in the event of complete or partial communication failures. The implementation specifically affects two key terms in Eq. 1. First, the $\dot{\epsilon}_i$ is modified to rely solely on speed data obtained from radar. Second, the gap_des is scaled up by a factor of 10, ensuring a longer vehicle spacing only for the period in which the communication is disrupted.

3.3 P1B Control Algorithm

In the P1B algorithm, the resilience of the platoon vehicles is enhanced by integrating a fallback mechanism that switches to the ACC algorithm upon detection

[1] We set the fallback trigger time to 100 ms, matching the beaconing interval at which the leader vehicle updates and transmits information.

of a communication failure. The switching mechanism is the same as P1A, which is described in the previous Sect. 3.2.

Vehicles equipped with ACC automatically decelerate to maintain a safe distance from the preceding vehicle, which is driving at a lower speed. This ACC implementation is available in SUMO. In our approach, the switchover from P1 to ACC occurs only for vehicles experiencing communication loss, while the rest of the platoon continues operating under P1. Once communication is restored, the affected vehicles seamlessly switch back to P1. The ACC determines the desired acceleration $\ddot{x}_{i\_des}$ for vehicle i by using Eq. 3 [5].

$$\ddot{x}_{i\_des} = -\frac{1}{T}(\dot{\epsilon}_i + \lambda\delta_i) \tag{3}$$

$$where$$

$$\delta_i = x_i - x_{i-1} + l_{i-1} + T\dot{x}_i$$

$$and$$

$$\dot{\epsilon}_i = \dot{x}_i - \dot{x}_{i-1}$$

In this equation, i represents the controlled vehicle, while T denotes the time headway in seconds. The term $\dot{\epsilon}_i$ captures the speed difference between the controlled vehicle and its preceding vehicle, which helps determine whether acceleration or deceleration is needed. The variable δ_i represents the deviation between the current distance to the preceding vehicle and the desired following distance. Lastly, λ is a design parameter that is always greater than zero (default value set to 0.1) [5]. The P1B algorithm we developed has fallback mechanisms similar to the one proposed by Ploeg et al. However, the P1B automatically switches to ACC upon experiencing poor communication.

P1A and P1B operate under the assumption that the timestamp included in each message, which indicates when the data is initially measured, remains accurate and has not been tampered with. This timestamp is essential for correctly aligning and interpreting the received data in time-sensitive control decisions. Although message falsification attacks could potentially violate this assumption by altering or forging timestamps, the detection and mitigation of such attacks fall outside the scope of this study and are left as future work.

4 Test Methodology and Experimental Setup

We adopt a simulation-based methodology to evaluate the CACC algorithms discussed in Sect. 3. The simulation environment integrates multiple frameworks to emulate a realistic platooning system, including cooperative vehicle controllers, vehicular dynamics, and wireless communication protocols and networks used for inter-vehicle communication. We use a four-vehicle platooning scenario to simulate a string of interconnected vehicles that accelerate and decelerate at specific frequencies. This setup allows us to test the controller under both nominal and stress conditions, such as jamming attacks. We introduce a barrage jamming attack model that uses the *'noise power'* parameter originally used in

SINR calculations on the incoming data frames at the physical layer. We analyze vehicle *deceleration profiles* and *collision incidents* to classify outcomes into four distinct categories and measure the impact. The following sections provide further details on the experimental setup and testing methodology.

4.1 Simulation Environment

To evaluate the jamming resilience of CACC algorithms, we used a simulation-based testing environment [7] that is built on four open-source simulators and an attack simulation engine:

- Plexe [5], a platooning extension of Veins that supports realistic vehicle dynamics and several CACC models that we evaluated. The framework includes the vehicle dynamics and cruise control logic. This enables the accurate simulation of longitudinal control behavior and inter-vehicle communication in platoons.
- Veins [9], a vehicular network simulation framework designed for vehicular network research, including Vehicle-to-Vehicle (V2V) and Vehicle-to-Everything (V2X). It couples OMNeT++ for simulating communication networks with SUMO for simulating vehicle movement. This allows co-simulation of realistic vehicle dynamics and wireless communication.
- OMNeT++ [21], a discrete event network simulator that is primarily used for simulating communication networks.
- SUMO [22], a microscopic traffic simulator. SUMO models the movement of individual vehicles in road networks.
- ComFASE [7], a fault and attack simulation engine. To model jamming attack scenarios. ComFASE enables the injection of barrage jamming attacks and logs detailed simulation data. The data includes vehicle speed, acceleration, deceleration, and position from SUMO, as well as communication events from Veins.

We adopt a simulation-based testing approach because it enables controlled, repeatable, and cost-effective testing of the platooning application [23]. Rajamani et al. [24] demonstrated longitudinal and lateral control of a platoon on a highway in a controlled physical (not simulation) test environment. However, we target platoons with jamming attacks that are impractical or unsafe to stage physically, potentially endangering vehicles and the surrounding environment. Simulation-based testing enables time-synchronized logging across subsystems, allowing precise analysis of system behavior and capabilities.

4.2 Driving Scenario

We define a driving scenario as the specific driving pattern (e.g., acceleration and deceleration) of the vehicles under test. The Plexe simulation framework provides various predefined platooning driving scenarios, including *sinusoidal scenario*, *braking scenario*, *platoon merge*, and *platoon split*. Our simulations use

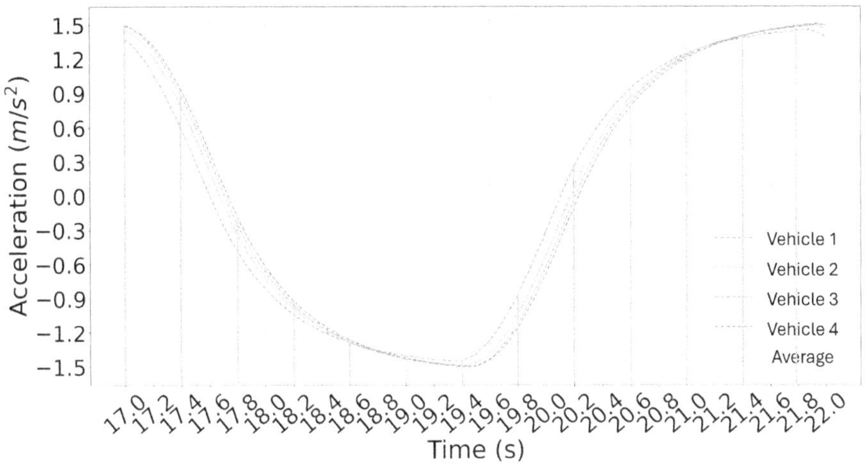

Fig. 1. A sample simulation period showing acceleration profiles of all vehicles in the platoon.

the *sinusoidal scenario* with a total simulation time of 45 s. In this driving scenario, the platoon of four vehicles drives in a sinusoidal driving pattern (see Fig. 1), where vehicles accelerate and decelerate at a fixed frequency of 0.2 Hz and an amplitude of 5.0 km/h. The lead vehicle's maximum speed is 100 km/h, and the inter-vehicle distance is kept to 5 meters.

We choose a four-vehicle platoon because it effectively captures dynamic highway conditions, including acceleration and deceleration phases, inter-vehicular dynamics, string-stability effects, and communication dependencies, which are critical for evaluating the impact of barrage jamming attacks on CACC algorithms. However, note that the platoon size is configurable in Plexe. Extending the study to larger platoon formations, such as ten vehicles or more, is a promising direction for future work to assess scalability under more severe communication load and disturbance propagation.

4.3 Attack Injection Methodology

We use the *barrage jamming* attack model from the ComFASE [7] attack model library. Our *barrage jamming* model injects equal noise across all vehicles simultaneously. However, its impact varies due to differences in the strength of the legitimate signal, which depend on factors such as the distance between vehicles and interference levels. These variations can lead to symmetric or asymmetric message losses. *Symmetric losses* affect all vehicles equally, whereas *asymmetric losses* result in uneven message losses based on distance and interference levels. Moreover, barrage jamming attacks often serve a more sinister purpose than mere denial-of-service. For example, a barrage jamming attack against a CDA application can cause vehicle collisions and traffic jams. Lichtman et al. [10]

classify *barrage jamming* as a *non-protocol-aware* attack since it neither requires prior knowledge of the communication protocol nor precision to be effective.

Table 3. Outcome categories defined to classify the simulation results.

Severe	Emergency braking activation (deceleration of higher than 5.0 m/s^2) or collisions recorded.
Benign	None of the vehicles perform an emergency braking, but at least one brakes with a rate higher than the highest deceleration recorded in the golden run corresponding to 1.53 m/s^2.
Negligible	The recorded maximum deceleration is less than or equal to 1.53 m/s^2.
Non-effective	The vehicles drive exactly as they did in the golden run.

Attack Injection Tool. We use ComFASE [7] to inject a *barrage jamming* attack into vehicle-to-vehicle communication. In ComFASE, barrage jamming is modeled by increasing the noise power used in the Veins Signal-to-Interference-plus-noise ratio (SINR) calculation. SINR captures contributions from channel interference from other channels and external noise (see Eq. 4).

$$SINR = \frac{Signal\ Power}{Interference\ Power + Noise\ Power} \tag{4}$$

Attack Model Parameters. The attack model is defined by three key parameters: *attack start time*, *attack duration*, and *attack value*. The start time specifies when the attack begins in the driving scenario, the duration sets how long it remains active, and the attack value determines its severity by specifying the additional noise injected into the channel.

Attack Injection Configuration. To configure the attack injection campaigns, we vary the attack value from 0.04 to 1×10^{-5} mW, in steps of 0.04×10^{-5} mW, resulting in 25 experiments. We selected 13 attack-start times within the range of 17.0 s to 21.9 s with a step size of 0.4 s (see Fig. 1) to analyze the vehicle's response under different driving situations, such as acceleration and deceleration phases. We conducted simulations with 11 different attack durations for each attack start time. In total, we performed 3575 attack simulations for the sinusoidal scenario, calculated as: 13 $(attack\text{-}start\ times)$*11 $(attack\ durations)$*25 $(attack\ values)$.

Outcome Classification. To classify the outcomes of our simulation results, we define four outcome categories based on the vehicles' *deceleration profiles* and *collision incidents*. These categories are described in Table 3.

Our classification scheme captures the impact of jamming attacks on vehicles in terms of collisions and severe and comfortable braking. That said, other classification metrics can also be used for assessment. Examples include time-to-collision (TTC) and inter-vehicle distance to measure the amplification of string stability disturbances along the platoon. In prior work, such as in [17], authors used ΔV to quantify collision impact, while in [25], authors use packet delivery probability as a classification metric to evaluate string stability under jamming.

Moreover, different attack surfaces may require different sets of classifications; for example, sensor spoofing or data manipulation attacks are better evaluated using perception accuracy, tracking consistency, and control deviation metrics rather than deceleration or collision alone.

5 Results

In this section, we first present the results of our simulations based on the outcome classification. We then analyze severe outcomes and their correlation with noise power levels. To do so, we evaluate and compare the jamming resilience of the P1 algorithm against its enhanced variants, P1A and P1B. Additionally, we extend our analysis by comparing the resilience of P1A and P1B with other CACC algorithms available in Plexe (Consensus, Ploeg, and Flatbed).

5.1 P1 Simulation Results

Results of the experiments conducted on the P1 algorithm show that this control algorithm is highly susceptible to jamming attacks causing communication failures (see Fig. 2); this confirms the results from the previous studies [7,17,19].

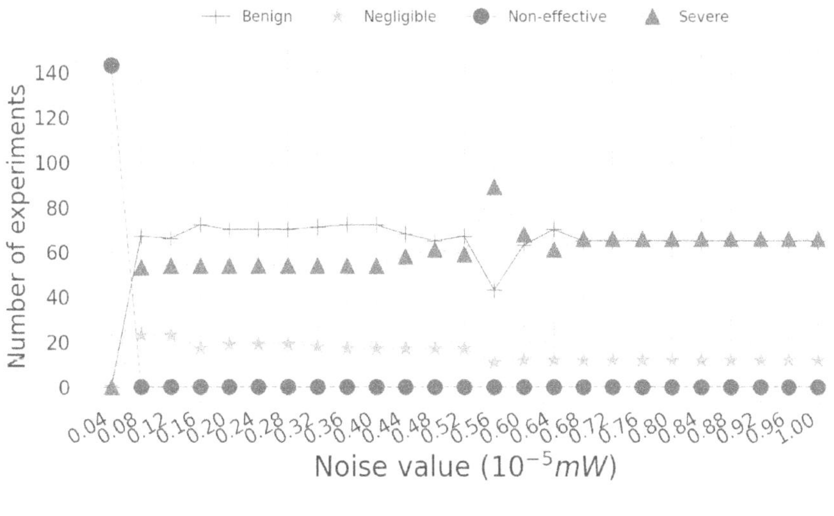

Fig. 2. Outcome distribution for the P1 algorithm w.r.t. the noise values.

The benign outcomes (represented by the blue curve) and the negligible outcomes (depicted by the orange curve) remain relatively stable across all attack values, indicating minimal variation in their occurrence. Additionally, for attack values at 0.04×10^{-5} mW, all attacks are classified as non-effective (represented by the green curve), implying that the message losses are not significant enough to deviate the trajectory of the vehicles. The proportion of severe outcomes remains relatively constant at around 42% across all noise values.

From 3575 simulation outcomes, 1475 results in collisions when P1 is subjected to barrage jamming attacks. This vulnerability of P1 is due to its lack of resilience against such attacks, as it does not incorporate any fallback mechanisms to mitigate communication failures. In the following sections, we analyze the severe outcomes of the two extensions to P1 that we presented in Sect. 3.

5.2 P1A Simulation Results

Figure 3a illustrates the impact of barrage jamming on vehicle behavior when using the P1A algorithm. We observed that the severe outcomes are substantially reduced from 42% to 14% for noise values greater than 0.62×10^{-5} mW. This is because the fallback mechanism implemented by $P1A_a$ is triggered by a complete communication loss, which is more likely to occur at higher noise values. For lower noise values, specifically the ones between 0.04×10^{-5} mW and 0.48×10^{-5} mW, certain vehicles experience partial communication failures due to the asymmetrical message losses, which do not meet the activation threshold for the $P1A_a$ fallback mechanism. Due to this reason, not all collisions are avoided when $P1A_a$ is active. However, the figure still shows significant improvements in the severe results when compared with those obtained for P1. The figure also shows a negative correlation between severe and benign outcomes. In other words, as the severe outcomes decrease, the benign outcomes increase.

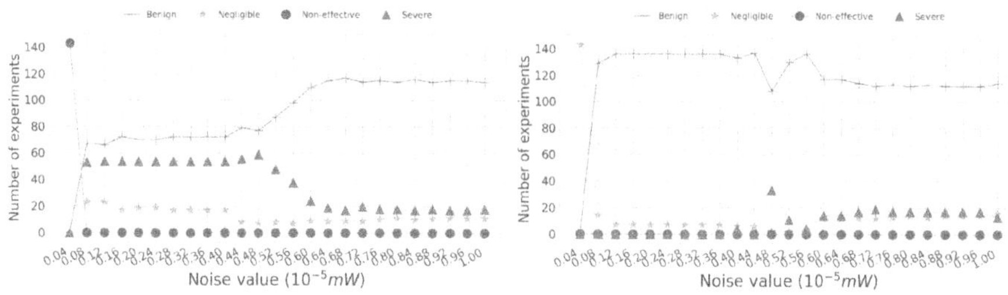

(a) Outcome of $P1A_a$ algorithm when the fallback mechanism is activated only on complete communication loss.

(b) Outcome of $P1A_b$ algorithm where the fallback mechanism covers both partial and complete communication loss.

Fig. 3. Outcome distribution for the P1A algorithms w.r.t. the noise values.

To further improve the jamming resilience of P1A, we decided to detect partial communication failures for every vehicle and activate the fallback mechanism upon such detections, in addition to those connected to complete communication failures. This enhancement ensures a more responsive CACC algorithm, reducing the likelihood of collisions under varying levels of communication failures.

$P1A_b$, that is, the improved version of P1A, significantly reduces collision incidents. As shown in Fig. 3b, no collisions are observed within the noise range of 0.04×10^{-5} mW to 0.36×10^{-5} mW. This highlights the effectiveness of the $P1A_b$ fallback mechanism, which detects both complete and partial communication failures and proactively switches to fallback mode for as long as a vehicle experiences a communication failure.

In summary, $P1A_b$, with the ability to handle partial communication failures, can significantly reduce collision incidents. The collisions are reduced to zero in 0.04×10^{-5} mW to 0.36×10^{-5} mW range (see Fig. 3b). For noise values greater than 0.48×10^{-5} mW the collision incidents are reduced to 14% from 42% compared to the P1 algorithm. The remaining 14% collisions cannot be mitigated by the P1A, as the fallback mechanism of this algorithm is not a completely redesigned one, but rather a change that uses vehicle onboard radar when the fallback activation condition is satisfied. Coming to why they occur in the first place in the P1A, we speculate that the degraded fallback mechanism itself is not sufficient to prevent collisions at such high noise values for long attack durations. To further enhance the jamming resilience against the remaining collisions, we extended P1 to P1B.

5.3 P1B Simulation Results

This section presents the outcomes of the P1B algorithm when subjected to barrage jamming attacks with varying noise levels. When the P1B algorithm is employed, the affected vehicle switches to ACC as a fallback mechanism upon detecting either partial or complete communication failure. As a result, the number of collisions is reduced to zero in both cases, as shown in Fig. 4. This significant improvement is due to ACC's sole reliance on onboard sensors for speed and distance measurement, eliminating dependence on V2V communication. These results highlight the effectiveness of using ACC as a fallback mechanism in enhancing vehicle resilience against barrage jamming attacks.

5.4 Discussions

To assess the jamming resilience of our enhanced P1A and P1B algorithms compared to other widely used CACC algorithms, we conducted targeted barrage jamming attack injection campaigns for the Consensus, Ploeg, and Flatbed. Our analysis revealed that both Consensus and Ploeg algorithms demonstrate high resilience against barrage jamming attacks, successfully avoiding collisions compared to the P1. These control algorithms incorporate robust mechanisms using onboard sensors to maintain stability and safety even during communication failures. While both Consensus and Ploeg effectively mitigated severe outcomes, Consensus recorded a higher number of benign outcomes than P1B, whereas Ploeg experienced more severe outcomes than P1B. In contrast, the Flatbed

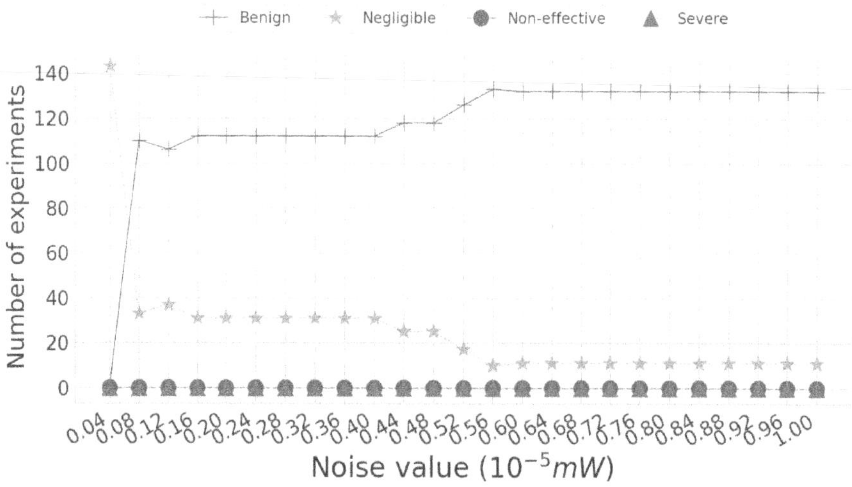

Fig. 4. Outcome distribution for when the fallback mechanism in the P1B algorithm is activated on partial communication failure.

algorithm demonstrated significant sensitivity to barrage jamming attacks, with 1764 out of 3575 simulations resulting in severe outcomes, out of which 1238 are collisions and 526 are emergency braking. Flatbed performs slightly better than the P1 in handling the impact of jamming attacks. A ranking of the CACCs based on their resilience to barrage jamming attacks is provided in Table 4.

Table 4. Ranking of CACC algorithms w.r.t the outcome classification.

Rank	CACC	Severe	Benign	Negligible	Non-effective
1	P1B	0	2947 (82.4%)	628 (17.6%)	0
2	Consensus	0	3551 (99.3%)	0	24 (0.7%)
3	Ploeg	9 (0.3%)	2840 (79.4%)	711 (19.9%)	15 (0.4%)
4	P1A	231 (6.5%)	2973 (83.2%)	371 (10.3%)	0
5	Flatbed	1764 (49.3%)	1530 (42.8%)	281 (7.9%)	0
6	P1	1475 (41.3%)	1591 (44.5%)	366 (10.2%)	143 (4%)

Our results show that it is possible to improve the jamming resilience of CVS-based CACC algorithms. However, this strengthens only one layer of defense. In real-world scenarios, the most effective approach is to adopt a *cyber-physical co-design defense methods* [18] that couples communication strategies with control-level fallbacks and sensing redundancy. For example, use frequency hopping or adaptive channel selection when one or more channels experience interference. Enable graceful degradation by switching from CACC to ACC or by increasing time gaps when packet delivery degrades. Moreover, increase reliance on local sensors while down-weighting V2V data when there is severe interference. Together, these measures provide a coordinated defense rather than isolated fixes.

6 Summary and Future Work

This paper investigates the vulnerability of CACC algorithms to barrage jamming attacks, a prevalent cybersecurity threat in V2V communication [10]. Barrage jamming disrupts V2V communication by injecting high-powered noise-like energy across the entire portion of the spectrum occupied by the vehicle with 100% duty cycle in time [10], effectively hindering the reliable exchange of information critical for CACC functionality.

As our focus is on assessing the jamming resilience of CACC algorithms, we chose the P1 (Plexe 1) algorithm due to its heavy reliance on V2V communication to maintain close inter-vehicle spacing and platoon string stability. In contrast, other CACC algorithms, such as Consensus and Ploeg, are more jamming resilient but use onboard sensors and maintain larger inter-vehicle distances based on the platoon's speed. P1 relies on V2V communication to obtain the distance and speed of the predecessor and the leader vehicle, making it particularly susceptible to jamming attacks. To enhance its jamming resilience, we extended it to P1A and P1B. The difference between P1A and P1B algorithms is that the former uses degCACC fallback while the latter uses ACC fallback. $P1A_a$ accounts for *symmetrical message losses*, while $P1A_b$ accounts for both *symmetrical* and *asymmetrical message losses* when triggering their fallback mechanisms. Symmetrical losses refer to complete communication failures, where no messages are received, while asymmetrical losses result from partial communication failures, where only some messages are lost.

P1A incorporates the vehicle's onboard radar and increases inter-vehicle spacing to mitigate the impact of communication failures. In contrast, P1B implements the ACC algorithm as a fallback mechanism, which triggers in the event of V2V communication failures. $P1A_b$ significantly improves jamming resilience, reducing the number of severe outcomes. $P1A_b$ mitigates collisions caused by both partial and complete communication failures. However, while significantly improved, P1A cannot entirely prevent collisions during complete communication failures. P1B, however, achieves the most robust performance by leveraging the ACC as a fallback mechanism, thereby eliminating severe incidents in both partial and complete communication failures.

Our study demonstrates that the jamming resilience of CACC algorithms based on a constant vehicle spacing (CVS) policy can be effectively enhanced through the careful design of fallback mechanisms and their activation criteria. We also subjected the Consensus, Ploeg, and Flatbed to barrage jamming attacks to provide a comparative analysis. Our findings reveal that the Consensus and Ploeg algorithms exhibit greater jamming resilience than the Flatbed and P1 algorithms. However, the P1B is the best-performing algorithm against barrage jamming attacks in terms of collision mitigation and reduced benign outcomes. Moreover, P1B achieves both closer inter-vehicle spacing, resulting in higher traffic density, and string stability. In contrast, the Consensus and Ploeg algorithms maintain string stability by allowing variable spacing between vehicles, which adjusts based on the platoon's speed.

As part of our **future work**, we design and implement a physical testing methodology for barrage jamming attacks to validate the attack model we used in the simulations. This validation helps bridge the gap between simulation-based and physical testing. Studying inter-vehicle distance variations, the impact of collisions caused by jamming attacks, and evaluating the impact of sensor failures used by algorithms like ACC is beyond the scope of this work, but represents a valuable direction for future research.

Acknowledgments. The work of this paper has been done in the context of the AGRARSENSE and SUNRISE projects. AGRARSENSE is supported by the Chips JU and its members, including top-up funding from Sweden, Czechia, Finland, Ireland, Italy, Latvia, Netherlands, Norway, Poland and Spain under grant agreement no. 101095835. SUNRISE is funded by the European Union's Horizon Europe Research and Innovation Actions under grant agreement no.101069573. The views expressed in this document are the sole responsibility of the authors and do not necessarily reflect the views or position of the European Commission. Neither the authors, the AGRARSENSE consortium, nor the Chips JU are responsible for the use which might be made of the information contained in this document.

References

1. Peppard, L.: String stability of relative-motion PID vehicle control systems. IEEE Trans. Autom. Control **19**(5), 579–581 (1974)
2. Shuo Feng, Yi Zhang, Shengbo Eben Li, Zhong Cao, Henry X. Liu, Li Li.: Definitions and analysis methods: string stability for vehicular platoon control. Annu. Rev. Control, **47**, pp. 81–97 (2019)
3. Ploeg, J., Semsar-Kazerooni, E., Lijster, G., van de Wouw, N., Nijmeijer, H.: Graceful Degradation of Cooperative Adaptive Cruise Control. IEEE Trans. Intell. Transp. Syst. **16**(1), 488–497 (2015)
4. Santini, S., Salvi, A., Valente, A.S., Pescapè, A., Segata, M., Cigno, R.L.: A consensus-based approach for platooning with Intervehicular communications and its validation in realistic scenarios. IEEE Trans. Veh. Technol. **66**(3), 1985–1999 (2016)
5. M. Segata, S. Joerer, B. Bloessl, C. Sommer, F. Dressler, and R. L. Cigno. Plexe: A Platooning Extension for Veins. In 2014 IEEE Vehicular Networking Conference (VNC), pp. 53–60 (2014)
6. Ali, A., Garcia, G., Martinet, P.: The Flatbed Platoon Towing Model for Safe and Dense Platooning on Highways. IEEE Intell. Transp. Syst. Mag. **7**(1), 58–68 (2015)
7. M. Malik, M. Maleki, P. Folkesson, B. Sangchoolie, and J. Karlsson. ComFASE: a Tool for Evaluating the Effects of V2V Communication Faults and Attacks on Automated Vehicles. In :52nd Annual IEEE/IFIP International Conference on Dependable Systems and Networks (DSN2022), pp. 1–12. IEEE (2022)

8. RISE Dependable Transport Systems. ComFASE GitHub repository for code access. https://github.com/RISE-Dependable-Transport-Systems/ComFASE/, Accessed: 2025 Oct 2025
9. Sommer, C., German, R., Dressler, F.: Bidirectionally Coupled Network and Road Traffic Simulation for Improved IVC Analysis. IEEE Trans. Mobile Comput. (TMC) **10**(1), 3–15 (2011)
10. Lichtman, M., et al.: A communications jamming taxonomy. IEEE Secur. Priv. **14**(1), 47–54 (2016)
11. Kalogiannis, K.: Investigating Attacks on Vehicular Platooning and Cooperative Adaptive Cruise Control. KTH Royal Institute Of Technology **12**(2020). PhD thesis
12. J. Ploeg, B.T.M. Scheepers, E. van Nunen, N. van de Wouw, and H. Nijmeijer. Design and experimental evaluation of cooperative adaptive cruise control. In :2011 14th International IEEE Conference on Intelligent Transportation Systems (ITSC), pp. 260–265 (2011)
13. S. Santini, A. Salvi, A.S. Valente, A. Pescapè, M. Segata, and R. Lo Cigno. A Consensus-based Approach for Platooning with Inter-Vehicular Communications. In: d34th IEEE Conference on Computer Communications (INFOCOM 2015), pp. 1158–1166. IEEE (2015)
14. T. C. Clancy. Efficient OFDM denial: pilot jamming and pilot nulling. In: 2011 IEEE International Conference on Communications (ICC), pp. 1–5 (2011)
15. Jirjees, A.: Vehicular ad hoc networks: growth and survey for three layers. Int. J. Electr. Comput. Eng. (IJECE) **7**(1), 271–284 (2017)
16. J. A. Mahal, C. Shahriar, and T. C. Clancy. Emulated cp jamming and nulling attacks on sc-fdma and two novel countermeasures. In: MILCOM 2015 - 2015 IEEE Military Communications Conference, pp. 275–280 (2015)
17. R. Van der Heijden, T. Lukaseder, and F. Kargl. Analyzing Attacks on Cooperative Adaptive Cruise Control (CACC). In: 2017 IEEE Vehicular Networking Conference (VNC), pp. 45–52 (2017)
18. Alipour-Fanid, A., Dabaghchian, M., Zeng, K.: Impact of Jamming Attacks on Vehicular Cooperative Adaptive Cruise Control Systems. IEEE Trans. Veh. Technol. **69**(11), 12679–12693 (2020)
19. M. Maleki, M. Malik, P. Folkesson, B. Sangchoolie, and J. Karlsson. Modeling and evaluating the effects of jamming attacks on connected automated road vehicles. In: 2022 IEEE 27th Pacific Rim International Symposium on Dependable Computing (PRDC), pp. 12–23. IEEE Computer Society (2022)
20. Amoozadeh, M., et al.: Security vulnerabilities of connected vehicle streams and their impact on cooperative driving. IEEE Commun. Mag. **53**(6), 126–132 (2015)
21. OMNeT++. OMNeT++ Manual. https://doc.omnetpp.org/omnetpp/manual/. Accessed: 30 Oct 2025
22. P. Alvarez Lopez, M. Behrisch, L. Bieker-Walz, J. Erdmann, Y.-P. Flötteröd, R. Hilbrich, L. Lücken, J. Rummel, P. Wagner, and E. Wießner. Microscopic Traffic Simulation using SUMO. In: The 21st IEEE International Conference on Intelligent Transportation Systems, pp. 1–12. IEEE (2018)
23. M. F. Drechsler, G. Seifert, J. Peintner, F. Reway, A. Riener, and W. Huber. How Simulation based Test Methods will substitute the Proving Ground Testing? In: 2022 IEEE Intelligent Vehicles Symposium (IV), pp. 903–908 (2022)

24. Rajamani, R., Tan, H.-S., Law, B.K., Zhang, W.-B.: Demonstration of integrated longitudinal and lateral control for the operation of automated vehicles in platoons. IEEE Trans. Control Syst. Technol. **8**(4), 695–708 (2000)
25. Alipour-Fanid, A., Dabaghchian, M., Zeng, K.: Platoon stability and safety analysis of cooperative adaptive cruise control under wireless Rician fading channels and jamming attacks. arXiv preprintarXiv:1710.08476 (2017)

Inter-technology Application Data Exchange Based on Advertisement Packets

Mariam Issa[1(✉)], Paul Couderc[2], and Jean-Marie Bonnin[3]

[1] Université de Rennes, Rennes, France
mariam.issa@inria.fr
[2] Centre INRIA de l'Université de Rennes, Rennes, France
paul.couderc@inria.fr
[3] IMT Atlantique / IRISA, Rennes, France
jean-marie.bonnin@irisa.fr

Abstract. Ephemeral, spontaneous interactions like proximity-based alerts and short-lived data exchanges, are becoming central to mobile and IoT applications. Traditional wireless systems, designed for persistent connections, are often too heavy for these use cases. We present in this paper a unified framework that enables opportunistic, connectionless data exchange across BLE and Wi-Fi advertisements. Our system, deployed on ESP32 hardware, serves as a proof-of-concept and as a performance study for a middleware that abstracts low-level protocol details. It requires no firmware modification and supports local and context-aware communication. We provide an in-depth experimental study highlighting the power consumption, coexistence constraints, and design trade-offs of concurrent BLE and Wi-Fi beaconing. Our results demonstrate the framework's potential for enabling seamless, standard-compliant inter-technology communication tailored to ephemeral applications.

Keywords: Ephemeral Interaction · Local Communication · Dataspaces · Association-less Communication · Wi-Fi Beacon Stuffing · BLE Advertisements

1 Introduction

Recently, digital interactions have become increasingly ephemeral by nature. Examples could range from pop-up data sharing between smartphones in proximity, to dynamic alerts from wearables or sensors in a smart city such as Vehicle-to-Pedestrian (V2P) warnings. Many of these emerging use cases are characterized by short-lived, spontaneous, and context-dependent exchanges of information. The ephemeral nature [1] of these interactions requires systems that can exploit

B. Kihei et al. (Eds.): INTSYS 2025, LNICST 717, pp. 79–99, 2027.
https://doi.org/10.1007/978-3-032-38705-9_4

brief encounters and minimal user involvement. We can imagine such systems as being analogous to a whiteboard or a graffiti board. Anyone could freely read or write.

Such ephemeral and spontaneous interactions are not only useful in IoT or mobile applications, but also form the foundation of awareness services in Intelligent Transport Systems (ITS). In this domain, technologies such as ITS-G5 or IEEE 802.11p (also referred to as 802.11 OCB) enable direct, connectionless broadcasts of Cooperative Awareness Messages (CAMs) to support safety-critical applications [2].

Traditional wireless systems, designed for long-lived, stable sessions, often impose unnecessary overheads and complex setups that are ill-suited for these scenarios. Therefore there is a need for communication paradigms that are tailored to the requirements and constraints of the short-lived nature of the interactions.

In this direction, association-less or connection-less communication paradigms [3–5] were investigated. They are based on the idea of embedding messages within discovery packets. Such packets are broadcasted whenever a node wants to announce itself. At the receiver side, scanning is done to extract the messages. Such paradigms proved to be efficient and served the purpose of context-related ephemeral interactions. Two popularly existing technologies that implement this concept are based on Wi-Fi and BLE, in particular Wi-Fi Beacon Stuffing [3], and BLE connectionless mode [6]. They have been applied in different application domains due to their abundance and ease of use. Through communicating over advertisements, they showed a high potential in different application domains including Vehicle to Pedestrian (V2P) safety systems [7,8], sensor networks [9] and proximity based messaging [10]. Bluetooth Low Energy (BLE) and Wi-Fi have become the dominant wireless standards in today's smart devices, powering a wide range of applications from mobile sensing to ubiquitous computing and IoT deployments. While each technology offers unique advantages such as BLE's low-power and latency, and Wi-Fi's higher throughput and coverage; the challenge of enabling direct, connectionless application data exchange between heterogeneous BLE and Wi-Fi devices persists [11]. From a networking perspective, bridging the gap between these protocols has required centralized gateways, protocol conversion layers, or connection-oriented handshakes , often adding latency, complexity, and extra energy cost to the system [12]. Moreover, the adoption of such approaches at an application level has been limited by the lack of simple, high-level software models and APIs that abstract away the low-level details. Existing works often propose systems that are complex to replicate or to use. Many reported complexities come from facing constraints on system parameters due to device specificity, vendor limitations, and developmental complexities.

Given the increasing need for inter-technology communication in diverse, real-world deployments, and motivated by the growing integration of both BLE and Wi-Fi in off-the-shelf devices, we extend our prior work in [5] to develop a unified, standard-compliant, broadcast framework that seamlessly spans both protocols. A unified framework that bridges BLE and Wi-Fi broadcast offers several practical advantages: it enhances reliability through redundancy and enables wider coverage and adaptability. However, practical implementation reveals important trade-offs and technical hurdles.

The proposed framework provides application-level data filtering and secure payload integrity using a lightweight hashing mechanism, supporting ephemeral, local, and battery-efficient scenarios, where classic connection-based approaches are unsuitable or too costly. Furthermore, our work delivers a detailed experimental characterization of radio coexistence, power consumption, and interoperability challenges when concurrently using BLE and Wi-Fi in beacon mode.

Unlike prior solutions (that will be discussed in the following section), which focus on high-level device discovery or rely on platform-specific APIs, our framework supports low-level, cross-radio broadcast over off-the-shelf ESP32 without requiring firmware modification. To our knowledge, this is the first work to evaluate dual-radio ephemeral messaging with integrated hash-based filtering on constrained hardware, in a connectionless environment.

In summary, our contributions can be summarized as follows:

- We design and implement an opportunistic broadcast framework enabling seamless, direct data exchange between BLE and Wi-Fi devices via advertisement packets, with no radio firmware modification required.
- We deploy the system on commercial ESP32 hardware and conduct an in-depth empirical study, characterizing energy consumption, payload constraints, and the interplay between BLE and Wi-Fi advertisement scheduling.

The rest of this paper is organized as follows: Sect. 2 provides a background and some of the related works. Section 3 details the proposed framework. Then the experimental procedure is explained in Sect. 4. Finally, the paper is concluded in Sect. 5.

2 Related Work

Understanding the basis of connectionless communication, or as we refer to it in our works as "Association-less Communication" is crucial for developing applications tailored to ephemeral interactions. In this section, we first present a brief background on BLE connectionless mode and on Wi-Fi Beacon Stuffing. We then review some works that compare Wi-Fi against BLE advertisements. Having such comparisons is important to identify the strengths and weaknesses of one technology over the other. This is particularly necessary when deciding on which technology to use for a certain application use-case. Finally, we provide some papers that have implemented frameworks that bridge the gap between the two technologies, allowing inter-technology communication. We summarize such frameworks, and discuss their limitations in terms of standard compliance, hardware requirements, and real-world applicability.

2.1 Association-Less Communication

A technology that allows devices to communicate without prior configuration, to act in a decentralized manner, to discover and broadcast data to devices in range, while not being affected by node mobility, would be a suitable enabler for association-less communication. Wi-Fi and BLE are two strong candidate technologies to implement association-less communication. This is motivated by the facts that both of the technologies allow to embed data within packets that are already exchanged among communicating peers. The data to be embedded is small, and usually acts as some state description, some identifier, or even could correspond to some sensor measurements. The other fact is the reliance on existing technologies without the need to deploy and install new equipment or apply major changes to the current infrastructure. For the case of Wi-Fi Beacon Stuffing, the Wi-Fi is accessible in a highly ubiquitous and dense manner. For BLE beacons, they come at a low cost and are easy to deploy and move. In what follows we provide a brief background on the operation of the two technologies.

Wi-Fi Beacon Stuffing. In Wi-Fi infrastructure mode, when an AP wants to announce its existence, it sends periodically beacon frames. Client devices perform active or passive scans to detect these beacons. In default mode of operation, advertisement beacons are broadcasted by APs every 100ms [14]. Wi-Fi Beacon Stuffing was first introduced in [3]. This was motivated by the fact that these beacons are exchanged among APs and clients despite of their connection state. Despite the fact that beacon stuffing has been proposed more than 15 years ago (2007), it continues to be a strong candidate for utilization in recent applications. Different implementations of this technique include embedding of the messages within the SSID (Service Set Identifier), BSSID (Basic Service Set Identifier) or the VSIE (Vendor-Specific Information Element) fields of beacon frames, a.k.a management frames.

BLE Connectionless Mode. BLE has gained popularity for its energy efficient and short range capabilities. It stands as a promising candidate wireless technology to realize association-less communication. The terms used in literature to describe such mode of communication are "Connectionless communications" or "Legacy advertising". BLE was designed with the attempt to support ephemeral interactions, due to the introduction of two modes: connectionless and connection-oriented modes. In the connection-less, the broadcaster (advertiser) periodically sends advertising packets to any device able to receive them. On the other side, the observer (scanner) continuously scans for these advertisements at periodic intervals [15]. Advertisement packets can take four forms: *Connectable undirected Advertising*, *Connectable Directed Advertising*, *Non-connectable Undirected Advertising* or *Scannable Undirected Advertising* [16].

Our previous work in [4] presents a comprehensive experimental comparison between Wi-Fi Beacon Stuffing and BLE Connectionless mode as mechanisms for association-less (connectionless) communication in smart environments. The paper focuses on evaluating both technologies on the ESP32 platform in terms of power consumption, delivery rate, and range, with the goal of guiding technology selection for ephemeral and local interactions.

To illustrate the trade-offs, consider two typical scenarios: (1) An event-driven alarm system in a smart building, where battery-powered sensors must signal emergencies rapidly and efficiently to nearby nodes; here, BLE's low power consumption and rapid advertising intervals are essential. (2) A video surveillance network, where Wi-Fi Access Points and always-powered cameras periodically announce status and metadata; here, Wi-Fi's greater payload and range, combined with data persistence on always-on devices, are more valuable.

Our results show that while Wi-Fi Beacon Stuffing theoretically offers higher payload capacity and longer transmission range, it suffers from higher power consumption compared to BLE. BLE connectionless mode, on the other hand, demonstrates lower power consumption and easier implementation thanks to standardized APIs, making it more suitable for energy-constrained and time-critical applications, despite its smaller payload and shorter range.

In [17], the authors conducted a comparative study of Wi-Fi and BLE advertisements for their application in vehiclepedestrian collision warning systems. The authors evaluated these technologies in various real-world scenarios, focusing on their reliability and responsiveness for proximity detection. Their findings showed that BLE outperformed Wi-Fi in terms of signal stability, responsiveness, and robustness under different environmental conditions. As a result, the study concludes that BLE is the most suitable technology for vehiclepedestrian safety applications due to its consistent performance and operational resilience.

In [18] the authors establish an experimental comparison between BLE and Wi-Fi. They compared the power consumed when advertising BLE beacons, to that by Wi-Fi when advertising as an access point and when it is listening in scanning modes. They demonstrate that BLE advertisements indeed consume significantly less power than Wi-Fi beacons. However, they do not establish a comprehensive study that takes into consideration the different parameters such as advertising and scanning intervals.

Despite the fact that the mentioned works compared Wi-Fi to BLE advertisements while providing important design insights, however they did so for each technology independently. To our current knowledge, there is no work that attempts to evaluate the performance of having both technologies operating concurrently on the same hardware for the same application.

We now provide some of the works that have proposed solutions for communication among technologies.

The work of [12] proposes BL-Fi, a combined BLEWi-Fi link-management protocol designed to enable high-data-rate sensing on low-power devices such as the ESP32-S3. Their system uses BLE solely for lightweight signaling, opening connections, waking up Wi-Fi, and shutting it down. While delegating all bulk data transmission to custom low-level Wi-Fi frames. Despite the fact that this work is not for connection-less settings, the protocol achieves high throughput but remains operationally complex due to multi-stage BLE negotiations, cross-radio synchronization, and linear scaling in network size.

Table 1. Comparison of middleware frameworks with respect to cross-technology support, connectionless operation, and constrained hardware/energy awareness.

Framework	Cross-Technology Support	Connectionless Mode	Energy / Constrained HW
Hyrax [19]	Wi-Fi Direct, Bluetooth, Cellular	No (mesh, connection-based)	No energy eval; mesh routing & persistent Wi-Fi Direct ⇒ likely power-hungry.
MIM [20]	Wi-Fi Direct, Bluetooth (D2D)	No (group sessions)	No energy eval; sync/group mgmt. ⇒ moderatehigh power use.
WARBLE [21]	BLE, Wi-Fi, vendor hubs (adapters)	No (bindings rely on connections)	No energy eval; continuous discovery & binding updates ⇒ likely energy-consuming.
Venice [11]	Wi-Fi, Bluetooth, NFC, QR, RFID	No (abstracted connections)	No constrained-HW eval; smartphone/PC focus ⇒ moderate energy, not optimized.
Our Framework	**BLE Advertisements + Wi-Fi Beacon Stuffing (ESP32)**	**Yes (native broadcast)**	**Explicitly evaluated on ESP32 with current profiling; lightweight & power-aware for ephemeral use.**

Wi-BLE [13] proposes a sophisticated multi-radio architecture that orchestrates BLE and Wi-Fi under IPv6 to achieve both high throughput and low energy consumption in multi-hop IoT networks. The system introduces MABLE, a custom BLE-based ad-hoc routing protocol. Then leverages these BLE routes to wake up Wi-Fi radios, construct optimized Wi-Fi paths, and dynamically switch between radios based on traffic load. Because it spans IPv6, routing, radio wake-up, BLE connection management, Wi-Fi route construction, and kernel-level driver modification, Wi-BLE is significantly complex both architecturally and operationally. The protocol introduces extra control-plane and connection-management overhead

The authors in Hyrax [19] propose a inter-technology platform that enables mobile devices to form self-organizing mesh networks, automatically discovering and connecting over Wi-Fi-Direct, Bluetooth, or similar radios to relay data without central infrastructure.

The design and implementation of the Multiuser Interaction Middleware (MIM) presented in [20], enables direct interaction among mobile devices in close proximity using D2D communication technologies, such as Wi-Fi Direct and Bluetooth.

WARBLE [21] introduces a middleware that abstracts away the complexity of discovering, selecting, and interacting with heterogeneous IoT devices by providing developers with high-level programming constructs called selectors and bindings. Developers use selectors to specify the functional and contextual requirements for devices (such as device type, user proximity, or location), and WARBLE automatically discovers and manages connections to matching devices, regardless of their underlying protocol (e.g., BLE, mDNS).

Finally, the Venice framework in [11] introduces a device-to-device (D2D) abstraction that leverages established communication channels such as Wi-Fi and Bluetooth to enable seamless communication between heterogeneous devices, including Android smartphones and computers. The authors address the lack of a unified data link layer for direct mobile interactions, proposing Venice as a middleware that abstracts the heterogeneity of underlying physical channels and platforms. Venice's main contribution is its channel abstraction, which enables developers to implement D2D communication without concerning themselves with the specifics of each hardware stack. The framework supports multiple communication technologies and is implemented using Flutter, allowing cross-platform compatibility.

Table 1 compares the middlewares against our framework with respect to cross technology support, connectionless mode support, and energy awareness. The comparison shows that while Hyrax, MIM, WARBLE, and Venice all support multiple radios, they remain connection-oriented and overlook energy constraints, leading to high power usage. In contrast, our framework uniquely adopts a connectionless broadcast model (BLE advertisements + Wi-Fi beacon stuffing) and is explicitly evaluated on constrained hardware, demonstrating lightweight and energy-aware operation suited for ephemeral interactions.

These works however, highlight the need for a middleware-based approach. A middleware can act as a mediator between applications and underlying network technologies, offering several advantages. First, it enables arbitration: the middleware can observe requests from multiple applications, group events where appropriate, and schedule advertisements to minimize channel contention and optimize energy use—capabilities not possible with direct, application-level use of network APIs. Moreover, a middleware can adapt to performance goals such as low latency (for urgent events), data persistence (for reliable status propagation), and spatial coverage, depending on the interaction pattern and node capabilities.

As advertisement-based communication can lead to channel saturation, especially in dense environments, middleware-driven arbitration and scheduling are crucial to ensuring robust, efficient, and scalable ephemeral communication. For example, a middleware might aggregate several sensor alerts into a single BLE advertisement, or prioritize urgent events for Wi-Fi beacon stuffing, balancing latency, coverage, and power.

While existing middlewares such as Hyrax, MIM, WARBLE, and Venice have demonstrated the feasibility of inter-technology communication by abstracting lower-layer details and providing unified interfaces for heterogeneous radios, they primarily focus on high-level device discovery, dynamic mesh formation, or generalized data exchange across platforms, using established connection-oriented protocols (e.g., Wi-Fi-Direct, Bluetooth Classic, mDNS). In contrast, our work targets seamless inter-technology data exchange in the connectionless (association-free) domain, specifically leveraging BLE advertisements and Wi-Fi Beacon Stuffing on resource-constrained hardware such as the ESP32. This work is a preliminary step for developing a middleware that achieves application level seamless communication between Wi-Fi ad BLE devices, using advertising. Nevertheless, a performance study is necessary to decide on the tradeoffs that will result from having such a system.

Our contributions bridge the gap between theoretical middleware abstractions and practical, energy-aware deployments on real IoT platforms, enabling reliable and interoperable inter-technology broadcast without requiring connections or platform-specific drivers. Thus, the motivation and novelty of our work. In the next section, we provide and discuss the proposed framework.

3 Inter-technology Framework for Ephemeral Dataspaces over BLE and Wi-Fi

In [5], we proposed a BLE-only framework for connectionless application data exchange, supporting hash-based filtering and lightweight encoding, and demonstrated that for the same application, it offered energy benefits over GATT-based approaches. This work has emphasized the necessity of elevating data exchange to the application layer, decoupling it from the constraints of connection-oriented or packet-level operations. By implementing a shared ephemeral dataspace, the proposed framework allows applications to both publish and retrieve relevant information in a manner that is directly addressable at the application level. This enables dynamic filtering based on the actual data content—such as application codes or service types—instead of relying on lower-layer identifiers.

Another critical aspect of the framework is its independence from MAC address-based identification and filtering. As device MAC addresses are increasingly randomized for privacy and security reasons, any protocol dependent on MAC-based addressing becomes unreliable for robust and privacy-preserving communication. Our protocol instead leverages content-based identification, using embedded application codes and cryptographic hashes to unambiguously classify and filter packets. This approach ensures that only the data pertinent to a given application or use case is processed, while completely abstracting away device identities at the network level. As a result, the system supports fully anonymous, association-less, and context-driven interactions, and enables a more flexible and scalable means of coordinating transient data exchanges among heterogeneous devices. In this we extend our lightweight BLE-based framework proposed, to support seamless communication over both BLE advertisements and Wi-Fi Beacon Stuffing. By leveraging both radios on the ESP32 platform, our protocol enables nodes to broadcast and retrieve application data without requiring connections or MAC-based addressing, while providing redundancy and broader device compatibility. We study the performance of such extension in terms of the power profile of the new combined system.

Framework Overview: For the sake of space, we provide the extended framework in a summarized form. We adopted a publish-subscribe (pub/sub) paradigm for our middleware because it provides strong decoupling between data producers and consumers. In pub/sub, applications publish events or data without knowledge of which nodes (if any) will receive them, and consumers subscribe to the data types or events they are interested in—this is known as process decoupling. By contrast, low-level approaches based directly on network message APIs (such as sockets or direct BLE/Wi-Fi advertising APIs) require explicit knowledge of endpoints and tight coupling between sender and receiver. They lack these decoupling properties and typically do not scale well for complex, event-driven, or dynamic IoT scenarios.

Adopting a data-mediation approach abstracts away the details of network communication, enabling modular, flexible, and robust applications. This is especially important in inter-technology systems where data should mediate interactions, not device addresses or static connections.

Nodes act as providers (publishers) or requesters (scanners), broadcasting or listening for context-relevant data simultaneously over both BLE advertisements and Wi-Fi beacons. Nodes operating in shared physical and temporal proximity can receive application data over either radio. In this proof of concept study, both radios are always on.

Unified Packet Structure: For both BLE and Wi-Fi, we use a common, technology-agnostic packet format (Fig. 1), enabling cross-decoding and unified verification. Packets are structured as follows:

- **Role (2 bits):** Indicates node function (e.g., provider/requester).
- **Application Code (2 bits):** Classifies the application (e.g., warning, sensor, etc.).
- **Generic Field (18 bits):** Reserved for extension and future use.
- **Payload (up to 11 bytes):** Encodes application data.
- **Hash Code (2 bytes):** MurmurHash2 output for membership verification.

Note that the total packet size in this extension becomes 16 bytes instead of 31 bytes. This will be discussed in details in the experimental results section.

Wi-Fi Beacon Encoding: Using the Vendor Specific Information Element (VSIE) in Wi-Fi management frames theoretically allows arbitrary data to be embedded in beacon or probe response frames, providing a higher payload capacity and avoiding some SSID limitations. However, in practice, most off-the-shelf mobile devices, laptops, and embedded Wi-Fi stacks do not expose VSIE content to user applications via standard APIs. Scanning applications on Android, iOS, Windows, and even many Linux distributions can typically only read basic AP fields like SSID, BSSID, RSSI, and security settings—while VSIE data remains inaccessible or filtered for security and privacy reasons. This lack of universal support and programmability makes VSIE unsuitable for widely-deployable inter-technology broadcast solutions, especially when the target devices and apps must operate without root or special drivers. As a result, encoding data in the

SSID, despite its constraints, remains the most interoperable option for such scenarios.

Directly embedding raw bytes into the Wi-Fi SSID for data broadcasting proved unreliable, as most operating systems, drivers, and device APIs treat the SSID as a printable string and truncate or mangle any non-UTF-8 or non-printable characters—especially null bytes—resulting in corrupted or incomplete payloads at the receiver. To ensure portability and reliability across all platforms, we encode the payload as a printable hex string before embedding it in the SSID. This approach universally preserves the data but reduces the maximum effective payload by half, since each byte now requires two characters. Despite this limitation, hex encoding is the most robust and widely adopted solution for SSID-based data channels in practical inter-technology scenarios.

Verification Mechanism: Upon receiving a packet (from BLE advertisement or extracted from Wi-Fi SSID), the node decodes the payload and recomputes the hash over all fields except the appended hash. A match validates membership in the ephemeral dataspace and ensures the integrity of the transmitted message (see Table 2). This process is technology-agnostic and works identically for both radios. Therefore, the scanner application will see the same data twice if it has both Wi-Fi and ble enabled.

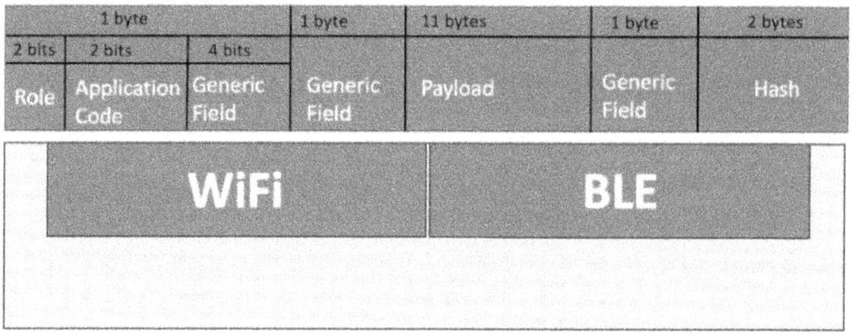

Fig. 1. Unified advertisement packet structure for BLE and Wi-Fi.

Table 2. Unified Packet Field Definitions (BLE/Wi-Fi)

Field	Description	Size
Role	Node role (provider/requester)	2 bits
App Code	Application class	2 bits
Generic Field	Reserved/Extension	18 bits
Payload	Application data	up to 11 bytes
Hash Code	MurmurHash2 output	2 bytes

With a 2-byte hash, the probability of collision remains below 2% for up to 50 concurrent transmitters, as was shown in [5]. If needed, the generic field can be partially reallocated to further extend the hash and reduce collision risk.

The integrated framework is implemented on ESP32, enabling devices to advertise and scan on both radios within a single application cycle. Application logic is agnostic to the underlying transport: data can be published or received via either BLE or Wi-Fi, and filtering is performed using the same hash-based verification.

4 Experimental Procedure

When enabling inter-technology communication (e.g., BLE advertisements or Wi-Fi using beacon stuffing) over the same hardware, it's not obvious how the combined use of these radios would affect the power draw and the overall output. There may be interactions, overhead, or unexpected inefficiencies that would only appear in real deployments. It is thus important to establish a performance study as a function of the input system parameters. In this section, we study the power consumption in terms of the current draw of the combined system, and compare it to a BLE only system. We then study the effect of the advertisement interval on the current draw of the combined system. Also, we study the boundary cases where the advertisement intervals of BLE and Wi-Fi are equal.

Table 3. Summary of experimental parameters.

Parameter	Value / Notes
BLE advertising interval	40 ms (baseline); varied in scheduling experiments
Wi-Fi beacon interval	100 ms (baseline); varied in scheduling experiments
Payload size (BLE & Wi-Fi)	11 bytes
Hash length & filtering	2-byte hash prefix, validated at receiver (hash validation)
Number of nodes	2 ESP32 nodes (1 advertiser, 1 scanner)
Measurement tool	Joulescope JS220, inline 5V supply

We implement the system using ESP WROOM32D. ESP32 is used within the scope of this project due to its cost-effectiveness, large community, and flexible development environment. Moreover, it features integrated Wi-Fi and dual-mode Bluetooth capabilities, thus allowing a dual functionality between the two techniques on the same hardware. The current draw is measured using a Joulescope JS220 Precision Energy Analyser[1]. We setup the experiment as shown in Fig. 2,

[1] https://www.joulescope.com/products/js220-joulescope-precision-energy-analyzer.

where the esp's are connected to the joulescope one at a time, and a DC power supply of 5V is used. Table 3 summarizes the parameters used throughout the experiments.

During the implementation of concurrent BLE and Wi-Fi advertisement and scanning on the ESP32, several challenges stemming from the hardware radio-sharing model were encountered. Notably, while it was possible to advertise over both BLE and Wi-Fi simultaneously, attempting to scan for BLE advertisements and Wi-Fi access points in parallel led to conflicts, system instability, or the need to explicitly suspend one stack to allow the other to function. This limitation is enforced by the ESP-IDF, which restricts simultaneous scanning operations to prevent resource contention on the shared radio.

To address this, the implementation adopted a serialized approach, whereby BLE scanning and Wi-Fi scanning were performed sequentially rather than concurrently. This was accomplished in the application code by explicitly deinitializing and disabling the BLE stack after a BLE scan completed, before reinitializing the Wi-Fi stack for scanning, and vice versa. By carefully orchestrating the radio usage and respecting the necessary setup sequences between BLE and Wi-Fi operations, it was possible to collect data from both technologies within a single application cycle, albeit at the cost of increased latency and complexity in the software flow. This solution enables inter-technology applications, but highlights the need for careful radio management on platforms with shared wireless hardware.

4.1 Functional Validation

The main questions to be answered in this subsection is whether both BLE and Wi-Fi advertisements could be received and decoded? Is the hash-based filtering working correctly?

For verifying the successful reception and data decoding, we use a dummy data vector to be advertised.

Figure 3 presents the terminal output of a inter-technology BLE-Wi-Fi broadcast and scan session on the ESP32, demonstrating the successful end-to-end propagation and detection of a custom payload across both radios. The BLE scan result at the top highlights the reception of a raw advertising packet (43 FF FF 56 31 37 32 35 38 30 34 2E 33 31 79 8C), which is recognized as belonging to the shared dataspace, and the relevant data is extracted and displayed. Subsequently, in the Wi-Fi scan output, the same payload is observed after being hex-encoded and broadcast as an SSID, which is then decoded back into its original byte sequence (43 FF FF 56 31 37 32 35 38 30 34 2E 33 31 79 8C). The system correctly identifies this SSID as part of the shared dataspace and parses out the advertised role, app code, and the intended data payload. The highlighted sections illustrate the seamless interoperability between BLE and Wi-Fi advertisement and scanning, validating the framework's ability to carry and verify a custom payload end-to-end across both radio technologies, while also confirming the effectiveness of the encoding/decoding and hash-matching process (Fig. 4).

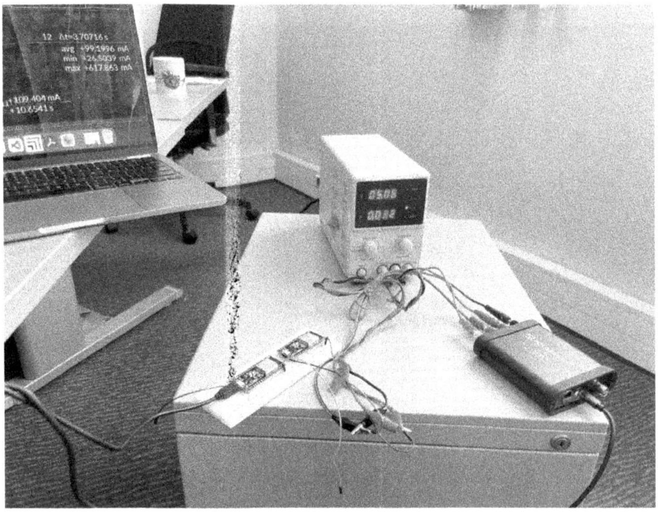

Fig. 2. Setup.

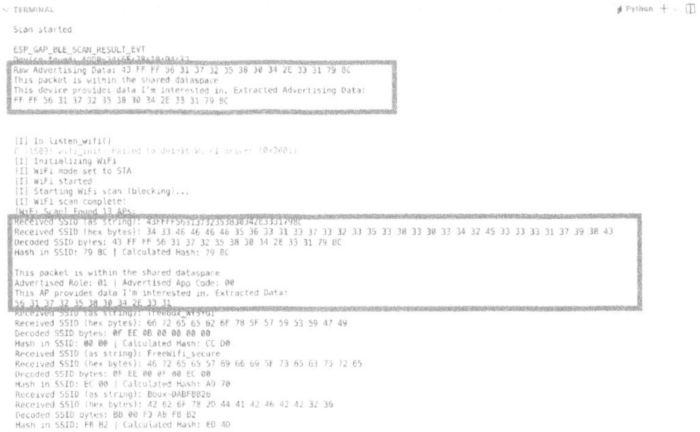

Fig. 3. Output.

4.2 Power Profiling

Power consumption remains a critical metric for wireless communication systems, especially in mobile and wearable devices that are power-constrained (Fig. 5). Thus, knowing the actual power consumption under different modes (BLE-only, Wi-Fi-only, BLE+Wi-Fi concurrently, etc.) is essential for choosing the best technology for a given application scenario, optimizing the battery life, and informing the decision on when and how to activate both Wi-Fi and BLE, or to operate only one of them. Finally, we provide some insights on the performance and tradeoffs of having both radios to operate concurrently.

[b]0.7

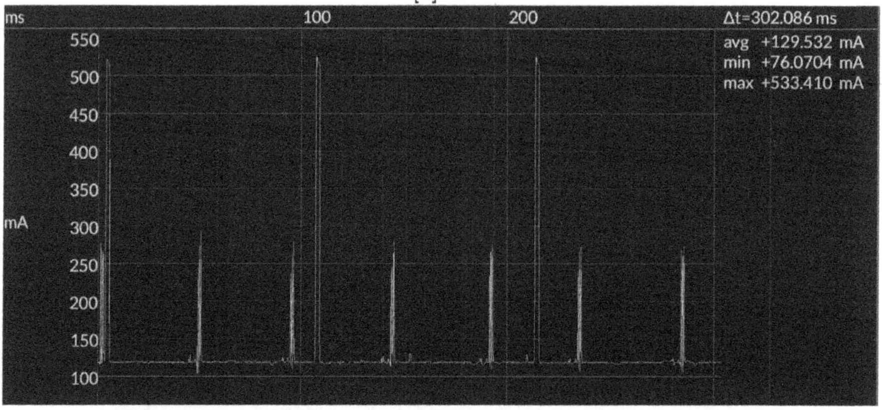

Fig. 4. Advertiser BLE+Wi-Fi

[b]0.7

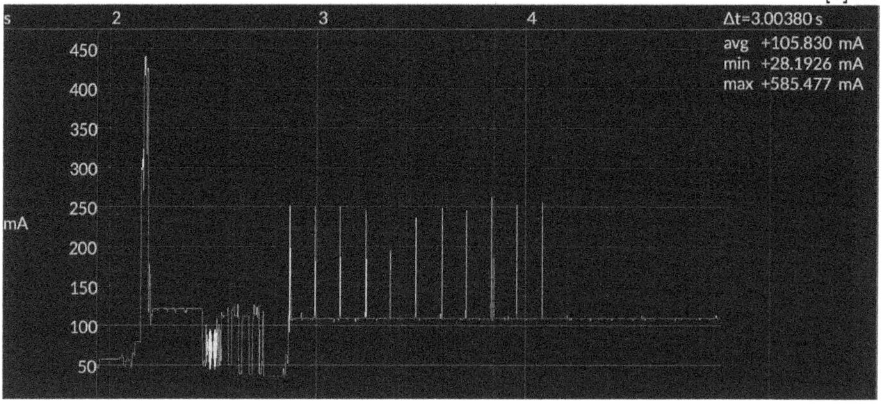

Fig. 5. Scanner BLE+Wi-Fi

To begin with the power profile study, we measure the average currents for advertising and scanning for BLE and for the composite system (Wi-Fi+BLE). We put the results in Table 4.

Examining in Table 4, the measured current values for BLE only and BLE+Wi-Fi operation modes reveal several important trends. When BLE operates alone and over the advertisement interval of 40ms, the average current consumption during advertising is 54.37 mA, with a minimum of 38.59 mA and a peak of 317.32 mA. For scanning over the scan interval of 40ms, the BLE-only mode shows an average of 87.39 mA, a minimum of 36.95 mA, and a maximum of 191.58 mA.

In contrast, when BLE operates concurrently with Wi-Fi (BLE+Wi-Fi), the average current during advertising rises substantially to 129.6 mA over the adver-

Table 4. Current consumption (mA) comparison for BLE and Wi-Fi in different operating modes.

	BLE Only		BLE+Wi-Fi	
	Adv	Scan	Adv	Scan
Avg (mA)	54.37	87.39	129.6	97.47
Min (mA)	38.59	36.95	76.45	26.3
Max (mA)	317.3	121.58	545.31	559.28

tising interval of Wi-Fi (100ms), and scanning jumps to 97.47 mA over the whole scan period. The minimum currents also increase, with advertising at 76.45 mA and scanning at 26.3 mA. Most strikingly, the maximum observed current surges to 545.31 mA for advertising and 559.28 mA for scanning—nearly doubling the peaks seen in BLE-only mode.

Then, to zoom over what is happening with more details, we trace in Fig. 6(a,b) the current of the advertiser and the scanner while operating both Wi-Fi (AP mode) and BLE. In Fig. 6-a, we observed the current trace for 300ms. I.e, 3 advertisement intervals of Wi-Fi. Each is advertising at a distinct interval—100 ms for Wi-Fi and 40 ms for BLE. The current trace shows a steady baseline of around 100–150 mA, punctuated by periodic spikes. The largest spikes, reaching up to approximately 533 mA and occurring every 100 ms, correspond to Wi-Fi advertisements, which are known for their higher power consumption. In between these, smaller yet regular spikes appear at roughly 40 ms intervals, representing BLE advertisements that consume less current but occur more frequently. The overall average current is elevated due to these periodic transmissions, and the pattern confirms that both Wi-Fi and BLE are operating at their configured intervals without overlap. This demonstrates the additive impact of concurrent wireless advertising on power consumption.

Figure 6-b shows the current trace of the scanner. As will be explained in the observations subsection, we operate the scanner sequentially between BLE and Wi-Fi. Over a 3-second window, the trace starts with a brief idle phase at a low baseline (around 50 mA), followed by a large spike peaking at nearly 585 mA when scanning activity begins—likely corresponding to the initial activation or a Wi-Fi scan, which typically draws significant current. After this spike, the current settles to a higher idle level (100150 mA), reflecting the system being in an active scanning state. Then, a sequence of periodic smaller current spikes at regular intervals can be seen. These repeated pulses represent the bursts of activity as the device performs active scanning for BLE advertisements. Throughout this period, the overall average current consumption is elevated (about 120 mA). Then, as Wi-Fi scanning starts as can be seen for the 11 spikes, the current is elevated to 250mA for each spike. This indicates the significant energy cost of Wi-Fi scanning. We can deduce the cumulative energy impact of concurrent wireless scanning for both Wi-Fi and BLE, where the baseline never fully returning to the pre-scan idle level during active operation.

The comparison between the power profiles of the advertiser and scanner in the dual mode, clearly demonstrates that scanning (especially Wi-Fi scanning) is more energy-intensive than advertising, both in average and peak current, due to longer radio-on times and the need to listen across multiple channels. Furthermore, while BLE advertising produces short, low-power pulses, Wi-Fi advertising and scanning both introduce significant current surges, but scanning sustains a higher power envelope for longer durations. This comparative observation underlines the asymmetry in power costs between broadcast and receive operations across BLE and Wi-Fi, which is a key design consideration for inter-technology middleware.

4.3 Scheduling Effects

Having observed the elevated power profile for the composite system, we experiment with varying the advertising intervals. This is to explore how does the alignment (or misalignment) of BLE and Wi-Fi advertisement intervals affect performance of the system.

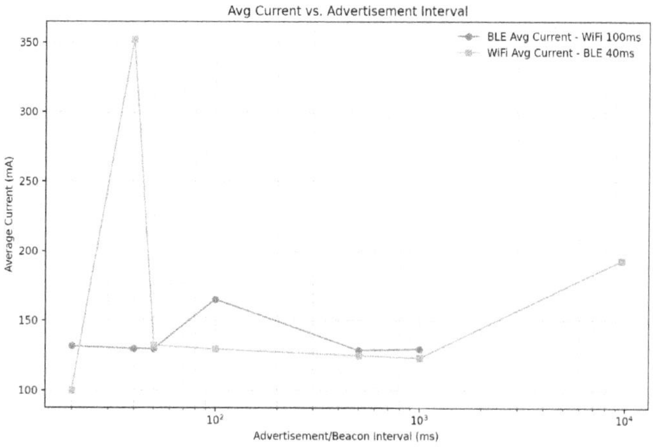

Fig. 6. Average current drawn as a function of different advertisement periods.

Figure 6 plots the average current drawn as a function of different advertisement periods. This experiment was done over two steps. In the first step, we fixed the Wi-Fi advertisement interval to 100ms (the default value), and varied that of the BLE. The measured current was always between 128mA and 131mA, except for one point where the advertising period of BLE matched that of the Wi-Fi, i.e., 100ms. At this instant, the average current raised to 165.122mA, indicating that a higher amount of processing was being done at the esp. In the next step, we repeated the same procedure but with fixing the advertisement interval of the BLE this time to 40ms, and varying that of the Wi-Fi. We observed that when the advertisement intervals matched at 40ms, the average current raised significantly to 352.216 mA, almost doubling its value. Also, we observed that the peak current raised up to 2.52A. This indicates that more processing is being done at the esp, and even higher than the case of BLE. Then it was observed that the current drawn started to decrease as the advertisement interval was going beyond 100ms. We can deduce from this figure that Wi-Fi affects the energy cost for a more frequent advertising, more than BLE.

Finally, to understand better what is happening when the advertisement intervals match (at 40ms, and at 100ms), we traced the current trace for these values in Figs. 7 and 8.

[b]0.7

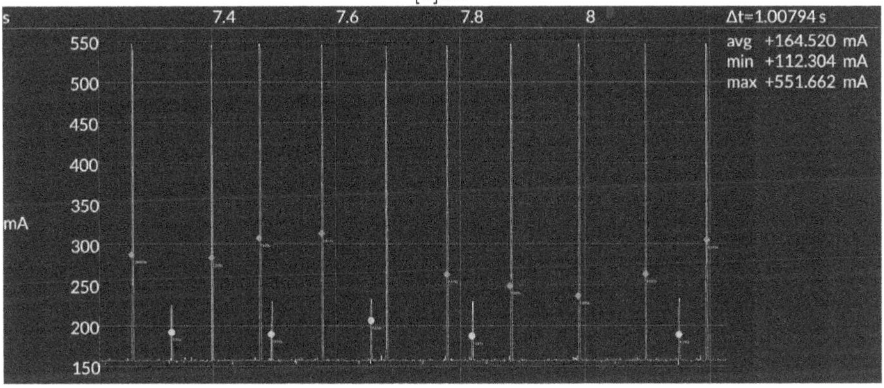

Fig. 7. BLE+Wi-Fi 100ms

[b]0.7

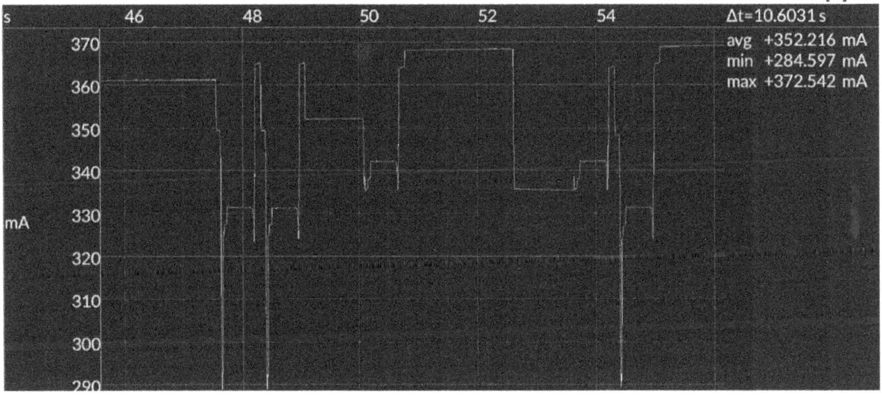

Fig. 8. BLE+Wi-Fi 40ms

Table 5. Trade-offs between BLE-only, Wi-Fi-only, and combined BLE+Wi-Fi operation.

Mode	Pros	Cons
BLE-only	Low power, standardized, medium payload (31bytes)	Limited range (~20 m)
Wi-Fi-only	Medium payload (31bytes), longer range (~100 m), widely available	Higher power consumption, costly scanning
BLE+Wi-Fi	Redundancy, cross-technology coverage, robustness	More power than BLE-only; requires careful scheduling to avoid contention; smaller effective payload for correct decoding (11bytes)

When both advertisement intervals are set to 100ms and over a period of 1 s, it can be seen from Fig.10a that the advertisements are no more uniformly spaced. During this period, 10 Wi-Fi advertisements were advertised, whereas only 5 BLE advertisements were observed (Table 5). This indicates that the direct effect of this overlap on the radio scheduling and sharing at the esp32. We mitigated this problem at the scanner by making the scans occur sequentially, and by de-initializing one tech when the other is listening. Moreover, the values of the min and max currents drawn are of high values compared to the values when the advertisement intervals are different and apart.

We also set both advertisement intervals to 40ms, and observed in Fig10-b that the resulting current trace reveals a highly irregular and elevated current profile, with the average current sustained at approximately 352 mA and very little time spent at lower baseline levels. Unlike traces with longer intervals, which show distinct, periodic peaks corresponding to individual advertisement events, this configuration produces a continuous plateau-like pattern with rapid fluctuations, indicating that the ESP32's radio is almost constantly active. This behavior is characteristic of severe resource contention, where the BLE and Wi-Fi advertisement events frequently overlap or even collide, preventing the radio from entering idle or low-power states between transmissions. Such inefficient scheduling not only causes significantly higher average power consumption—greatly diminishing battery life—but also increases the likelihood of packet loss and scheduling errors. Overall, this trace demonstrates that aggressive, synchronized advertisement intervals on both BLE and Wi-Fi lead to inefficient radio coexistence, underscoring the necessity of careful interval configuration or the implementation of staggered schedules to optimize energy efficiency and reliability.

Finally, we highlight in 5 the final trade-offs resulting from operating in each mode. BLE-only provides the most energy-efficient option with standardized support, but its limited range restricts applicability. Wi-Fi-only extends communication distance and offers larger payloads, yet incurs higher power costs, especially during scanning. BLE+Wi-Fi combines the strengths of both, delivering redundancy and broader coverage, but at the expense of greater power consumption and the need for careful scheduling to avoid contention on shared hardware. It thus depends on the application to choose the operational mode.

Combining BLE and Wi-Fi provides complementary benefits that neither technology achieves alone. BLE excels at lightweight, low-latency broadcasts ideally suited for ephemeral interactions in the immediate vicinity, but its limited payload size and range restrict more complex exchanges. Wi-Fi, on the other hand, offers longer reach and larger payloads but at a higher power cost. Applications such as vehicular-to-pedestrian safety alerts, crowd and event management, smart campus IoT, or healthcare wearables can benefit from operating both radios: BLE ensures fast discovery and local alerts, while Wi-Fi enables an extended coverage. This synergy makes dual-radio operation attractive for scenarios where immediacy, robustness, and interoperability must coexist with broader communication capabilities.

5 Conclusions

In this paper, we have proposed a unified, advertisement-based communication framework enabling direct, inter-technology data exchange over BLE and Wi-Fi without requiring radio-level modifications. Our implementation on ESP32 hardware revealed non-trivial interactions in power consumption during concurrent operation, highlighting the need for careful tuning of advertisement intervals and coexistence parameters. Experimental results show that power draw under hybrid BLE+Wi-Fi modes is not simply additive, with contention and scheduling dynamics introducing measurable inefficiencies. Also, we have showed that the effective payload of broadcasted data decreases by half when interoperability among devices is crucial. These findings are critical for ephemeral, energy-sensitive applications, where communication must be opportunistic yet efficient. Our work sets the basis for a middleware layer that abstracts away low-level protocol complexity, harmonizes BLE and Wi-Fi behavior, and exposes a simple, unified API to application developers—bridging the gap between heterogeneity and deployability in real-world scenarios. By tailoring the communication system to the requirements of ephemeral, opportunistic exchanges; prioritizing low latency, simplicity, and open access, we can enable new classes of applications that are lightweight, flexible, and responsive to the dynamics of the environment.

References

1. Chin, A., Wang, H., Xu, B., Zhang, K., Zhu, L.: Connecting people in the workplace through ephemeral social networks. In: IEEE 3rd International Conference on Privacy, Security, Risk and Trust and 2011 IEEE 3rd International Conference on Social Computing, pp. 527–530. IEEE (2011)
2. Bonnin, J.-M., Couturier, C.: Local interactions for cooperative ITS: opportunities and constraints. In: Cooperative Intelligent Transport Systems: Control and Management, pp. 1–xx. John Wiley & Sons (2024)

3. Chandra, R., Padhye, J., Ravindranath, L., Wolman, A.: Beacon-stuffing: Wi-Fi without associations. In: 8th IEEE Workshop on Mobile Computing Systems and Applications, pp. 53–57. IEEE (2007)
4. Issa, M., Espinel-Galviz, P., Couderc, P., Bonnin, J.M.: Wi-Fi beacon stuffing vs. BLE connectionless mode for ephemeral interactions in smart environments. In: 2024 20th International Conference on Wireless and Mobile Computing, Networking and Communications (WiMob), pp. 402–407. IEEE (2024)
5. Issa, M., Couderc, P., Bonnin, J.M.: Supporting an ephemeral shared dataspace with a BLE connectionless protocol. In: 21st EAI International Conference on Mobile and Ubiquitous Systems, Springer (2024)
6. Zachariah, T., Jackson, N., Ghena, B., Dutta, P.: ReliaBLE: towards reliable communication via Bluetooth Low Energy advertisement networks. In: Proc. 2022 International Conference on Embedded Wireless Systems and Networks (EWSN), vol. 22 (2022)
7. Wu, M., Ma, B., Liu, Z., Xiu, L., Zhang, L.: BLE-horn: a smartphone-based Bluetooth low energy vehicle-to-pedestrian safety system. In: 2017 9th International Conference on Wireless Communications and Signal Processing (WCSP), pp. 1–6. IEEE (2017)
8. Gu, F., Niu, J., Jiang, L., Liu, X., Hancke, G.P.: SafePath: exploiting ubiquitous smartphones to avoid vehicle-pedestrian collision. IEEE Int. Things J. **9**(9), 6763–6777 (2021)
9. Abedi, A., Abari, O., Brecht, T.: WI-LE: can Wi-Fi replace Bluetooth? In: Proceedings of 18th ACM Workshop on Hot Topics in Networks, pp. 117–124 (2019)
10. Ng, P.C., Spachos, P., Plataniotis, K.N.: COVID-19 and your smartphone: BLE-based smart contact tracing. IEEE Syst. J. **15**(4), 5367–5378 (2021)
11. Raes, R., Luxey-Bitri, A., Rouvoy, R., Frey, D., Taïani, F.: Venice: eschewing the cloud by leveraging local communication channels. In: ICT4S 2024 - International Conference on Information and Communications Technology for Sustainability, pp. 1–4 (2024)
12. Chatharajupalli, N.S., Rotta, R., Karnapke, R., Nolte, J.: Assessing the feasibility of combined BLE and Wi-Fi communication for high data sensing applications. In: Proceedings of the 2023 International Conference on Embedded Wireless Systems and Networks (EWSN), pp. 56–59 (2023)
13. Lee, M., Lee, T., Kim, H.-S., Bahk, S.: Wi-BLE: On cooperative operation of Wi-Fi and Bluetooth Low Energy under IPv6. *J. Commun. Netw* **24**(4), 489–502. KICS (2022)
14. Couderc, P., Maurel, Y.: Location corroboration using passive observations of IEEE 802.11 access points. In: 2019 16th IEEE Annual Consumer Communications & Networking Conference (CCNC), pp. 1–7. IEEE (2019)
15. Tosi, J., Taffoni, F., Santacatterina, M., Sannino, R., Formica, D.: Performance evaluation of Bluetooth low energy: a systematic review. Sensors **17**(12), 2898 (2017)
16. Townsend, K., Cufí, C., Davidson, R.: Getting started with Bluetooth low energy: Tools and techniques for low-power networking. O'Reilly Media (2014)
17. Mohammadi, S., Ismail, K., Ghods, A.H.: Investigating Wi-Fi, Bluetooth, and Bluetooth low-energy signal characteristics for integration in vehicle-pedestrian collision warning systems. Sustainability **13**(19), 10823 (2021)
18. Dede, J., Förster, A.: Comparative analysis of opportunistic communication technologies. In: International Conference on Interoperability in IoT, pp. 3–10. Springer (2016)

19. Rodrigues, J., Marques, E.R.B., Lopes, L.M.B., Silva, F.: Towards a middleware for mobile edge-cloud applications. In: Proceedings of 2nd Workshop on Middleware for Edge Clouds & Cloudlets, pp. 1–6 (2017)
20. Yun, Y.H., Choi, H.: Development of a multiuser interaction middleware based on D2D communications. In: 2017 International Conference on Information Networking (ICOIN), pp. 480–485. IEEE (2017)
21. Saputra, Y., Hua, J., Wendt, N., Julien, C., Roman, G.C.: Warble: programming abstractions for personalizing interactions in the internet of things. In: 2019 IEEE/ACM 6th International Conference on Mobile Software Engineering and Systems (MOBILESoft), pp. 128–139. IEEE (2019)

Security, Forensics, and Trust in Connected Mobility Systems

Reflections on the Security of In-Vehicle Connectivity

Xiangji Chen[1], Jingqi Wu[1(✉)], Shengzhi Zhang[1], and Wu Zhou[2]

[1] Department of Computer Science, Boston University Metropolitan College, Boston, MA, USA
{cxjcn,wjq2002,shengzhi}@bu.edu

[2] Meta Platforms, Menlo Park, CA, USA
wu1zhou@meta.com

Abstract. The framework that links mobile devices with automotive head units, such as SmartDeviceLink (SDL), facilitates smooth interaction between mobile applications and in-vehicle infotainment platforms. However, their open interfaces significantly expand the attack surface and raise unresolved security concerns. We analyzed SDL's transport and policy layers on both the mobile device and the head unit, uncovering attack vectors including compromising mobile systems, hijacking SDL sessions, etc. Our experiments demonstrate that these weaknesses can be exploited to spoof GPS navigation and manipulate projected information on head units. To address these vulnerabilities, we discuss the necessity of defense strategies incorporating app signature authentication, device integrity checks, and end-to-end encryption.

Keywords: Infotainment System · Vehicle Security · SmartDeviceLink

1 Introduction

In recent years, the automobile has been steadily evolving from a largely mechanical conveyance to a software-defined, network-connected platform. Central to this shift is the infotainment system running on the head unit, which now lets drivers/passengers project their familiar smartphone apps, like navigation, media, voice assistants, etc., onto the head unit display, and even directly control the vehicle functionalities, including air conditioning, volume, etc., on their smartphones. Early open standards such as MirrorLink [5] blazed the trail, and later, Ford and Toyota backed SmartDeviceLink (SDL) [16], which continues to be deployed in over five million Ford vehicles. Recently, two proprietary ecosystems dominate: Apple CarPlay, factory-fitted on over 800 vehicle models worldwide [1], and Google's Android Auto, which Google reported at I/O 2025 to

X. Chen and J. Wu—Equal contribution.

B. Kihei et al. (Eds.): INTSYS 2025, LNICST 717, pp. 103–118, 2027.
https://doi.org/10.1007/978-3-032-38705-9_5

be supported on approximately 250 million vehicles on the road [3]. Analysts therefore expect the global automotive smartphone integration market to grow from $10.2 billion in 2023 to over $18.5 billion by 2031 [24].

However, the security issues associated with such frameworks have become a significant concern. Most closed-source frameworks, such as Apple CarPlay and Android Auto, rely on proprietary design to obscure system details and limit attackers' knowledge. But the security-by-obscurity approach has long been criticized for its ineffectiveness. For instance, in 2025, a zero-click remote code execution vulnerability was discovered in Apple CarPlay, which allowed attackers to exploit a wireless connection to gain control over the vehicle's infotainment system without user interaction [8]. Similarly, Android Auto also faced security flaws, where malicious apps could elevate privileges to access and manipulate vehicle functionality [7]. In contrast, open-source frameworks like SDL expose their design and implementation, relying on public scrutiny to address security issues. Zhang et al. [26] analyzed the attack vectors against early SDL design and proposed a security model to mitigate these risks.

This paper focuses on identifying and analyzing potential security flaws within the new SDL framework implementation. We analyze SDL's transport and policy layers on both the smartphone and the Human-Machine Interface (HMI) of the head unit, and validated the real-world impact of these issues with two types of attacks. First, in a breached mobile environment, we use Xposed to hook Glympse's **getLatitude()** call to send forged GPS coordinates to the head unit, thus misleading drivers with manipulated navigation services. Second, by advertising a spoofed SDLRouterService over Bluetooth, a Man-In-The-Middle Attack (MITM) can be launched to manipulate the traffic between the smartphone and the infotainment system.

Contributions. The contributions of this paper are summarized as follows:

- We perform the security analysis of SDL's transport and policy layers on both mobile devices and head units, revealing protocol and configuration weaknesses, including plaintext Bluetooth communication, unauthenticated service discovery, and coarse-grained RPC (Remote Procedure Call) permissions, which may compromise message integrity, endpoint authentication, and access control.
- We developed two exploits: a mobile location forgery attack to spoof GPS data, and a Bluetooth MITM session hijacking that allows a remote adversary to manipulate the data projected onto the head unit, demonstrating the realistic risks exposed to drivers.
- We discussed potential defenses against security vulnerabilities of SDL to mitigate those identified security issues, leading to a dependable design and implementation of a similar framework.

The rest of the paper is organized as follows: Sect. 2 provides background information on the SDL framework and the Xposed hooking technique. Section 3 analyzes the potential security vulnerabilities in the SDL framework. In Sect. 4, we present two experimental case studies, one involving a compromised mobile system and the other demonstrating an MITM attack. In Sect. 5, we discuss possible defense mechanisms against the identified security issues. Section 6 reviews related works, and Sect. 7 concludes the paper.

2 Background

2.1 SDL Framework

SmartDeviceLink [21] is a standard set of protocols that connects smartphone applications to a vehicle's head unit. It enables drivers to interact with their application using common in-vehicle interfaces such as a touch screen display, embedded voice recognition, steering wheel controls, and various vehicle knobs and buttons. The SDL ecosystem has two main components, as shown in Fig. 1. The core component is the software running on the Vehicle Manufacturers (OEMs) to support SDL functionalities on the vehicle. Integrating this component into their head units and HMI enables access to various smartphone applications. App developers implement the iOS and Android libraries into their applications to facilitate command and control via the connected head unit. The policy table is maintained on the OEM's policy server and defines the permissions and security rules for connected mobile applications. When an app attempts to connect to SDL Core, the system consults the policy table to verify whether the app is allowed to access specific vehicle data, perform certain RPC functions, or interact with the HMI. This ensures compliance with OEM-defined safety and security policies before granting the app access to in-vehicle features.

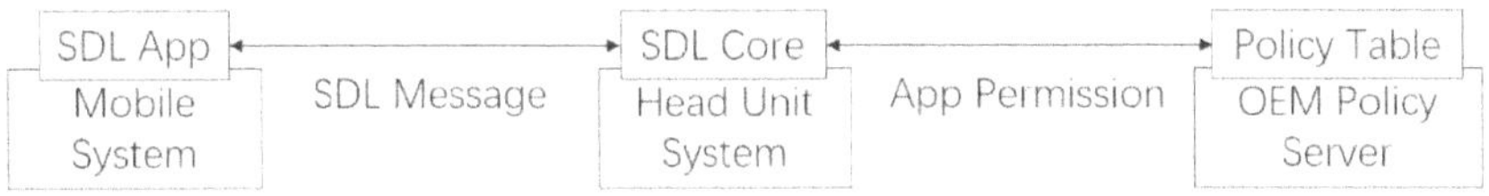

Fig. 1. SDL Framework.

SDL Core. SDL core is a C++ implementation running on the In-Vehicle Infotainment (IVI) system, acting as the central message broker between the vehicle HMI and the connected smartphone. It is mainly divided into six parts, which are transport manager controlling different transport types (Bluetooth, USB, etc.), protocol handler parsing the binary messages into SDL protocol messages, RPC service interpreting and processing the RPCs, HMI interface bridging SDL Core with the vehicle's HMI, policy manager ensuring app permissions and security compliance, and app manager controlling connected apps, their states, and events.

Android Libraries. SDL on Android is implemented using a Proxy Library, which enables third-party mobile apps to communicate with SDL Core running in a vehicle's IVI system over various transport mechanisms. It is used to manage transport connections (Bluetooth, USB, TCP), handle serialization/deserialization of SDL messages (RPCs), and provide thread-safe queues and callbacks for communication. In particular, a message goes from the app to the SDL Manager, the proxy layer, the RPC layer, and finally the transport layer.

SDL Communication. SDL establishes bi-directional communication between a mobile app and the SDL Core via Bluetooth, USB, or the Internet. Among these methods, Bluetooth is the most commonly used. A mobile phone with SDL functionality registers an SDL service. When the phone connects to the vehicle via Bluetooth, the vehicle detects the service and accepts the connection. Upon a successful connection, the name of the phone appears in the device list of the SDL HMI display, allowing drivers to select that connection.

2.2 Xposed

The Xposed Framework is a tool that allows developers to change how Android apps behave, without modifying the app binaries directly. Instead, it uses hooking to intercept and alter app behavior during runtime.

Xposed Overview. Android uses a process called **Zygote** to launch apps, which loads the core parts of the Android system into memory and copies itself to start new app processes. Xposed modifies the Zygote process, which allows Xposed to load its own code into every app that it starts. Therefore, Xposed becomes part of the app's process from the beginning. With full access to the app's code, Xposed can then run custom logic before or after any method in the app. Once Xposed is resident inside each app process via Zygote, it influences the app's behavior through hooking, a technique that rewires method entry points so Xposed code can execute before, after, or in place of the original logic. The Xposed developer can write a module to define what logic should be manipulated, with one or more apps targeted. The module uses the **Xposed API** [25] to find and hook specific methods (we use API Level 53), thus changing their behavior. When an app starts, Xposed checks if any modules have registered a hook to it to deviate the execution flow if necessary.

Permission Bypass Using Xposed. Xposed modules can bypass Android permission checks. Each module hooks methods like **checkPermission** and forces a "granted" result. The target app then gains GPS, camera, or signature-level access without permissions granted by users. Xposed can also track and alter data in transit. A developer hooks key methods, logs network payloads, rewrites intents, or masks SharedPreferences values. The same mechanism enables the addition of new features to closed-source apps. The hooks can inject UI elements, expose hidden settings, and call blocked system APIs at runtime. Note that users still receive official updates because the APK remains untouched. Security researchers use Xposed as a live test harness, developing modules to feed crafted inputs into internal APIs and observe responses.

3 Security Analysis of SDL Framework

SDL greatly enlarges the attack surface between a mobile device and the in-vehicle head unit. In this section, we discuss several representative threats against the SDL framework.

3.1 Mobile Application Spoofing

SDL's permission management primarily relies on the appID and, when permissions are device-specific, the deviceID. However, the appID can be easily obtained by intercepting messages exchanged between the application and the SDL Core. This allows attackers to develop apparently legitimate applications and distribute them through third-party app stores. By impersonating the target application and sending the same appID to the SDL Core, the malicious application can obtain the same set of permissions as the original app. Once installed on the user's device, such a rogue application could gain access to vehicle data, issue HMI commands, or exfiltrate sensitive driver information, posing significant security and privacy risks.

3.2 Breached Mobile Operating Environments

For Android mobile phones, the malware can gain root permissions. Once the OS is compromised, any SDL-enabled app can have its outbound RPC calls modified, or new ones injected from inside the same process. Malware can therefore modify the data from the SDL application. A prominent example is the use of frameworks like Xposed, which allow malicious modules to hook into application-level functions at runtime. Using this technique, attackers can intercept, alter, or inject RPC messages sent from the app to the SDL Core. For instance, a compromised SDL app may have its GPS location data, such as that shared by navigation or location-sharing apps, replaced with spoofed values before transmission. The head unit still trusts that data and uses it for navigation, as it originates from within the trusted app context.

3.3 Head Unit System Compromise

Compromising the vehicle's head unit infotainment system is another significant attack vector. As vehicles become increasingly connected and run complicated embedded systems, attackers can exploit vulnerabilities in the infotainment system to access critical vehicle components, including the CAN bus. Once the head unit is compromised, malicious actors can tamper with middleware operations or control vehicle functionalities remotely. Pwn2Own Automotive 2024 showed a fresh zero-click bug, which allows network-adjacent attackers to execute arbitrary code on affected installations of Alpine Halo9 devices. A compromised head unit can rewrite any SDL traffic and bridge to the CAN bus [9]. Generally, patches to fix those issues arrive slowly because many vehicles lack over-the-air updates.

3.4 DoS / DDoS Attacks

Denial of Service (DoS) and Distributed Denial of Service (DDoS) attacks against vehicle middleware are increasingly common. These attacks can target mobile apps, vehicle control systems, or even vehicle manufacturers' infrastructure. Attackers may flood vehicle systems with requests, disrupting the normal operation of vehicle functions such as navigation or vehicle control through the CAN bus. DDoS attacks against the manufacturer's cloud infrastructure can also disrupt vital services like software updates or credential management. While there are defenses in place, DDoS attacks remain effective in certain scenarios, particularly in high-volume, resource-constrained environments.

3.5 Man-in-the-Middle-Attack (MITM)

Bluetooth BR/EDR devices with Secure Simple Pairing and Secure Connections Pairing in Bluetooth Core Specification 4.2 through 5.4 allow certain man-in-the-middle attacks when a short key is forced, leading to the disclosure of the encryption key and live injection, i.e., BLUFFS [13]. Because default SDL deployments accept Bluetooth profiles without mutual TLS, an attacker who registers a spoofed SDL service can intercept or even manipulate the connection between the phone and the vehicle.

4 Security Flaws Exploration

In this section, we demonstrate two of the above-mentioned security flaws, i.e., compromised Mobile System and Man-In-The-Middle attack.

4.1 Compromised Mobile System

We assume that the Android phone hosting the SDL apps has already been compromised. In practice, the attacker can gain persistent root privileges through a variety of well-documented channels, including: (i) exploiting publicly disclosed kernel vulnerabilities (e.g., CVE-2022–0847 showed that attacks can write to pages in the page cache backed by read-only files to escalate their privileges on the system [18]), (ii) flashing an unlocked boot-image obtained from grey-market firmware sites (e.g., firmware.mobi - an online boot image patcher[1]), or

[1] https://desktop.firmware.mobi/.

(iii) deploying turnkey rooting toolkits such as Magisk or KingRoot. With full control of the OS, the attacker installs the Xposed Framework so that malicious code can be injected at runtime into any target app without repackaging its APK. Xposed is ideal for this scenario because it (a) hooks Dalvik/ART method calls with single-line APIs, (b) leaves the original app binary and signature intact, avoiding Play-Store tamper checks, and (c) can be toggled on or off without reflashing the device, reducing forensic traces.

Attack Description. Modern smartphones often include strict controls on location data to prevent tampering. To make the attack concrete, we focus on **Glympse**[2], a popular live-location sharing app officially listed among SDL-compatible titles by several OEMs. Glympse polls GPS coordinates via the standard `LocationManager` API and forwards them through SDL to the vehicle's HMI by Bluetooth or Network, so that passengers can view their trip in real time.

However, the standard Android APIs can be intercepted or modified at runtime using dynamic instrumentation frameworks. Leveraging Xposed, the attacker registers hooks on the methods that Glympse calls, i.e., `getLatitude()` and `getLongitude()`. In our demonstration, we hook into these methods using an Xposed module, which allows us to intercept the method that Glympse uses to access location data. Our module replaces the real location with a manipulated one. The manipulation is limited to the Glympse app's process memory, leaving the actual system location untouched, so the attack can bypass system-wide integrity checks and location-based security features. The manipulated location is then sent to the vehicle system over the network, as if it were legitimate.

Because Glympse can transmit its data via the internet, no additional network configuration is required. The app continues to function normally. From the perspective of both the vehicle and the Glympse user interface, the location data appears authentic. However, the underlying values are controlled by the attacker. Consequently, the vehicle HMI displays the attacker-chosen position while the phone's other apps (e.g., Google Maps) still show the real location (see Fig. 2), making the attack stealthy and difficult to detect.

Attack Demonstration. The experimental setup consists of Glympse version 3.38.13, a rooted Nexus 6 smartphone running Android with the Xposed framework (API Level 53), an Ubuntu 20.04 workstation that simultaneously hosts the SDL Core service and an HMI running in an emulator. The attack only modifies Glympse's GPS coordinates, leaving the Android system's canonical location data intact. We implemented the attack as an Xposed module packaged in an APK called `Xposed Toolkit`. At boot time, Xposed supplies the module with a package-specific `lpparam.classLoader`; the code then: (i)resolves `getLatitude()` and `getLongitude()` with that loader, (ii) registers hooks that return attacker-chosen coordinates, and (iii) launches

[2] https://www.glympse.com/.

Fig. 2. Modified Only Glympse Location.

`sendLocationDataViaHttp()` in a background thread to POST the original and modified data to a fixed server endpoint. The module lists the Xposed APK as a `compileOnly` dependency. Once the user enables it in the Xposed Installer and reboots, the hooks fire before Glympse's first activity.

Figure 2 confirms that only Glympse shows the manipulated location, while Google Maps still displays the true GPS location. The method **sendLocationDataViaHttp** transmits both the true and the spoofed coordinates to the HMI by using HTTP. The code launches this task in a background thread. The thread keeps the user interface responsive. It constructs a simple POST request with three form fields: **type**, **original**, and **modified**. It then targets the server endpoint, sets the proper Content-Type header, and writes the payload to the connection. After the request is dispatched, the thread records the HTTP response code. This log confirms a successful transfer or flags any failure.

To visualise the effect on the vehicle side, we extended the head-unit HMI to print both sets of coordinates and their resolved place names[3]. Figures 3 and 4 show the resulting dashboard, making the manipulation measurable while the rest of the HMI remains unchanged.

[3] The stock HMI only reported a "Glympse connected" flag. We added a lightweight HTTP parser plus UI elements that call the Google Geocoding API, so we can see the exact latitude/longitude pairs and human-readable addresses for both the original and manipulated values.

4.2 MITM

Attack Description. Attackers can exploit known vulnerabilities in older Bluetooth implementations, as vehicles are often used for many years without hardware or software upgrades [4,6,19] to launch MITM attacks. Alternatively, an attacker-controlled device could be used to impersonate the phone and the head unit to establish connections directly. If the victim does not carefully verify the Bluetooth pairing codes, is unaware of the risks associated with mismatched codes, or incidentally accepts the pairing request (e.g., due to repeated prompts), the attack is likely to succeed. When the attacker's device connects to the vehicle, the SDL Core on the vehicle automatically establishes a connection with the fake service. The attacker's device then relays messages between the vehicle and the phone, forwarding messages from the vehicle to the phone and vice versa, effectively placing itself between the two endpoints.

Fig. 3. HMI Displays the Original Data.

Fig. 4. HMI Displays the Modified Data.

Attack Demonstration. The experimental setup consists of a Nexus 6 smartphone running Android, an SDL Core instance operating on Ubuntu 22.04, and an attacker's device running Ubuntu 20.04. The attack begins by scanning for nearby Bluetooth devices to obtain the MAC address of the target phone. Once the MAC address is acquired, a service discovery is performed to identify the services hosted by the device. Among the listed services, SdlRouterService is found, along with its associated details. Using this information, the attacker registers a spoofed service that mimics the legitimate one, also named SdlRouterService. With the fake service in place, the attacker's device first changes its Bluetooth name to match that of the target phone and repeatedly attempts to initiate pairing. Once successful, the attacker's device then changes its name to that of the vehicle and similarly attempts to pair with the phone.

After establishing the necessary pairing, the attacker's device proceeds to connect to the SDL Core running on Ubuntu 22.04. Once the SDL Core initiates a connection to the spoofed service, the attacker intercepts the messages and forwards them to the actual phone hosting the legitimate service. From that point on, all messages between the phone and the SDL Core pass through the attacker's device, allowing the attacker to read, modify, or manipulate the communication. We demonstrate two types of attacks in this paper: modifying application names and hiding specific applications. The original SDL HMI display is shown in Fig. 5 as a reference.

Fig. 5. Original HMI.

For the application name modification attack, the relevant field in the message payload is identified as "appName". The attack code scans for this field and extracts the corresponding string value. If the extracted name matches the target application, the name is modified to a desired value. As a result, the manipulated application name is reflected on the SDL HMI interface. as shown in Fig. 6.

For the application hiding attack, the attack monitors messages sent from the phone to the vehicle and inspects them for the target application's name. If a message containing the target name is detected, it is blocked and not forwarded to the vehicle. As a result, the SDL Core receives no information about the application, effectively making it invisible on the HMI as shown in Fig. 7.

Fig. 6. Manipulating App Names.

Fig. 7. Hiding Connected Apps.

5 Discussion

Mobile-App Masquerading Defense. Since each app has a unique signature that can be obtained from the system, it is recommended to use the signature together with appID as a pair to verify the app. As the signature is directly from the system instead of from the app, it cannot be stolen unless the system is compromised.

Secure Mobile Platform. SDL should be permitted to run only on devices that successfully pass remote attestation. The head unit can query the Google Play Integrity API or Apple DeviceCheck at every pairing. If the service reports root, jailbreak, or a known malware build, SDL should refuse the session. Encryption keys should be kept inside the phone's trusted execution environment, so even privileged malicious code cannot access them.

Head Unit Hardening. Secure boot can be used to lock the infotainment system firmware to a vendor-signed image. Runtime memory protection (e.g., ARM PXN, MPU) isolates the SDL process from the CAN gateway. A host-based IDS can watch for abnormal RPC rates and new sockets. Critical fixes should be shipped as deltas over an OEM TLS channel, so owners need no workshop visit.

DoS / DDoS Mitigation. The gateway can be utilized to enforce per-app quotas, e.g., several RPCs per second and several bytes per minute. It drops traffic that exceeds the quota and logs the event. Cloud services can be deployed to sit behind autoscaling proxies and apply upstream rate-limiting CAPs. Together, these controls keep critical system components and back-end APIs responsive.

Encryption Against MITM. The phone and head unit can derive a session key with ECDH at pairing. They wrap every SDL frame in an AES-GCM ciphertext, so an interceptor can only see random bytes, not able to read or alter the data. Any tampering breaks the authentication tag and triggers an error [2]. The system can refresh the key at each ignition cycle or after a period of time, thus blocking BLUFFS-style downgrades and hiding sensitive data.

6 Related Works

6.1 Android Auto/Apple Carplay

There are also some reflections regarding Android Auto and Apple CarPlay. Similar to SDL, these two frameworks may also have similar security problems that require further exploration.

Mandal et al. conducted a vulnerability analysis of Android Auto infotainment applications, revealing a concerning prevalence of security flaws in widely used apps. Through static analysis of 20 Android Auto-related applications, they discovered that 25% of these apps improperly executed JavaScript code from untrusted sources, and many suffered from insecure inter-component communication (ICC) channels. This left them open to privilege escalation and unauthorized data access attacks. Moreover, a lack of robust cryptographic protections and improper input validation contributed to these risks, demonstrating that even applications distributed through official channels may expose sensitive user and vehicle data to exploitation [11]. Their next study, expanding on this work, applied comprehensive static analysis techniques to both Android Auto infotainment and OBD-II diagnostic applications. Their findings revealed that approximately 60% of the analyzed apps contained critical vulnerabilities, emphasizing the systemic nature of security weaknesses in automotive apps [12].

Shin et al. extended this work by performing forensic case studies on actual IVI systems supporting Android Auto and Apple CarPlay. Their methodology included capturing HCI and Wi-Fi traffic and analyzing mobile and head unit storage via forensic imaging. They found that paired mobile devices store artifacts such as activation timestamps, GPS logs, message histories, and contact data. However, forensic investigations often focus only on device storage—the wireless communication channels, especially over BT/Wi-Fi, remain underexplored [20].

6.2 Head Unit System Security

Studies show that the head unit system in vehicles can also be attacked, causing issues such as data leakage, permission theft, and more. Since head unit systems are often used for extended periods without updates, they are more susceptible to persistent vulnerabilities and pose a greater risk.

Moiz and Alalfi introduced a static-analysis method to detect information leakage in infotainment apps by fuzzing intents and analyzing Android Auto modules. Their study revealed that insecure intent-based communications enabled malicious components to intercept sensitive user data within the head unit, such as location and contact information, with many apps susceptible to spoofed or hijacked intents [14]. In their 2022 survey, Moiz and Alalfi further assessed vulnerabilities across Android Auto and Automotive apps. They reproduced 11 out of 14 platform-level vulnerabilities, showing that apps running on in-vehicle head units share the same insecure programming practices found in mobile platforms [15].

Pesé et al. provided a comprehensive high-level architecture of Android Automotive, coupling it with systematic security analyses. Their experiments confirmed that third-party apps in Android Automotive often contain JavaScript flaws and other vulnerabilities that could lead to remote compromise, highlighting that the native head unit environment itself is a weak link, not just external companion apps [17]. Mallojula et al. analyzed 125 Android-based automotive companion apps, finding that 70% possessed critical flaws allowing unauthorized access through open OBD dongles, arbitrary CAN injection, or unauthenticated data flows. They demonstrate how companion apps can act as unintentional backdoors into the vehicle network, compromising both data confidentiality and control-plane integrity [10]. Wu et al. proposed CANGuard, an unsupervised CAN-bus intrusion detection system that leverages autoencoder-based feature learning to identify anomalous in-vehicle traffic without requiring labeled data, achieving performance comparable to state-of-the-art supervised IDS approaches [27].

6.3 Android Root/Xposed

Several flaws in the Android system have been identified and can be exploited to obtain root permissions. Studies show that with (or even without) root permissions, attackers can modify packets sent and received by using some frameworks like Xposed. Totosis and Patsakis present Ronin, a hooking tool that enables analysts to inject and manage dynamic hooks on unmodified Android devices by hijacking entries in the Global Offset Table (GOT). In SDL scenarios, such inline hooks could be used to intercept key API calls [23]. Tan et al. propose an inline hooking framework that intercepts calls to native methods in shared libraries at runtime by modifying function pointers, and this works even on non-rooted devices using VirtualXposed. They show that attackers with root permissions can intercept SDL method calls or Bluetooth APIs, enabling real-time payload manipulation or facilitating MITM attacks [22].

6.4 Bluetooth Security

Numerous studies have explored MITM vulnerabilities in Bluetooth security, showing that there are multiple ways to carry out MITM attacks on different Bluetooth versions and connection modes. Figueroa Lorenzo et al. reviewed a range of Bluetooth vulnerabilities using open-source tools like Ubertooth, Btle-Juice, and Bleah. Their work highlighted at least three newly exploited weaknesses, including MITM attacks on "Just Works" pairing, encryption downgrade exploits, and fuzzing-based protocol crashes. These findings demonstrate that real-world Bluetooth communications remain highly exposed and can be instrumented using readily available hardware and software frameworks [6].

In the automotive context, Renganathan et al. introduced the "valet attack", showing that many head units accept automated Bluetooth reconnections without user awareness. Through a systematic STPA-Priv analysis and live experimentation on a vehicle's infotainment system, they demonstrated unauthorized data access, such as contact lists and call logs-via compromised Bluetooth interfaces. They revealed how assumptions in automotive Bluetooth implementations can unintentionally expose private user data, even when paired devices seem trusted [19]. Classen and Hollick's Happy MitM paper revealed yet another concern: none of the major Bluetooth stacks alert users to MITM attempts, even when authentication or encryption fails. This violation of the Bluetooth 5.2 specification means users remain unaware during pairing downgrades or key manipulations—common tactics used in automotive Bluetooth exploits [4].

7 Conclusion

In this paper, we targeted the security weaknesses of the SDL-based connection between mobile devices and automobile head units. We analyzed SDL's transport and policy layers on both the connection end devices. The uncovered plaintext Bluetooth links, unauthenticated data transmission, and over-permissive RPC policies together reveal the larger attack surface. We then demonstrated two attacks: (i) a compromised mobile attack that modifies Glympse's GPS location data on a rooted Nexus 6, and (ii) a Bluetooth man-in-the-middle attack that relays and alters SDL traffic to rename or hide apps on the HMI. These proof of concepts show that an adversary can covertly manipulate critical data and UI elements, deceiving drivers without triggering existing safeguards. Finally, we discussed various defense mechanisms to counter these security threats.

References

1. Apple: more than 800 models to choose from. https://www.apple.com/ios/carplay/available-models (2025)
2. Bellare, M., Tackmann, B.: The multi-user security of authenticated encryption: AES-GCM in TLS 1.3. In: Robshaw, M., Katz, J. (eds.) CRYPTO 2016. LNCS, vol. 9814, pp. 247–276. Springer, Heidelberg (2016). https://doi.org/10.1007/978-3-662-53018-4_10

3. Blog, A.D.: New in-car app experiences. https://android-developers.googleblog.com/2025/05/android-for-cars-google-io-2025.html (2025)
4. Classen, J., Hollick, M.: Happy MitM: fun and toys in every Bluetooth device. In: Proceedings of the 14th ACM Conference on Security and Privacy in Wireless and Mobile Networks, pp. 72–77 (2021)
5. consortium, C.: Mirrorlink operations sunsetting by September 30, 2023. https://carconnectivity.org/mirrorlink-operations-sunsetting-by-september-30-2023 (2021)
6. Figueroa Lorenzo, S., Añorga Benito, J., García Cardarelli, P., Alberdi Garaia, J., Arrizabalaga Juaristi, S.: A comprehensive review of rfid and bluetooth security: Practical analysis. Technologies **7**(1), 15 (2019)
7. Inc., G.: There exists a code execution vulnerability in the car app android jetpack library. https://nvd.nist.gov/vuln/detail/cve-2024-10382 (2024)
8. Katz, U., Lumelsky, A., Elbaz, G.: Airborne: Wormable zero-click remote code execution (RCE) in airplay protocol puts apple & IoT devices at risk. https://www.oligo.security/blog/airborne (2025)
9. Lab, C.R.: From Pwn2Own automotive: a high-severity zero-click RCE Bluetooth vulnerability in the Alpine Halo9 IVI system. https://vicone.com/blog/from-pwn2own-automotive-a-critical-zero-click-rce-bluetooth-vulnerability-in-the-alpine-halo9-ivi-system (2024)
10. Mallojula, P., Li, F., Du, X., Luo, B.: Companion apps or backdoors? On the security of automotive companion apps. In: European Symposium on Research in Computer Security, pp. 24–44. Springer (2024)
11. Mandal, A.K., Cortesi, A., Ferrara, P., Panarotto, F., Spoto, F.: Vulnerability analysis of android auto infotainment apps. In: Proceedings of the 15th ACM International Conference on Computing Frontiers, pp. 183–190 (2018)
12. Mandal, A.K., Panarotto, F., Cortesi, A., Ferrara, P., Spoto, F.: Static analysis of android auto infotainment and on-board diagnostics ii apps. Softw.: Pract. Exper **49**(7), 1131–1161 (2019)
13. MITRE: Bluetooth forward and future secrecy attacks and defenses. https://nvd.nist.gov/vuln/detail/CVE-2023-24023 (2024)
14. Moiz, A., Alalfi, M.H.: An approach for the identification of information leakage in automotive infotainment systems. In: 2020 IEEE 20th International Working Conference on Source Code Analysis and Manipulation (SCAM), pp. 110–114. IEEE (2020)
15. Moiz, A., Alalfi, M.H.: A survey of security vulnerabilities in android automotive apps. In: Proceedings of the 3rd International Workshop on Engineering and Cybersecurity of Critical Systems, pp. 17–24 (2022)
16. NEWSROOM, T.: Ford and Toyota establish smartdevicelink consortium to accelerate industry-driven standard for in-vehicle apps. https://pressroom.toyota.com/toyota-ford-smartdevicelink-consortium-vehicle-apps (2017)
17. Pese, M., Shin, K., Bruner, J., Chu, A.: Security analysis of android automotive. SAE Int. J. Adv. Current Pract. Mob. **2**(2020-01-1295), 2337–2346 (2020)
18. Red Hat, I.: There exists a code execution vulnerability in the car app android jetpack library. https://nvd.nist.gov/vuln/detail/cve-2024-10382 (2024)
19. Renganathan, V., Yurtsever, E., Ahmed, Q., Yener, A.: Valet attack on privacy: a cybersecurity threat in automotive Bluetooth infotainment systems. Cybersecurity **5**(1), 30 (2022)
20. Shin, Y., Kim, S., Jo, W., Shon, T.: Digital forensic case studies for in-vehicle infotainment systems using android auto and apple carplay. Sensors **22**(19), 7196 (2022)

21. SmartDeviceLink: Smartdevicelink core. https://github.com/smartdevicelink/sdl_core (2022)
22. Tan, Y.A., Feng, S., Cheng, X., Li, Y., Zheng, J.: An android inline hooking framework for the securing transmitted data. Sensors **20**(15), 4201 (2020)
23. Totosis, N., Patsakis, C.: Android hooking revisited. In: 2018 IEEE 16th International Conference on Dependable, Autonomic and Secure Computing, 16th International Conference on Pervasive Intelligence and Computing, 4th Intl Conf on Big Data Intelligence and Computing and Cyber Science and Technology Congress (DASC/PiCom/DataCom/CyberSciTech), pp. 552–559. IEEE (2018)
24. Verified Market Research: Automotive smartphone integration market size and forecast. https://www.verifiedmarketresearch.com/product/automotive-smartphone-integration-market (2024)
25. Vollmer, R.: Xposed module repository API reference. https://api.xposed.info/reference/packages.html (2017)
26. Zhang, S., Makke, O., Gusikhin, O., Shah, A., Vasilakos, A.V.: A security model for dependable vehicle middleware and mobile applications connection. In: Proceedings of the 4th International Conference on Vehicle Technology and Intelligent Transport Systems (VEHITS), pp. 379–386. (2018)
27. Zhou, W., Fu, H., Kapoor, S.: CanGuard: practical intrusion detection for in-vehicle network via unsupervised learning. In: 2021 IEEE/ACM Symposium on Edge Computing (SEC), pp. 454–458. IEEE (2021)

A Forensic Framework for Android Emulators in macOS Environments within Ad Hoc Network Scenarios

Sedat Şen[1(✉)] and Harun Artuner[2]

[1] Department of Forensic Sciences, Institute of Science, Hacettepe University, Çankaya Ankara, Türkiye
sensedat34@gmail.com

[2] Department of Computer Engineering, Faculty of Engineering, Hacettepe University, Çankaya Ankara, Türkiye

Abstract. Android emulators, widely used for development and testing, are increasingly involved in forensic investigations due to their misuse in device spoofing, credential manipulation, and evidence tampering. However, existing methodologies provide limited guidance for systematically acquiring and analyzing emulator artifacts within Apple's restrictive macOS ecosystem. This study proposes and validates a macOS-specific forensic framework for Android emulators, focusing on reliable imaging, artifact extraction, and integrity preservation. The framework is experimentally evaluated using Parallels, NoxPlayer, and Genymotion, and incorporates emulator-centric acquisition techniques—including dd, adb, and qemu-img—along with application-level artifact analysis (e.g., WhatsApp, Gmail).

To extend forensic capability beyond the endpoint, the framework includes an optional MANET-aware network-context layer that synchronizes emulator artifacts with packet captures and routing-state observations (AODV/OLSR). While not the primary focus of the study, this layer enhances attribution and timeline reconstruction in decentralized environments where emulator-based rogue nodes may exist.

Key contributions include: (i) a validated, macOS-aware emulator forensic workflow; (ii) a reproducible testbed supporting consistent artifact and image acquisition; and (iii) procedures for correlating emulator artifacts with network traces when required. The results provide practical, evidence-sound guidance for investigators analyzing Android emulators within macOS environments, supported by read-only imaging, hashing, and auditable privilege control.

Keywords: emulator forensics · macOS forensics · MANET · AODV · OLSR · timeline correlation · virtualization forensics

1 Introduction

The widespread adoption of mobile devices, particularly smartphones, has significantly transformed digital forensic investigations. As of 2024, the global number of smartphone users exceeds 4.6 billion and is projected to reach over 6 billion by 2029 [1]. This

B. Kihei et al. (Eds.): INTSYS 2025, LNICST 717, pp. 119–139, 2027.
https://doi.org/10.1007/978-3-032-38705-9_6

dramatic growth has elevated mobile devices to primary sources of digital evidence in cybercrime investigations. Law enforcement agencies and forensic units increasingly encounter mobile-related digital materials during examinations, with recent national and international statistics confirming this trend [2–4].

While Android-based systems dominate the mobile operating system market—holding approximately 72% share [5] digital forensic efforts often focus on the analysis of physical Android devices. However, Android emulators, originally designed for application development and testing, are also being exploited by cybercriminals for malicious purposes [6], including device spoofing, credential manipulation, proxy-based anonymity, and evidence tampering [7, 8]. A notable example is an IBM-reported incident where over 16,000 mobile identities were simulated using 20 different emulators to commit large-scale fraud [9]. Despite the growing relevance of emulator environments in both legitimate and illicit contexts, current digital forensic methodologies offer limited guidance for the acquisition and analysis of emulator artifacts—particularly within the macOS operating system. The macOS ecosystem poses unique challenges due to its restrictive architecture, file system protections, and limited tool compatibility. These constraints make it difficult to extract, preserve, and interpret forensic evidence without compromising its integrity and admissibility in legal settings.

Although there are extensive forensic frameworks for Android devices and traditional desktop systems, the literature lacks a systematic methodology for analyzing Android emulators operating on macOS platforms. Addressing this gap, the present study proposes a forensic framework specifically designed to detect, acquire, and analyze emulator-generated artifacts in macOS environments. This challenge is further complicated by Mobile Ad Hoc Networks (MANETs). These networks form spontaneously without fixed infrastructure, relying on multi-hop, peer-to-peer forwarding. While such flexibility is attractive for tactical and opportunistic communications, the transient nature of MANET nodes, intermittent connectivity, and volatile routing state introduce distinct forensic complications, including distributed traces and transient artifacts across multiple physical nodes [10, 11]. Crucially, Android emulators can be misused as potential rogue nodes within these networks to inflate device identities, evade attribution, or disrupt MANET traffic. Consequently, detecting these emulator-backed nodes and linking their endpoint artifacts to specific network behaviors becomes essential for reliable traceability and attribution. To address this complex challenge, this study extends the macOS-centric framework with a MANET-aware layer designed to bridge endpoint and network evidence by combining emulator imaging, hashing, and artifact analysis with synchronized packet capture and routing-state observation (AODV/OLSR). Cross-layer correlation is vital for reconstructing accurate timelines and supporting node attribution.

In light of these objectives, this research seeks to answer three core questions: First, How can Android emulators on macOS be reliably detected and forensically acquired with integrity? Second, How can emulator artifacts be effectively correlated with MANET traffic to reconstruct comprehensive timelines and support accurate node attribution? Finally, How can the proposed methodology be rigorously validated for reliability in both standalone emulator environments and live ad hoc network scenarios? The framework aims to support practitioners by providing structured procedures, validated toolchains, and practical techniques for reliable data extraction and interpretation across these complex, interconnected environments.

This dual-layer approach—which couples macOS-specific emulator acquisition with MANET-oriented network correlation—addresses a methodological gap not covered in existing literature and establishes a foundation for unified endpoint-network forensic analysis in virtualized environments.

2 Related Studies

Digital forensic analysis is inherently shaped by the examiner's technical expertise, contextual understanding of incidents, and the methodological rigor applied throughout the evidence acquisition and analysis stages. While traditional forensic approaches often prioritize physical devices, there is a growing recognition in the literature of the value of virtualization and emulation environments in modern investigative contexts.

The foundational literature in **emulator-based forensics** highlights the transition from physical device analysis to the examination of virtual environments. Studies have validated the use of live system analysis techniques to examine volatile memory and transient data in virtualized settings. For instance, Makate et al. conducted extensive forensic investigations using the Genymotion emulator, applying tools like SIFT and FTK Imager to emphasize the critical role of memory snapshots and temporary file structures when analyzing emulated mobile environments on desktop systems [12]. Similarly, Kurtca and Samet highlighted that live memory analysis can significantly improve evidence extraction outcomes, especially on systems with dynamic state transitions [13]. Furthermore, the forensic examination of **Android application artifacts** is crucial; Azfar et al. proposed a forensic taxonomy for Android communication apps, stressing that accurate timeline reconstruction and contextual interpretation hinge on timely data acquisition [14]. These findings collectively demonstrate that while the interpretation of Android data is understood, the methodology for reliably acquiring the underlying virtual disk images and volatile data from the *host* machine, especially one with unique protection features, is a key unresolved challenge.

Beyond core acquisition, emulators are increasingly utilized in **proactive forensics and training environments**. Ceballos Delgado et al. introduced the FADE tool to automate the generation of realistic forensic scenarios by populating emulators with synthetic usage data, underscoring the emulator's role in replicating real-world usage patterns in a controlled manner [15]. Additionally, Machaka and Bălan proposed an adversary emulation approach that mirrors threat actor behaviors using virtual setups, aiding in vulnerability discovery and attack path reconstruction from both endpoint and network perspectives [16]. This application of emulation in defensive research necessitates robust forensic capabilities to accurately trace malicious activity within the virtual machine. Moreover, the increasing complexity of modern digital infrastructures, including the migration to cloud-based virtualization [17]. and the adoption of technologies like Software Defined Networking (SDN) [18], further stresses the need for customized forensic protocols capable of accommodating non-static architectures and utilizing tools like **Artificial Intelligence** for automated anomaly detection and artifact classification [19].

The literature on **Forensics in Ad Hoc and MANET Environments** introduces a separate layer of complexity. Mobile ad hoc networks (MANETs) are extensively studied for routing and security, but their forensic implications remain relatively underexplored. Existing research highlights challenges such as ephemeral connections, dynamic topologies, and the absence of centralized logging, which complicate evidence acquisition and correlation [10, 11]. While some works consider MANET forensics from the perspective of traffic analysis, comprehensive methodologies that integrate endpoint artifact collection with network-layer traces are still lacking. Crucially, adversaries may deploy emulator-backed nodes to inflate network membership, launch attacks, or manipulate routing. However, systematic frameworks that explicitly align emulator-specific artifacts (e.g., application databases, configuration files) with MANET packet captures remain absent in the literature.

2.1 Comparative Summary and Research Gap

In summary, current research provides valuable insights into generic emulator forensics and the difficulties of MANET environments. However, a significant **research gap** persists: few studies offer a consolidated, systematic methodology for acquiring and analyzing emulator-based artifacts specifically in **macOS environments**, which pose unique challenges due to APFS, SIP restrictions, and Time Machine configurations. Furthermore, the combination of **macOS host forensics** with **MANET network correlation** has not been addressed. Table 1 outlines how existing frameworks—which are either Al-Dhaqm et al. broad reviews [20] or Şen and Artuner's EFIM [21] cross-platform generalizations fall short of providing the specialized, validated procedures necessary for reliable forensic investigation in the macOS-emulator-MANET nexus. This gap motivates our study, which proposes a specialized, systematic framework for macOS-based Android emulators, validated for both standalone and MANET-integrated scenarios.

Table 1. Comparative overview of related forensic frameworks

Study	Scope	Platform	Validation	Limitations
Al-Dhaqm et al. (2020) – Review of Mobile Forensic Models [20]	Systematic review of 100+ mobile forensic investigation models; proposes Harmonized Mobile Forensics Investigation Process Model (HMFIPM)	General mobile forensics (platform-agnostic, literature-driven)	Comparative literature analysis; no experimental validation	No practical validation; does not address emulator-specific challenges

(continued)

Table 1. *(continued)*

Study	Scope	Platform	Validation	Limitations
Şen & Artuner (2025) – Emulator Forensics Investigation Model (EFIM) [21]	Nine-phase emulator-specific forensic model; operationalized with Emulator Forensics Tool (EFT); platform-agnostic (Windows, Linux, macOS)	Cross-platform (Bluestacks, NoxPlayer, Waydroid across Windows/Linux/macOS)	Controlled experiments; EFT tool validation; statistical performance comparison with Magnet Axiom	Tool limited in Linux IMG parsing; EFT supports only Windows OS currently; limited app set
This Study (2025) – macOS Emulator Framework	Forensic framework tailored for macOS-based Android emulators, addressing APFS, SIP, Time Machine, and emulator disk artifacts	macOS-specific (Parallels, NoxPlayer, Genymotion tested)	Controlled experiments on macOS Ventura testbed; emulator artifacts collected and validated via adb, dd, qemu-img, FTK Imager	Focused only on macOS; excludes some popular emulators (Bluestacks, LDPlayer); limited cross-platform generalization

3 Methodologies

3.1 Framework Design and Digital Forensics Model

The methodology presented in this study is based on the four-stage model defined in NIST Special Publication 800–86: collection, examination, analysis, and reporting [22]. The proposed forensic framework is specifically designed for identifying, acquiring, and analyzing artifacts generated by Android emulators operating within the macOS ecosystem. This framework has been empirically tested through structured experiments and validated using controlled forensic scenarios.

Building on this four-stage process model, the following subsections describe the experimental environment and acquisition workflow used to operationalize the framework on macOS. An overview of the proposed macOS-centric forensic framework—and its alignment with the NIST four-stage model—is illustrated in Fig. 3, which presents the conceptual workflow guiding all acquisition, processing, and correlation steps used in this study.

3.2 Environment Setup

The Test Platform (TP) was established on macOS Ventura 13.5 (APFS) with Parallels, NoxPlayer, and Genymotion emulators, where WhatsApp, Gmail, and Chrome were installed to generate synthetic activity over ten days. A separate Analysis Station (AS), running Windows 10 and equipped with high-capacity CPU, RAM, and storage, was used for forensic imaging and analysis. Consolidated specifications of both TP and AS are provided in Table 2.

Table 2. TP features analysis station

Platform	Test Platform	Analysis Station
OS & FS	MacOS Ventura 13.5 APFS	Windows 10 64 Bit NTFS
Hardware	Macbook Air A1932	HP workstation
CPU	1.6 GHz Intel Core i5 (Dual-Core)	Intel Xeon 2.3 GHz (8 cores)
Disk Size	128 GB	2 Tbyte
RAM	8 GB	64 GB

Fig. 1 provides a detailed view of the Test Platform (TP), showing the macOS host, installed Android emulators, and the set of communication and browsing applications deployed for data generation. The illustration clarifies the experimental environment and supports the reproducibility of forensic acquisition procedures described in this study.

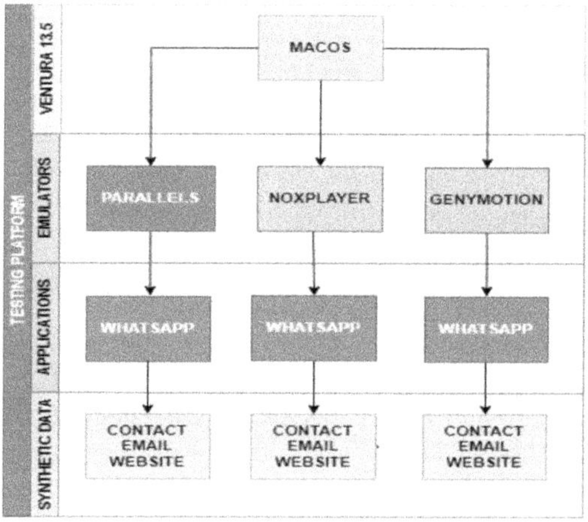

Fig. 1. Test platform showing the macOS host, installed emulators, and deployed applications used for data generation and forensic acquisition

3.3 Preparation of Test Platform

Three emulators—Parallels, NoxPlayer, and Genymotion—were selected based on popularity and compatibility with macOS. Each was installed and initialized with Android environments. Information regarding the monitors used in the test platform and the applications loaded on these emulators are summarized in Table 3.

Table 3. Emulator and application information

Emulator and Version	Parallels 20.2.0 (55872)	NoxPlayer 3.8.5.7.	Genymotion 3.8.0
OS Ver.	Android 9-r2	Android 7.1.2	Android 9.0
Brand Model	Google Android	SM-N950N	Note10+
App. Name	WhatsApp, IMO, Gmail	WhatsApp, IMO, Gmail	WhatsApp, IMO, Gmail
App. Ver.	Ver. 2.24.	Ver.2.23.25.78v2	Ver. 2.24.25.77

Test scenarios included typical user behavior such as messaging, email access, and browsing to generate logs and databases representative of real usage. Applications were monitored for data persistence and trace generation.

3.4 Acquisition Process and Tool Selection

Acquisition involved using dd for bitwise imaging and qemu-img for format conversion; emulator-specific virtual disks (e.g., HDS, QCOW2, VMDK) were extracted and—where necessary—converted to RAW (.img) for downstream analysis.

A curated set of forensic tools was employed to ensure methodological integrity and repeatability. Table 4 lists the selected tools, their categories, platforms, and roles. Tools such as **dd** and **qemu-img** provided low-level imaging and format conversion, while **FTK Imager** and **SQLite Browser** enabled artifact review. Hashing utilities (e.g., HashCalc) were used to calculate SHA-256 and MD5 values before and after acquisition, ensuring evidentiary integrity. Together, these tools supported a reliable, emulator-aware workflow adapted to macOS environments.

Table 4. Tool summary and functional role

Tool Name	Category	Platform Used	Purpose in Workflow	Output Type
macOS Timemachine	Backup Tool	macOS GUI	Logical-level disk imaging	Logical Data
dd	Imaging Tool	macOS Terminal	Physical-level disk imaging	RAW disk image (.img)
adb	Logical Acquisition	Android Emulator CLI	Pulling app data, file trees	APK, SQLite, logs
qemu-img	Format Converter	macOS Terminal	Converting QCOW2/HDS/VMDK to raw for analysis	RAW image
FTK Imager	Forensic Analyzer	Windows (AS)	Mounting, previewing and exporting artifacts	Reports, file exports
SQLite Browser	Database Viewer	Windows/macOS	Viewing app databases (e.g., msgstore.db)	Table exports, screenshots

(*continued*)

Table 4. *(continued)*

Tool Name	Category	Platform Used	Purpose in Workflow	Output Type
DCode	Timestamp Decoder	Windows	Converting binary and Unix timestamp formats	Human-readable timestamps
Hex Editor	Hex Editor	Windows	Manual artifact verification and low-level data parsing	Binary/hex data views
HashCalc	Hashing Tool	Windows	Generating SHA-256 and MD5 values	Hash values

As a complementary method, macOS Time Machine was used to recover emulator data from historical backups. Restored directories (e.g., */Users/*, emulator images, configs, logs) were examined with forensic tools to detect deleted or modified files and enrich timelines. While not a substitute for disk imaging, Time Machine snapshots—stored in APFS format under *Macintosh HD – Data*—provide valuable access to earlier system states. This method enables recovery of deleted artifacts but requires prior backup activity and does not capture volatile session data.

3.5 Analysis

All acquired disk images were mounted read-only to preserve integrity. Analysis followed three steps: (i) file-system survey of emulator images to identify sandboxes, logs, and directory structures; (ii) mapping key artifacts (e.g., WhatsApp, Gmail databases, caches, config files) to canonical paths for cross-emulator comparison; and (iii) extracting/normalizing data using tools such as FTK Imager, SQLite Browser, and DCode, with selective handling of encrypted containers. All actions, hashes, and tool versions were logged, ensuring reproducibility and minimal privileged access.

3.6 Validation and Reliability Checks

Experiments were repeated on a controlled testbed with synchronized clocks and pre/post hash verification. Workflows were rerun across emulators to confirm image integrity, stable artifact locations, and consistent timelines. Independent re-analysis verified tool-independence, while discrepancies (e.g., encryption, transient logs) were documented with causes and mitigations, ensuring reliable and transferable results.

3.7 Ad Hoc Network Scenario (Network-Context Layer)

A network-context layer was added for synchronized acquisition of emulator and MANET evidence. Emulator instances (Parallels, NoxPlayer, Genymotion) acted as nodes in a virtual testbed running AODV and OLSR. Network traffic was captured with tcpdump/tshark/Wireshark, while emulator artifacts (e.g., SQLite DBs, logs, configs) were acquired with adb, dd, and qemu-img. All systems were NTP-synchronized to align pcaps with emulator events. Packet traces were cross-correlated with artifacts—e.g., WhatsApp messages matched to TCP/UDP flows, OLSR events aligned with logs—supporting attribution, timeline reconstruction, and rogue-node detection. Repeatability tests confirmed consistent results across runs. Fig. 2 shows the extended framework. As summarized in Table 1, while prior works such as Al-Dhaqm et al. (2020) and Şen & Artuner (2025) proposed generalized or cross-platform frameworks, the present methodology is tailored to the macOS environment.

Fig. 2. Extended forensic framework integrating the test platform (TP), analysis station (AS), acquisition workflow, MANET network-context layer, and cross-layer correlation with validation/reporting

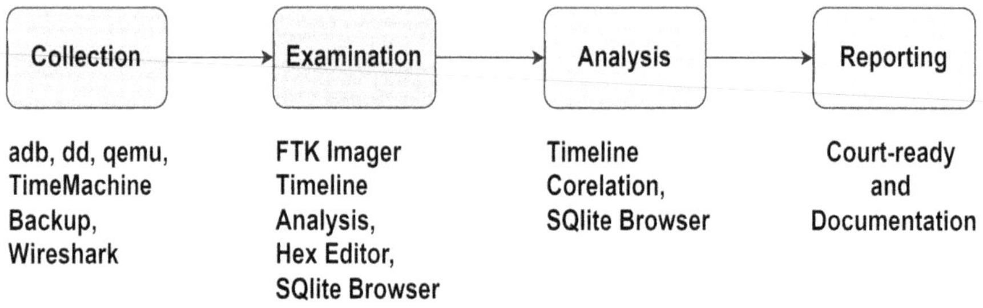

Fig. 3. Conceptual overview of the proposed macOS-centric forensic framework, aligned with the NIST four-stage model and adapted for emulator-specific acquisition and analysis

4 Results

This section presents the empirical findings obtained from the acquisition, imaging, and analysis of emulator artifacts across Parallels, NoxPlayer, and Genymotion on macOS Ventura. The results cover (i) forensic imaging and integrity verification, (ii) recovery of application-level artifacts, (iii) emulator performance evaluation, (iv) handling of storage formats, (v) challenges in data interpretation and encryption, and (vi) cross-layer correlation in MANET scenarios.

4.1 Forensic Imaging and Data Integrity

All three emulators were successfully imaged using **dd**, **adb**, and **qemu-img**, depending on the storage format and acquisition constraints of each platform. The corresponding forensic methods, the emulators they apply to, and their typical file paths on macOS are summarized in Table 5, which highlights the heterogeneity of storage structures across Parallels (HDS/PVM), NoxPlayer (VMDK), and Genymotion (QCOW2). These differences required emulator-aware acquisition strategies to ensure consistency and forensic soundness.

Virtual disks stored in **HDS** (Parallels), **VMDK** (NoxPlayer), and **QCOW2** (Genymotion) were acquired and, when necessary, converted to **RAW** images for downstream analysis. Example commands demonstrating these acquisition and conversion procedures are provided in Table 6, illustrating reproducible workflows for each emulator type.

Integrity was verified through **SHA-256** and **MD5** hashes calculated both before and after acquisition, confirming that no modifications occurred during imaging. Additionally, **Time Machine snapshots** provided complementary recovery capability, enabling access to deleted or overwritten emulator files. These snapshots enriched timeline reconstruction but were dependent on prior backups and did not capture volatile states.

Table 5. Tools applicable for forensic acquisition (methods, emulator type, and file paths)

Forensic Method / Emulator	DD	ADB	QEMU	Typical Emulator File Path and File Names
Parallels	–	–	√	/Users/testplatform/Parallels/ Android9.pvm (Android x86–0.hdd) **(Android x86–0.hdd.hds)**
NoxPlayer	√	√	–	/Users/testplatform/Library/ApplicationSupport/NoxAppPlayer/BignoxVMS/nox/ **nox-disk-1.vmdk ve nox-disk-2.vmdk**
Genymotion	–	√	–	/Users/testplatform/.Genymobile/Genymotion/deployed/Samsung Galaxy Note 10+/ **data.qcow2**

Table 6. Example commands for forensic acquisition

Emulator	Example Command / Procedure
Parallels	qemu-img convert -O raw "Android x86–0.hdd.0.hds" imaj.dd C:\Program Files\qemu>qemu-img convert -O raw "Android x86–0.hdd.0.{*}.hds" imaj.img
NoxPlayer	VMDK Acqusition adb Shell /dd if=/dev/block/sdb3 of=/sdcard/image/imaj.dd
Genymotion	adb pull / /Users/testplatform/adlikopya/ qemu-img convert -f data.qcow2 -O raw data.qcow2 imaj.dd adb shell "su -c dd if=/dev/block/vdb3 bs = 4096 | pv > /Users/testplatform/adlikopya/imaj.dd

4.2 Recovery of Application-Level Artifacts

Artifacts from WhatsApp, Gmail, and IMO were recovered consistently across all emulators. Key databases such as:

- **WhatsApp:** msgstore.db,
- **Gmail:** bigtopdata.db,
- **IMO:** application logs and caches,

were successfully extracted and parsed. Recovered records included chat messages, timestamps, contacts, and metadata, providing a reliable basis for behavioral reconstruction. The results demonstrate that emulator-hosted applications generate artifacts structurally comparable to those on physical Android devices.

4.3 Emulator Performance Evaluation

The forensic suitability of emulators was evaluated using six metrics: imaging feasibility, data access difficulty, macOS security impact, analysis feasibility, artifact interpretability, and encryption handling. Parallels achieved the highest overall score (47/60), demonstrating strong compatibility with forensic tools and stable extraction routines. NoxPlayer (39/60) offered moderate accessibility but was affected by macOS privilege restrictions. Genymotion (40/60) exhibited reliable imaging but required more time and effort due to encryption layers and complex container structures.

The comparative scores for all three emulators across these six criteria are presented in Table 7, and Fig. 4 visualizes these results using a performance bar chart for clearer comparison. These findings indicate that no emulator is uniformly superior; each requires tailored acquisition strategies to ensure forensic soundness.

Table 7. Comparative metrics table

Criteria / Emulator	Parallels	NoxPlayer	Genymotion
Imaging (Data Collection)	9/10	7/10	8/10
Data Access Difficulties	6/10	8/10	7/10
Security Settings (MacOS)	8/10	5/10	7/10
Data Analysis (Review)	9/10	7/10	6/10
Data Meaning	9/10	6/10	7/10
Decryption (Decipherment)	8/10	6/10	5/10
Total Score	47/60	39/60	40/60

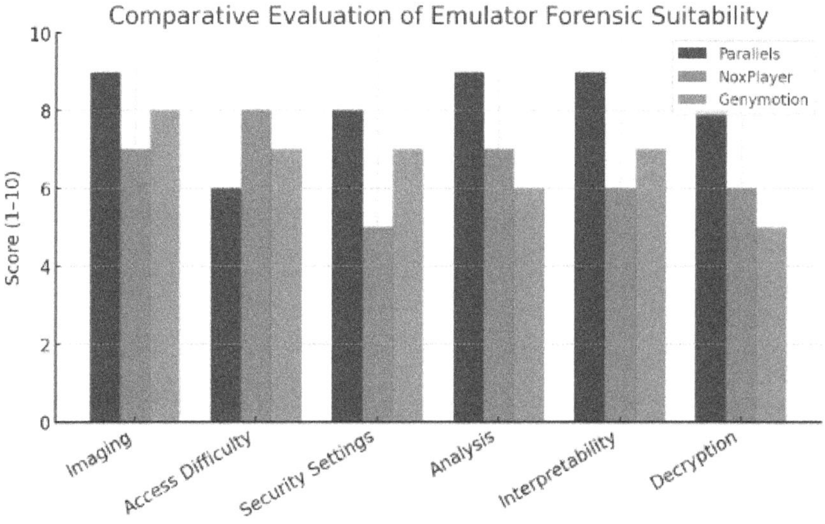

Fig. 4. Comparative bar chart of emulator performance metrics

4.4 Storage Format Handling and Pre-Analysis Processing

The three emulators used distinct storage formats, requiring different preprocessing steps: Parallels (.hds / .pvm) required HDS segments to be combined and converted to RAW via qemu-img; NoxPlayer (.vmdk) images were directly mountable and required no format conversion; and Genymotion (.qcow2) images often required conversion and, in some cases, decryption prior to analysis. These differences highlight the need for emulator-aware preprocessing, particularly when dealing with layered or encrypted container formats.

A consolidated overview of emulator-independent forensic methods applicable across these formats is provided in Table 8, demonstrating that disk imaging, integrity verification, cross-layer correlation, and backup-based recovery remain applicable regardless of the emulator product.

Table 8. Emulator-independent forensic methods in macOS environments

Method	Emulator-Independent Capability
Disk Imaging & Format Conversion (dd, qemu-img)	Enables bit-stream acquisition and RAW conversion from diverse emulator disk formats (.hds, .vmdk, .qcow2), ensuring tool interoperability across platforms.
Data Integrity & Hash Verification (SHA-256/MD5)	Verifies pre/post-acquisition integrity of images and exports to maintain evidentiary admissibility and repeatability.
Application/Data-Layer Analysis (FTK Imager, SQLite Browser)	Extracts and interprets app artifacts (e.g., WhatsApp msgstore.db, Gmail databases), independent of emulator vendor or version.
Time Synchronization & Cross-Layer Correlation	Aligns emulator artifacts (logs, DB timestamps) with packet captures (pcap) and routing events to strengthen timelines and attribution (incl. MANET scenarios).
macOS Security Controls Management (SIP, Privilege Handling)	Applies controlled procedures for System Integrity Protection (SIP) and root/ACL access to safely reach low-level artifacts across all emulators.
Backup & Temporal Analysis (Time Machine)	Recovers historical states of emulator files and configs from APFS snapshots to detect deletions/modifications and enrich timelines.
Manual Verification & Hex-Level Review (Hex editors, DCode)	Validates automated findings, decodes timestamps, and inspects low-level structures for hidden or corrupted artifacts.
Automation & AI-Assisted Triage	Speeds triage and anomaly detection with scripted acquisition/parsing and ML-based classification, without coupling to a specific emulator.
Chain of Custody & Documentation	Maintains standardized logs of actions, tools, hashes, and versions to ensure legal defensibility across heterogeneous setups.

(continued)

Table 8. *(continued)*

Method	Emulator-Independent Capability
Validation & Repeatability Testing	Re-runs acquisitions/analyses under controlled conditions to confirm consistent outcomes regardless of emulator product.

4.5 Interpretation Challenges and Encryption Findings

Data interpretation was straightforward in Parallels images, where artifacts appeared in expected Android directory structures. By contrast, Genymotion introduced significant challenges: encrypted containers, non-standard mount points, and nested file systems slowed extraction and required manual verification using hex-level inspection.

NoxPlayer presented moderate difficulty due to macOS System Integrity Protection (SIP), which restricted access to certain directories until privilege adjustments were made. Across all emulators, automated tools occasionally failed to parse encrypted or partially corrupted artifacts, confirming the need for examiner-driven validation.

4.6 Cross-Layer Correlation in MANET Scenarios

To evaluate the framework within decentralized network environments, emulator instances were deployed as MANET nodes running AODV and OLSR. Packet captures collected via tcpdump/tshark/Wireshark were synchronized with emulator artifacts through NTP-aligned timestamps.

The results showed:

- WhatsApp activity recorded in msgstore.db was temporally correlated with observed TCP/UDP traffic flows in MANET packet captures.
- OLSR neighbor discovery and topology updates aligned with emulator logcat entries, confirming emulator-originated routing activity.
- Emulator-based nodes could be distinguished from physical devices through characteristic traffic patterns and timing correlations.

These findings demonstrate the feasibility and reliability of cross-layer correlation between endpoint artifacts and MANET network traces, supporting both timeline reconstruction and node attribution.

4.7 Summary of Experimental Findings

Overall, the results confirm the robustness of the proposed framework across heterogeneous emulator environments. Despite differences in storage formats, encryption schemes, and macOS security restrictions, consistent imaging, artifact recovery, and network-artifact correlation were achieved. The MANET experiments further validated that emulator-originated activity can be accurately attributed through synchronized endpoint and network-level evidence.

5 Discussion

5.1 Comparison with Existing Frameworks

This study complements and extends existing work by positioning a macOS-specific emulator forensic workflow against both survey-based and cross-platform models. Unlike Al-Dhaqm et al. [20], whose comprehensive review remains platform-agnostic and largely theoretical, our framework is operationalized and experimentally validated on macOS. Compared to the cross-platform EFIM [21], which emphasizes performance and generalized phase design, our approach targets environment-specific constraints—APFS snapshots, System Integrity Protection (SIP), root/ACL handling, and Time Machine recovery—that materially affect acquisition repeatability and evidentiary integrity under macOS. In short, EFIM generalizes across OS families, whereas our contribution deepens the methodology where EFIM is comparatively shallow: the constrained macOS ecosystem and emulator-specific artifact handling therein.

5.2 Environment-Specific Adaptations for macOS

A key contribution is the systematic treatment of macOS controls that directly influence forensic soundness: (i) APFS snapshot semantics and their role in historical state recovery; (ii) SIP-aware acquisition pathways that minimize system modification while preserving access to low-level artifacts; and (iii) Time Machine–assisted timeline enrichment, enabling recovery of deleted/overwritten emulator files (.hds, .vmdk, .qcow2). These adaptations translate into procedural reliability (pre/post hash verification, read-only mounting, reproducible conversion pipelines) that are often assumed—but not detailed—in generalized models. Our findings indicate that macOS-aware procedures reduce analyst time spent on ad-hoc workarounds and lower the risk of evidentiary inadmissibility due to invasive system changes.

5.3 Cross-Layer Correlation in MANET Scenarios

By extending the workflow with a network-context layer for MANETs (AODV/OLSR), we show that emulator artifacts (e.g., WhatsApp msgstore.db, app logs, config files) can be synchronized with packet captures and routing events through NTP-aligned timestamps. This cross-layer alignment improves (i) timeline reconstruction (linking database events to TCP/UDP flows), (ii) node attribution (associating routing behavior with emulator-backed hosts), and (iii) rogue-node detection in decentralized, intermittently connected networks. Prior work either examines emulators or MANETs in isolation; our results demonstrate practical interoperability between endpoint and network evidence where centralized logging is unavailable. Although real-time traffic monitoring could further enhance MANET-oriented forensic analysis, it was not implemented in the present study due to several methodological and technical constraints. Real-time capture streams distributed across multiple emulator instances introduce timestamp drift, performance overhead, and volatility that can compromise evidentiary reliability on macOS. Furthermore, maintaining synchronized live feeds within decentralized MANET topologies requires additional instrumentation not native to emulator environments. Nevertheless, the proposed framework remains compatible with real-time extensions—such as remote tcpdump streams, Wireshark live interfaces, or SDN-assisted telemetry—which constitute a promising direction for future work.

5.4 Practical Implications for Investigators

For practitioners, three implications follow:

Method portability: Disk-image conversion (qemu-img), integrity checks, and SQLite-level artifact parsing remain stable across Parallels, Genymotion, and NoxPlayer, yielding a vendor-agnostic core.

Risk management under macOS: SIP/privilege handling can be planned as bounded, **auditable** steps, reducing legal/operational exposure.

Ad-hoc readiness: The network-context layer offers actionable procedures to correlate emulator behavior with MANET traffic, useful for field operations where infrastructure is absent.

5.5 Where this Study Stands Relative to EFIM

While EFIM formalizes a nine-phase, tool-supported pipeline and reports strong performance across OS families, its treatment of macOS-specific acquisition hurdles (APFS, SIP, Time Machine) is limited. Our study narrows scope to macOS to deliver depth: fine-grained paths, conversion recipes, integrity routines, and legal/ethical guardrails specific to Apple platforms. Conversely, EFIM's broader toolchain and performance analysis suggest avenues we can adopt (e.g., automation, formal process proofs, and larger-scale benchmarking) to scale our approach beyond macOS.

5.6 Limitations and Alignment with Future Work

Two limitations frame future extensions. First, the emulator set—while representative—excludes some popular options (e.g., BlueStacks/LDPlayer) in macOS contexts due to compatibility constraints. Second, encryption and IMG/Container peculiarities occasionally demand manual intervention. In alignment with EFIM's roadmap, future work should prioritize (i) automated parsing for additional disk/container formats, (ii) plugin-based decryption for BLOB artifacts, (iii) scripted acquisition and AI-assisted triage, and (iv) replication across multiple macOS versions to strengthen external validity.

5.7 Key Takeaways

Overall, the findings of this study highlight three overarching insights regarding the forensic examination of Android emulators on macOS and their integration into MANET environments. First, the research demonstrates that a macOS-aware forensic workflow—one that explicitly accounts for APFS characteristics, System Integrity Protection (SIP), and Time Machine snapshot semantics—provides a reliable basis for acquiring and analyzing emulator-based evidence. Incorporating these platform-specific considerations into a systematic procedure reduces the reliance on ad-hoc workarounds and strengthens evidentiary integrity.

Second, the results show that cross-emulator consistency can be achieved through an emulator-independent set of core forensic practices, including bit-stream imaging, integrity verification, database-level artifact extraction, and manual validation techniques. These practices remain effective despite differences in storage formats, encryption schemes, or emulator-level security implementations, thereby enhancing the portability and reproducibility of forensic workflows.

Finally, by integrating a network-context layer for MANET scenarios, the study illustrates that emulator artifacts can be meaningfully correlated with packet-level routing activity using synchronized time references. This capability enables more complete timeline reconstruction and supports node attribution in decentralized environments where centralized logging is absent. Together, these insights underline the broader significance of the proposed framework, demonstrating its value for both forensic practitioners and researchers working with virtualized Android environments under macOS.

In addition, while a dedicated cross-emulator correlation module was beyond the scope of this study, the results indicate that consistent alignment of timestamps, artifact paths, and routing events across Parallels, NoxPlayer, and Genymotion is feasible. These observations suggest that a unified correlation layer—normalizing event structures across multiple emulator platforms—could be developed in future research to further strengthen attribution and temporal analysis.

6 Limitations and Recommendations

This study has several limitations that should be considered when interpreting the findings and planning future research. The evaluation was conducted on macOS Ventura 13.5 using a representative but limited emulator set (Parallels, NoxPlayer, and Genymotion). Although these emulators cover widely used categories, the results may vary across other products—such as BlueStacks or LDPlayer—or across different macOS releases and hardware configurations. Additionally, some emulator containers, particularly those employing layered QCOW2 structures or file-based encryption, required manual intervention. These procedures may be difficult to scale in time-critical investigations and may introduce examiner-dependent variability. Furthermore, macOS security controls, including System Integrity Protection (SIP) and application-level privilege restrictions, occasionally required carefully monitored adjustments. While these steps were necessary for comprehensive acquisition, they highlight the need for standardized, auditable privilege-handling routines.

A tool-level comparison with commercial forensic suites (e.g., Magnet Axiom, Oxygen, Cellebrite UFED) was not included because these products lack native support for macOS-based emulator containers such as HDS, QCOW2, and layered VMDK formats. As a result, any direct benchmark would produce incomplete or misleading results, and was therefore considered outside the methodological scope of this study.

From an operational standpoint, challenges were encountered when accessing low-level storage artifacts, parsing encrypted containers, and synchronizing emulator artifacts with network traces in MANET scenarios. Although these issues were mitigated through repeatable workflows, hashing practices, and NTP-based time alignment, they indicate areas where tooling and automation support are still evolving. In particular, automated handlers for encrypted BLOBs, multi-layer disk formats, and cross-layer event alignment would benefit both practitioners and researchers.

Based on these limitations, several recommendations can be made. First, forensic practitioners working with Android emulators on macOS should adopt controlled acquisition strategies that include read-only imaging, pre–/post-hash verification, and careful documentation of any privilege elevation required during the process. The use of Time Machine snapshots can substantially improve temporal reconstruction but should be supplemented with full disk imaging to avoid reliance on user-initiated backups. Second, researchers are encouraged to extend the framework to additional emulator platforms and to evaluate its applicability across multiple macOS versions, enabling broader generalizability. Future studies should also explore automation of disk parsing, decryption routines, and MANET traffic correlation, including the use of machine-learning–based anomaly detection to support triage. Finally, integrating both emulator-backed and physical Android nodes into hybrid MANET testbeds would provide valuable insights into cross-platform attribution and routing behavior.

Legal and ethical considerations must also guide forensic investigations involving emulator environments. Evidence acquisition should proceed under appropriate legal authority, with a well-documented chain of custody and minimal system modification to ensure admissibility. Processing of personal data—particularly communication logs, account metadata, or contact information—must comply with principles of lawfulness, data minimization, and purpose limitation. Where feasible, non-case-relevant data should be excluded or anonymized, and investigators should remain aware of software licensing constraints and terms of service associated with emulator platforms. These considerations are essential for maintaining both procedural integrity and compliance with regulatory frameworks governing digital evidence.

From a legal-admissibility perspective, the framework reinforces data provenance through read-only imaging, pre- and post-acquisition hashing, APFS snapshot preservation, and auditable privilege elevation. These procedures align with widely accepted chain-of-custody principles by minimizing system alteration and ensuring transparent documentation of each acquisition step. Such safeguards are essential for maintaining evidentiary integrity when emulator environments are used as investigative sources in formal legal proceedings.

7 Conclusions

7.1 Key Contributions

This study introduces a structured and validated forensic framework specifically tailored for the acquisition and analysis of Android emulator artifacts in macOS environments. By focusing on widely used emulators such as Parallels, NoxPlayer, and Genymotion, the methodology addresses a critical gap in current forensic practices—namely, the lack of reliable, emulator-specific approaches within Apple's restrictive macOS ecosystem. The framework was experimentally tested on a controlled testbed and evaluated through six core forensic metrics. Specifically, the key contributions include: (i) the identification of emulator-specific storage formats and file paths, (ii) procedures for extracting forensic disk images while maintaining data integrity, (iii) practical guidance for interpreting encrypted and application-level artifacts, particularly from communication apps such as WhatsApp and Gmail, and (iv) the integration of emulator forensics into ad hoc network scenarios, enabling cross-layer correlation between endpoint artifacts and MANET packet captures.

7.2 Practical Recommendations

Forensic practitioners working with virtualized Android environments on macOS should adopt emulator-aware acquisition protocols, ensuring compatibility with formats such as .vmdk, .qcow2, and .hds. Standard operating procedures should be established to guide the safe handling of kernel-level settings—such as SIP disabling via recovery mode (csrutil disable)—and to ensure compliance with digital evidence admissibility standards. Additionally, future investigations should expand the emulator set beyond the current sample, include multiple macOS versions, and explore the integration of automation (e.g., scripted acquisition), artificial intelligence for artifact classification, and live forensic review capabilities. A continuous update cycle for forensic tools and procedures is essential as emulator platforms evolve.

7.3 Emphasis on Reliability and Data Integrity

Data integrity was prioritized at every stage of the framework—from acquisition using adb, dd, and qemu-img to post-acquisition validation via SHA-256 and MD5 hash checks. Emulator artifacts were extracted without altering their native structure, and each tool was selected for its forensic soundness and replicability. The study also demonstrated that forensic results cannot rely solely on automated output: manual verification, log comparison, and encrypted file examination remain essential. Where applicable, cross-validation with network traces should also be performed to strengthen evidentiary defensibility. This reinforces the foundational principle that the reliability of forensic evidence hinges on methodological rigor and examiner oversight.

7.4 Importance of a Systematic and Emulator-Independent Methodology

The macOS environment introduces unique technical and procedural challenges for digital forensics. Without a structured methodology, critical artifacts may be missed or compromised. This study's framework—aligned with NIST's four-stage forensic process (collection, examination, analysis, reporting)—offers a repeatable model that supports consistency across forensic cases. Its systematic nature ensures that even complex emulator configurations can be handled with reliability, enabling investigators to collect and interpret volatile and persistent data from emulated Android environments with confidence. Importantly, the findings confirm that the strength of emulator forensics is not limited to vendor-specific performance but is grounded in emulator-independent methods that apply across heterogeneous platforms (see Table 7). Techniques such as disk imaging, integrity verification, cross-layer correlation, and Time Machine–based recovery remain valid regardless of the emulator product, thereby enhancing portability, reproducibility, and legal defensibility. Furthermore, this structured approach facilitates the integration of emulator forensics into MANET contexts, ensuring that both endpoint and network artifacts can be consistently correlated in decentralized environments. In doing so, the study provides not only a product-aware evaluation but also a methodological foundation for future research in emulator-based MANET forensics.

References

1. Statista: Global: number of smartphone users 2014–2029| Statista, https://www.statista.com/forecasts/1143723/smartphone-users-in-the-world, Accessed 28 Sep 2025.
2. IOCTA: Intsernet Organised Crime Threat Assessment (IOCTA) 2023 (2023). https://doi.org/10.2813/587536.
3. TNP: EGM 2024 Yılı İdari Faaliyet Raporu (2025).
4. J.Gn.K.lığı: Jandarma Genel Komutanlığı 2024 Yılı Faaliyet Raporu (2025).
5. Statista: Smartphone OS market share worldwide 2009–2017| Statista, https://www.statista.com/statistics/263453/global-market-share-held-by-smartphone-operating-systems/, Accessed 28 Sep 2025.
6. Akshaya Asokan: Hackers Use Mobile Emulators to Steal Millions, https://www.bankinfosecurity.com/attackers-use-mobile-emulators-to-steal-millions-a-15623, Accessed 28 Sep 2025.
7. Alzaylaee, M.K., Yerima, S.Y., Sezer, S.: EMULATOR vs REAL PHONE: android malware detection using machine learning. In: CODASPY '17: Seventh ACM Conference on Data and Application Security and Privacy, pp. 65–72. ACM (2017). https://doi.org/10.1145/3041008.3041010
8. Imaginationtech: imaginationtech, https://www.imaginationtech.com/glossary/emulation/, last accessed 19 Jan 2025.
9. Gritzman Shachar, Kessem Limor: securityintelligence, https://securityintelligence.com/posts/massive-fraud-operation-evil-mobile-emulator-farms/, Accessed 29 Jan 2025.
10. Perkins, C., Belding-Royer, E., Das, S.: Ad hoc on-demand distance vector (AODV). Routing., https://www.rfc-editor.org/info/rfc3561. (2003). https://doi.org/10.17487/rfc3561
11. Clausen, T. and Jacquet, P. (2003) Optimized link state routing protocol (OLSR). Ietf Rfc3626, 75. - References - Scientific Research Publishing, https://www.scirp.org/reference/referencespapers?referenceid=2253964, Accessed 28 Sep 2025.
12. Makate, A., Muduva, M., Chiwariro, R., Agrawal, A.K., Khatri, P.: Android Smart Phone Forensics using Open Source Tools. **11** (2023). https://doi.org/10.22214/ijraset.2023.56106
13. Kurtca, T., Samet, R.: Examination of MAC address records of phones connected to the macOS computer. J. Fac. Eng. Archit. Gazi Univ. **39**, 1637–1647 (2024). https://doi.org/10.17341/gazimmfd.1140690
14. Azfar, A., Choo, K.K.R., Liu, L.: An android communication app forensic taxonomy. J. Forensic Sci. **61**, 1337–1350 (2016). https://doi.org/10.1111/1556-4029.13164
15. Ceballos Delgado, A.A., Glisson, W.B., Grispos, G., Raymond Choo, K.-K., Alberto Ceballos Delgado, C.A.: FADE: a Forensic Image Generator for Android Device Education, vol. 4, p. e1432. Wiley Interdisciplinary Reviews: Forensic Science (2022). https://doi.org/10.1002/wfs2.1432
16. Machaka, V., Balan, T.: Investigating proactive digital forensics leveraging adversary emulation. Appl. Sci. **12**, 9077 (2022). https://doi.org/10.3390/app12189077
17. Yang, R., Ren, J., Bai, S., Tang, T.: A digital forensic framework for cloud based on VMI. DEStech Transactions on Computer Science and Engineering. **0** (2017). https://doi.org/10.12783/DTCSE/CST2017/12595

18. Spiekermann, D., Eggendorfer, T.: Challenges of network forensic investigation in virtual networks. J. Cyber Secur. Mobility **5**(2), 15–46 (2016). https://doi.org/10.13052/jcsm2245-1439.522
19. Gujar, P., Sabale, A., Shaha Ayurved Mahavidyalaya, S.: Role of artificial intelligence in forensics. International Journal of Advanced Research in Science, Communication and Technology (IJARSCT) International Open-Access, Double-Blind, Peer-Reviewed, Refereed, Multidisciplinary Online Journal. **4** (2024). https://doi.org/10.48175/IJARSCT-19859
20. Al-Dhaqm, A., Razak, S.A., Ikuesan, R.A., Kebande, V.R., Siddique, K.: A review of mobile forensic investigation process models. IEEE Access **8**, 173359–173375 (2020). https://doi.org/10.1109/ACCESS.2020.3014615
21. Şen, S., Artuner, H.: Emulator forensics investigation model (EFIM). IEEE Access. **13**, 134189–134211 (2025). https://doi.org/10.1109/ACCESS.2025.3585096
22. Kent, K., Chevalier, S., Grance, T., Dang, H.: Guide to Integrating Fo-Rensic Techniques into Incident Response. National Institute of Standards and Technology, Gaithersburg, MD (2006)

AI, Multimodal Learning, and Intelligent Mobility Applications

SYNAPSE: Synthesizing Narratives from Agentic Path Spatial Exploration

Prateek Gupta(✉), Daniel Antunes Pedrozo, Aleksandr Koviazin, Jorge Augusto Meira, and Antonio Ken Iannillo

SnT, University of Luxembourg, 29 Av. John F. Kennedy, 1855 Luxembourg City, Luxembourg

{prateek.gupta,daniel.antunes,aleksandr.koviazin,jorge.meira, antonioken.iannillo}@uni.lu

Abstract. We introduce Synapse, a modular, privacy-preserving framework for generating multilingual summaries of logistics routes, a task distinct from traditional routing optimization or forecasting. Our approach transforms static route definitions by synthesizing them with a variety of signals, including pre-computed failure predictions, real-time traffic, and weather, through a network of specialized AI agents, orchestrated using the FastMCP (Multi-Agent Communication Protocol) framework. To ensure GDPR compliance, we apply random perturbation to GPS coordinates before querying external APIs, a method that obfuscates precise locations while preserving local context. The system simulates the route's temporal progression via iterative calls to a traffic API, enabling time-aware queries for other agents gathering weather and urban context data. A generative agent fuses these multimodal signals into a core narrative. Parallel translation agents then render that narrative in multiple languages. This work presents a scalable pipeline for interpretable logistics intelligence, introducing an agentic architecture and a human-validated, multilingual evaluation benchmark.

Keywords: Multimodal Machine Learning · Privacy-Preserving Logistics · Route Summarization · Agent-Based Systems · Large Language Models (LLMs)

1 Introduction

The planning and execution of logistics routes in heterogeneous regions, such as Europe, involves navigating two persistent challenges: the synthesis of high-volume, multimodal data streams and the need for clear communication across multilingual teams. While substantial research has advanced route optimization planning, a complementary challenge is the automated generation of concise, multilingual narratives for real-time operational awareness. Such summaries can help human decision-makers adapt to dynamic conditions, a task that remains difficult to scale. The complexity of this task is enhanced by two primary obstacles. First, route data contains sensitive geolocations protected by frameworks

B. Kihei et al. (Eds.): INTSYS 2025, LNICST 717, pp. 143–153, 2027.
https://doi.org/10.1007/978-3-032-38705-9_7

like GDPR. This privacy constraint renders monolithic approaches impractical for real-world deployment, as they would require transmitting all raw, sensitive data to a single, often third-party, large language model. Second, the architectural challenge of reasoning across diverse data domains (e.g., service failure predictions, traffic, weather, workload) remains significant. A traditional approach would require a human planner or a monolithic application to manually query multiple REST APIs, each with its own unique payload structure, authentication, and data format. Our agentic framework is designed to abstract this complexity. It allows users to make requests in plain English, delegating the intricate task of data retrieval and synthesis to a network of specialized agents. This not only makes the system more scalable and easier to maintain but also democratizes access to complex logistics intelligence by removing the need for specialized API knowledge. In this work, we explore this problem space by introducing Synapse, a modular agentic framework built on the FastMCP library designed to navigate these constraints. To address privacy constraints, the framework applies random perturbation to GPS coordinates before they are sent to external services. The system's architecture uses specialized agents to reason over distinct data modalities; for instance, a traffic agent projects a route's temporal progression to enable time-aware queries for weather and urban context. These signals are then synthesized into a base narrative by a generative agent and localized by parallel translation agents. The contributions of this work are therefore twofold: (1) Synapse, a novel and extensible agentic architecture for multilingual narrative generation, and (2) a human-validated multilingual evaluation benchmark, which includes the challenging low-resource Luxembourgish language. We release both our framework and benchmark publicly to provide a foundation for future research and development in this new domain.[1]

1.1 Related Work

Logistics operations present numerous challenges stemming from the complexity and volume of multimodal data streams. Planners and drivers must continuously interpret inputs such as traffic conditions, weather forecasts, and delivery constraints to make time-sensitive decisions. However, raw streams of GPS coordinates and sensor signals often lack the semantic clarity required for intuitive, proactive risk assessment. This disconnect between low-level data and high-level situational awareness has positioned the automated summarization of geospatial data as a key research direction. Early work in this area explored the segmentation of GPS trajectories into semantically meaningful units, followed by the generation of textual summaries to highlight salient events along a route [15]. This concept was extended to summarizing network-level activity by identifying representative paths, such as the K-Main Routes approach used to cluster crime reports or traffic flows [13]. Subsequent efforts aimed to improve the human-centric utility of these summaries through personalization and multimodality;

[1] The evaluation benchmark and script are available at: https://github.com/Synapse-INTSYS2025/agentic-eval-benchmark.

frameworks like PerNav and PaRE generated more intuitive directions from historical data [11,12], while systems such as TREADS and Scenemash demonstrated the value of enriching summaries with real-time social media and image data [1,5,8]. While these foundational systems demonstrated the value of multimodal data integration, they predate the advanced cross-domain reasoning and synthesis capabilities of modern Large Language Models (LLMs), which have enabled a new paradigm for solving complex, multi-step problems through agentic workflows [4]. Advanced reasoning techniques like Chain-of-Thought (CoT) and its variants allows LLMs to function as orchestrators that can decompose problems and interact with external tools [3,17,19].

This has spurred the development of multi-agent systems built upon standardized communication frameworks like the Model Context Protocol (MCP), which provides a unified interface for model-tool interaction [7,9,16]. Applying these advanced systems to multilingual contexts, however, introduces significant challenges, particularly for low-resource languages, as comprehensive surveys of Neural Machine Translation (NMT) establish that model performance remains suboptimal for language pairs with scarce parallel data [14]. This limitation extends directly to generative tasks like summarization [10], with the difficulty being particularly acute for languages such as Luxembourgish, where even foundational NLP tasks require specialized models and human-in-the-loop validation to achieve acceptable performance [6]. Furthermore, the linguistic inequality in training data can degrade the effectiveness of safety mechanisms in LLMs, making robust evaluation in low-resource settings a critical area of study [2,18].

2 System Architecture and Model

2.1 Overview

We propose Synapse, a modular agentic framework designed for the automated generation of multilingual, human-centered summaries for logistics operations. The framework transforms static route definitions and dynamic, real-time signals into natural language narratives through a network of specialized AI agents. Our architecture explicitly models the distinct domains of logistics data, with individual agents handling real-time traffic, weather, workload assessment, and urban context. A core component of our approach is a privacy-preserving mechanism that applies random perturbation to all GPS coordinates before they are sent to external services, ensuring GDPR compliance. Furthermore, this modular design offers a significant scalability advantage: users can interact with the entire system through a single, natural language endpoint, completely obviating the need to understand or construct the complex, individual REST API payloads required by the downstream specialist agents. While the underlying MCP framework supports dynamic tool discovery, our implementation uses a static registration model. This is a deliberate design choice to enhance security and privacy; by manually registering a limited, necessary set of tools for each agent, we prevent the potential for the underlying LLM to discover and misuse other available tools in unintended ways.

2.2 Input Representations

The system ingests an unstructured natural language query, such as the example shown in Listing 1.1, via a JSON API endpoint. A Natural Language Understanding (NLU) module, powered by an LLM, parses this query into a structured `tool_call`. This decouples the ambiguity of natural language from the deterministic execution required by the downstream agentic workflow.

```
curl -X POST http://localhost:8088/natural_query \
     -H "Content-Type: application/json" \
     -d '{"query": "Briefing for Route-001 tomorrow at 2 PM."
   }'
```

Listing 1.1. Example user query via `curl`.

2.3 Workflow

Our system's architecture is a multi-agent framework designed to process a natural language query and generate a multilingual briefing, as illustrated in Fig. 1. The system comprises a user-facing API Gateway, a central `Pipeline Agent` orchestrator, and a suite of specialist agents for data retrieval and synthesis.

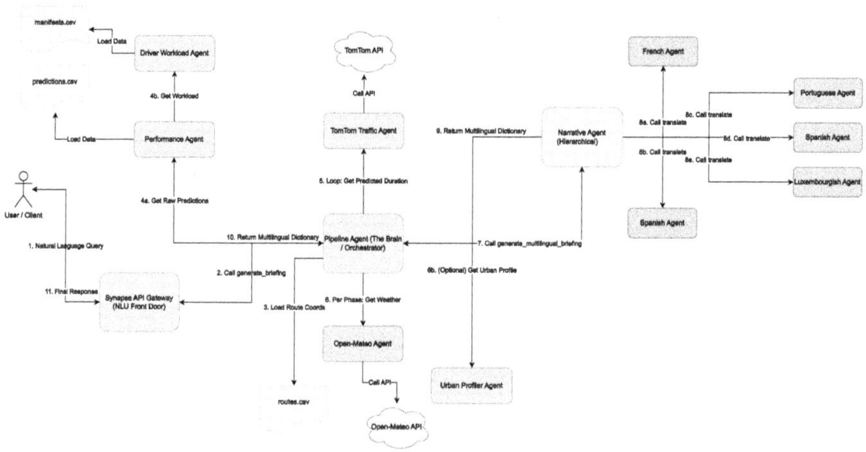

Fig. 1. Architecture and execution flow of the Synapse multi-agent system.

1. **Query Ingestion and Orchestration.** The workflow is initiated when a user's natural language request is ingested by the `Synapse API Gateway`, which performs initial NLU parsing. The gateway then invokes the central `Pipeline Agent`, a FastMCP service orchestrator, to begin the main workflow.

2. **Baseline Data and Prediction Loading.** The orchestrator begins by gathering the foundational data for the route. It calls the internal `Performance Agent`, which provides a set of pre-computed failure predictions for each stop based on a model using historical data. Concurrently, it loads the route's static geospatial coordinates and manifest details. This initial step provides the system with a complete baseline of the planned route and its historically-informed risks before querying for live, dynamic signals.
3. **Dynamic Agent Interrogation.** The orchestrator enriches the static data by querying its specialist agents. It first projects the route's temporal progression by sequentially calling the `TomTom Traffic Agent` for leg-by-leg travel times. This simulation assigns each stop to an operational phase (e.g., Morning, Afternoon), enabling phase-specific queries. A geospatial centroid is calculated for the stops in each phase to serve as a representative point for a targeted `Open-Meteo Agent` weather forecast, assuming minimal intra-phase weather variation. Concurrently, the `Driver Workload Agent` provides manifest details. This culminates in a multi-factor risk assessment: if a phase combines adverse weather with a challenging load (heavy/oversized items), the `Urban Profiler Agent` is invoked to provide proactive parking guidance, mitigating potential delays from increased manual handling in areas with limited parking.
4. **Hierarchical Synthesis and Multilingual Generation.** With the complete data context assembled, the orchestrator invokes the `Narrative Agent`. This agent exemplifies a key architectural pattern in our framework, acting as both a service provider and a service consumer. First, in its server role, it receives the data and synthesizes all information into a coherent base summary in English. Then, acting as a client, it broadcasts this English summary concurrently via FastMCP to five single-language translation agents (e.g., `French Agent`, `Spanish Agent`) for localization. This hierarchical delegation allows the primary orchestrator to remain simple while enabling specialized sub-tasks like translation to be managed by the appropriate agent.
5. **Response Aggregation.** Finally, the `Pipeline Agent` collects the outputs from all translation agents into a single multilingual dictionary, which is returned to the user through the API Gateway.

The final aggregated response is a JSON object containing the synthesized narrative in English and its translations. An example of the `Luxembourgish` output, which is generated by the `Narrative Agent` to match the golden standard format, is shown in Listing 1.2.

```
D'Route-003 huet 10 Arrêten mat 1 virausgesoten Ausfall. D'
    Haapterausfuerdorunge sinn Appartement-Arrêten: 2, Schwéier
    Artikelen: 1. --- Phasendetailer: - Moies: D'Wieder wäert kloer
    sinn mat Temperaturen ëm 27.9°C a mëttelméissegem Wand (39-43 km
    /h) an den éischten dräi Stonnen. 1 Ausfäll virausgesot op 7 Arr
    êten an dëser Phas.
```

Listing 1.2. Example of the final Luxembourgish narrative output

3 Experimental Setup

Experiments were conducted on a server with an NVIDIA RTX A6000 GPU (48 GB VRAM) running Ubuntu 24.04.2 LTS. The entire multi-agent system was containerized using Docker to ensure reproducibility. All generative agents were powered by local language models served via Ollama v0.9.6, and agent communication was managed by the FastMCP framework. To ensure temporal consistency for the evaluation, all queries to time-sensitive external APIs (e.g., traffic, weather) were anchored to a static date of **May 15, 2025**, although the framework is designed for live data streams.

3.1 Hyperparameters and Prompts

All generative tasks were performed using large language models served via the Ollama v0.9.6 framework. We evaluated two primary models: `Mistral-7B Instruct` and `Llama 3.2`. To ensure a reproducible baseline, we used the official default inference parameters for both models. For all experimental runs, the `seed` was not fixed to a static value.

System Prompts. Each generative agent was assigned a distinct system prompt tailored to its specialized function. The key prompts are summarized below:

- **Narrative Agent:** Instructed to act as an expert "Senior Logistics Editor," this agent's sole task is to synthesize the incoming JSON data into a single, factually perfect string. The prompt enforces a strict output template ('Overall, [route name] has...') and provides explicit step-by-step instructions for calculating totals and formatting the phase details. This ensures the output matches the golden standard format used for evaluation.
- **Translation Agents:** Given a simple, direct instruction to "Translate the following English logistics briefing into professional, formal [Language]," followed by the English text. The prompt explicitly commands the agent to respond ONLY with the translated text to ensure a clean output for the final response aggregation.
- **Weather Agent:** Prompted to act as a specialized meteorologist, this agent is provided with a suite of tools for accessing different types of weather data (e.g., 'get forecast 3 h', 'get daily summary', 'get forecast 6 h'). Its primary task is to perform LLM-driven tool selection based on the specific temporal and geospatial context provided by the orchestrator.
- **API Gateway:** This agent is prompted to act as an "API routing bot" with the sole function of parsing an unstructured user query. The prompt provides a clear example of both the input query and the required structured JSON output ("“tool": "generate briefing", "parameters": ...'), forcing the LLM to act as a reliable Natural Language Understanding (NLU) component.

3.2 Baselines

We evaluate the performance of our Synapse framework by comparing two distinct large language models serving as the core generative engines for all agents:

- **Mistral-7B:** A widely-used, high-performance 7-billion parameter model, selected as our primary baseline due to its strong performance and the clear visibility of its default inference parameters, which facilitates a reproducible experimental setup. We use the `mistral:7b-instruct-q4_K_M` variant.
- **Llama 3.2:** A recent, state-of-the-art model used for comparison against the established baseline. We use the `llama3.2:8b-instruct-q4_K_M` variant.

A third potential baseline, a monolithic approach using a single powerful external LLM (e.g., GPT-4), was considered but explicitly excluded. Such an approach is fundamentally incompatible with the GDPR constraints central to our problem formulation, as transmitting precise geolocations to a third-party service would constitute a privacy violation. Our agentic architecture is specifically designed to mitigate this risk, and our evaluation therefore focuses on comparing different LLMs within our privacy-preserving framework.

4 Evaluation

To assess the performance of our framework, we conducted a quantitative analysis of the multilingual translation quality produced by our agentic pipeline.

4.1 Evaluation Setup

Dataset. Our evaluation benchmark consists of 100 semi-synthetic, 10-stop logistics routes. To ensure linguistic and geographic diversity, stop locations were sampled from regions across Luxembourg, France, and Belgium, corresponding to the target languages of the system. For each route, a canonical English summary was first manually authored by the researchers. This text then served as the source for creating and validating with the help of native speakers, the golden reference translations for our five target languages: French, Spanish, Italian, Portuguese, and Luxembourgish.

Metrics. To provide a comprehensive assessment of translation quality, we employed three standard automated metrics, each capturing a different aspect of performance.

COMET. We use the `Unbabel/wmt23-cometkiwi-da-xl` model, a neural regression metric that estimates translation quality based on semantic similarity to the source and reference texts. It is trained on direct human judgments, and higher scores indicate better performance. As a neural model, it leverages contextual embeddings rather than relying on explicit word overlap.

METEOR. This metric computes a score based on the harmonic mean of unigram precision (P) and recall (R), with a penalty for fragmentation. The score is calculated as:

$$\text{METEOR} = F_{\text{mean}} \cdot (1 - \text{Penalty}) \quad \text{where} \quad F_{\text{mean}} = \frac{10PR}{9P + R}$$

The penalty term increases with the number of contiguous chunks of matched words, rewarding longer, more coherent matches.

TER (Translation Edit Rate). TER is an error metric that measures the minimum number of edits required to transform a system hypothesis into the reference translation. It is defined as:

$$\text{TER} = \frac{\text{Number of edits}}{\text{Number of words in reference}}$$

Edits include insertions, deletions, substitutions, and shifts. Lower scores indicate better translation quality.

5 Results and Discussion

The performance of the Llama 3.2 and Mistral-7B models within the SYNAPSE framework is presented in Table 1. A horizontal analysis of these results comparing a model's performance across tasks reveals a critical finding: a significant and consistent degradation in quality occurs when the synthesized English narrative is passed to downstream translation agents. This suggests a systemic challenge in maintaining quality across a multi-agent generative pipeline. With the superior Llama 3.2 model, the METEOR score drops from a high of 0.70 on the English synthesis task to an average of 0.47 across the four high-resource languages. This degradation is even more pronounced in the Translation Edit Rate (TER), which increases from 43.30 for the English output to as high as 78.68 for the Italian translation. For a logistics planner who must coordinate multilingual teams, such a high error rate transforms the system from a tool for clarity into a source of operational confusion, risking a loss of user trust and eventual abandonment of the system. This finding validates the necessity of a modular agentic architecture. The data clearly shows that a single, general-purpose LLM is insufficient for reliably executing all sub-tasks in this specialized pipeline. The poor performance of the translation components highlights the need for a system where underperforming agents can be individually fine-tuned or replaced.

6 Conclusion and Future Work

We introduced SYNAPSE, a modular, privacy-preserving agentic framework for generating multilingual logistics summaries. Our system demonstrates a scalable approach to synthesizing real-time multimodal data, including traffic, weather,

Table 1. Comparative performance of Llama 3.2 (L3.2) and Mistral-7B (M7B). COMET scores are reported as mean (std. dev.). Best results are in bold.

	COMET ↑		METEOR ↑		TER ↓	
Language	**L3.2**	**M7B**	**L3.2**	**M7B**	**L3.2**	**M7B**
English (en)	**0.34** (0.03)	0.25 (0.04)	**0.70**	0.39	**43.30**	64.51
Spanish (es)	**0.46** (0.08)	0.38 (0.06)	**0.48**	0.30	**65.43**	75.68
French (fr)	**0.40** (0.07)	0.30 (0.05)	**0.48**	0.30	**68.56**	74.75
Italian (it)	**0.41** (0.08)	0.31 (0.06)	**0.42**	0.24	**78.68**	82.90
Portuguese (pt)	**0.43** (0.09)	0.37 (0.07)	**0.49**	0.30	**65.45**	76.09
Luxembourgish (lb)	0.22 (0.06)	**0.26** (0.07)	**0.20**	0.08	**93.37**	97.80

and pre-computed failure predictions, into a coherent, human-centered narrative while ensuring GDPR compliance through coordinate perturbation. The quality of the final output, however, remains dependent on the capabilities of the underlying LLMs, and the microservices architecture presents a trade-off between modularity and latency.

Future work will focus on two primary directions. First, we plan to fine-tune the generative agents on domain-specific logistics texts to improve narrative quality and mitigate factual inconsistencies. Second, we will investigate agent optimization techniques and the integration of additional data streams, such as vehicle telematics, to enhance the system's real-time contextual awareness and overall robustness.

Competing Interests. The authors have no competing interests to declare that are relevant to the content of this article.

Acknowledgments. We wish to express our sincere gratitude to our colleagues at the SnT, University of Luxembourg. We are particularly indebted to our fellow researchers for their meticulous work in constructing our evaluation benchmark. Their efforts included curating the foundational logistics route data and, crucially, providing native-speaker validation for each of the target language translations. This research was greatly strengthened by their collaborative support and linguistic expertise.

References

1. van den Berg, J., Rudinac, S., Worring, M.: SceneMash: multimodal route summarization for City Exploration. In: Ferro, N., et al. (eds.) ECIR 2016. LNCS, vol. 9626, pp. 833–836. Springer, Cham (2016). https://doi.org/10.1007/978-3-319-30671-1_75
2. Buscemi, A., et al.: Mind the Language Gap: automated and augmented evaluation of bias in LLMs for high- and low-resource languages (2025).https://doi.org/10.48550/arXiv.2504.18560, http://arxiv.org/abs/2504.18560, arXiv:2504.18560
3. Chen, Q., et al.: Towards Reasoning Era: a survey of long chain-of-thought for reasoning large language models (2025). https://doi.org/10.48550/arXiv.2503.09567, http://arxiv.org/abs/2503.09567, arXiv:2503.09567

4. Chen, Q., Qin, L., Wang, J., Zhou, J., Che, W.: Unlocking the capabilities of thought: a reasoning boundary framework to quantify and optimize chain-of-thought. Adv. Neural Info. Process. Syst. **37**, 54872–54904 (2024). https://proceedings.neurips.cc/paper_files/paper/2024/hash/62ab1c2cb4b03e717005479efb211841-Abstract-Conference.html
5. Fu, K., Lu, Y.C., Lu, C.T.: TREADS: a safe route recommender using social media mining and text summarization. In: Proceedings of the 22nd ACM SIGSPATIAL International Conference on Advances in Geographic Information Systems, pp. 557–560. SIGSPATIAL '14, Association for Computing Machinery, New York, NY, USA (2014). https://doi.org/10.1145/2666310.2666368
6. Hosseini-Kivanani, N., Kühn, J., Schommer, C.: Mapping Sentiments: a journey into low-resource Luxembourgish analysis. In: Sousa-Silva, R., Lopes Cardoso, H., Koponen, M., Pareja Lora, A., Seresi, M. (eds.) Proceedings of the First LUHME Workshop, pp. 20–27. CLUP, Centro de Linguística da Universidade do Porto FLUP - Faculdade de Letras da Universidade do Porto, Santiago de Compostela, Spain (2024). https://aclanthology.org/2024.luhme-1.3/
7. Hou, X., Zhao, Y., Wang, S., Wang, H.: Model Context Protocol (MCP): landscape, security threats, and future research directions (2025). https://doi.org/10.48550/arXiv.2503.23278, http://arxiv.org/abs/2503.23278, arXiv:2503.23278 [cs]
8. Kanaya, Y., Kawanaka, S., Suwa, H., Arakawa, Y., Yasumoto, K.: Automatic route video summarization based on image analysis for intuitive touristic experience. Sens. Mater. **32**(2), 599 (2020). https://doi.org/10.18494/SAM.2020.2616, http://myukk.org/SM2017/article.php?ss=2616
9. Karimova, S., Dadashova, U.: The model context protocol: a standardization analysis for application integration. J. Comput. Sci. Digit. Technol. **1**(1), 50–59 (2025). http://journals.unec.edu.az/index.php/jcsdt/article/view/27
10. Li, J., Chen, J., Chen, H., Zhao, D., Yan, R.: Multilingual generation in abstractive summarization: a comparative study. In: Calzolari, N., Kan, M.Y., Hoste, V., Lenci, A., Sakti, S., Xue, N. (eds.) Proceedings of the 2024 Joint International Conference on Computational Linguistics, Language Resources and Evaluation (LREC-COLING 2024), pp. 11827–11837. ELRA and ICCL, Torino, Italia (2024). https://aclanthology.org/2024.lrec-main.1032/
11. Li, Y., Su, H., Demiryurek, U., Zheng, B., He, T., Shahabi, C.: PaRE: a system for personalized route guidance. In: Proceedings of the 26th International Conference on World Wide Web, pp. 637–646. WWW '17, International World Wide Web Conferences Steering Committee, Republic and Canton of Geneva, CHE (2017). https://doi.org/10.1145/3038912.3052717
12. Li, Y., Su, H., Demiryurek, U., Zheng, B., Zeng, K., Shahabi, C.: PerNav: a route summarization framework for personalized navigation. In: Proceedings of the 2016 International Conference on Management of Data, pp. 2125–2128. SIGMOD '16, Association for Computing Machinery, New York, NY, USA (2016). https://doi.org/10.1145/2882903.2899384
13. Oliver, D., Bannur, A., Kang, J.M., Shekhar, S., Bousselaire, R.: A K-main routes approach to spatial network activity summarization: a summary of results. In: 2010 IEEE International Conference on Data Mining Workshops, pp. 265–272 (2010). https://doi.org/10.1109/ICDMW.2010.156, https://ieeexplore.ieee.org/abstract/document/5693309, iSSN: 2375-9259
14. Ranathunga, S., Lee, E.S.A., Prifti Skenduli, M., Shekhar, R., Alam, M., Kaur, R.: Neural machine translation for low-resource languages: a Survey. ACM Comput. Surv. **55**(11), 229:1–229:37 (2023). https://doi.org/10.1145/3567592

15. Su, H., et al.: Making sense of trajectory data: a partition-and-summarization approach. In: 2015 IEEE 31st International Conference on Data Engineering, pp. 963–974 (2015). https://doi.org/10.1109/ICDE.2015.7113348, https://ieeexplore.ieee.org/abstract/document/7113348, iSSN: 2375-026X
16. Szeider, S.: MCP-Solver: integrating language models with constraint programming systems (2025). https://doi.org/10.48550/arXiv.2501.00539, http://arxiv.org/abs/2501.00539, arXiv:2501.00539
17. Wang, Y., Wu, S., Zhang, Y., Yan, S., Liu, Z., Luo, J., Fei, H.: Multimodal chain-of-thought reasoning: a comprehensive survey (2025). https://doi.org/10.48550/arXiv.2503.12605, http://arxiv.org/abs/2503.12605, arXiv:2503.12605 [cs]
18. Yong, Z.X., Menghini, C., Bach, S.H.: Low-resource languages jailbreak GPT-4 (2024). https://doi.org/10.48550/arXiv.2310.02446, http://arxiv.org/abs/2310.02446, arXiv:2310.02446
19. Zhang, X., Du, C., Pang, T., Liu, Q., Gao, W., Lin, M.: Chain of preference optimization: improving chain-of-thought reasoning in LLMs. Adv. Neural Info. Process. Syst. **37**, 333–356 (2024). https://proceedings.neurips.cc/paper_files/paper/2024/hash/00d80722b756de0166523a87805dd00f-Abstract-Conference.html

Multimodal Learning for Operational Risk Detection in Delivery Route Planning

Prateek Gupta[1(✉)], Daniel Antunes Pedrozo[1], Jorge Augusto Meira[1], Antonio Ken Iannillo[1], and Danilo D' Aversa[2]

[1] SnT, University of Luxembourg, 29 Av. John F. Kennedy, 1855 Luxembourg City, Luxembourg
{prateek.gupta,daniel.antunes,jorge.meira,antonioken.iannillo}@uni.lu
[2] Gulliver Luxembourg S.à r.l., Luxembourg City, Luxembourg
danilo.daversa@gullivernet.lu

Abstract. We propose a privacy-aware multimodal framework for detecting operational risks in last-mile delivery routes by integrating spatial, temporal, and semantic information. Our method fuses geospatial embeddings derived from latitude–longitude coordinates or representative zip-code centroids, ensuring GDPR compliance when precise locations are withheld, with temporal features from delivery attempt timestamps and semantic embeddings extracted by a locally hosted large language model (LLM). To capture localized delivery failure patterns, we incorporate sequence-to-pattern mining at the zip-code level, enabling the model to recognize high-risk operational contexts. This unified architecture is designed to maintain predictive robustness even when partial location data is missing, ensuring routes remain analyzable despite privacy constraints. Empirical evaluation on real-world logistics datasets comprising approximately 2,000 routes, each visiting between 2 and 26 customers, shows that multimodal embeddings significantly enhance precision in detecting early failures compared to random baselines during validation. However, test-set results reveal generalization challenges and overfitting risks, suggesting that further work is needed on data augmentation, embedding fine-tuning, and regularization strategies. By enabling early, data-driven risk detection, our approach has the potential to support more reliable and sustainable last-mile delivery operations.

Keywords: Multimodal Machine Learning · Privacy-Aware Modeling · Operational Risk Detection · Sustainable Logistics · Large Language Models (LLMs)

B. Kihei et al. (Eds.): INTSYS 2025, LNICST 717, pp. 154–165, 2027.
https://doi.org/10.1007/978-3-032-38705-9_8

1 Introduction

Last-mile logistics is one of the most challenging supply chain stages, which involves transportation from local depots to customer doorsteps. This final leg often represents a significant portion of total delivery costs, driven by routing complexity, urban congestion, and unpredictable customer behavior, such as customers being unreachable despite prescheduled time slots.

Accurate prediction of operational risks, such as delivery failures, is crucial to cost efficiency and service quality. We specifically measure precision around the first failure event to assess how reliably the model signals early warnings. This metric is particularly important in contexts involving large or heavy products that must be unloaded in a strict sequence, and early detection of potential failures can help prevent cascading disruptions to subsequent deliveries and mitigate costly downstream effects. This remains difficult for two key reasons. First, logistics data often contain private information, including precise customer locations and personalized delivery instructions, which are tightly regulated under frameworks such as the General Data Protection Regulation (GDPR) in Europe. Second, in practice, some customers withhold precise geographic location data for privacy reasons, leaving gaps that can render route-level machine learning models unusable if they rely exclusively on accurate spatial signals.

In this paper, we tackle both challenges with a privacy-aware multimodal architecture that integrates spatial, temporal, and semantic information to predict route-level risks. Even when precise coordinates are unavailable, we substitute them with representative latitude-longitude values derived from zip-code centroids, ensuring GDPR compliance and preserving model functionality. Our experiments on real-world logistics data show that this multimodal approach can improve early risk detection in modern last-mile delivery networks.

1.1 Related Work

Classical optimization approaches to last-mile delivery are modeled as variants of the Vehicle Routing Problem (VRP), which optimize cost-minimizing delivery routes subject to constraints such as vehicle capacity, time windows, or maximum tour length. These models provide strong theoretical guarantees, are computationally expensive, and do not take advantage of historical data collected during logistics operations. For example, previous work by Dettenbach et al. [2], proposed maintaining backup plans to handle interruptions before delivery begins. However, such strategies are limited in capturing real-world uncertainties, particularly those arising from delivery failures due to customer unavailability or localized risk patterns.

To address these limitations, recent research uses machine learning (ML) and deep learning (DL) techniques to leverage data-driven insights for predictive accuracy and adaptability in last-mile logistics. Sharma et al. [11], for instance, employed random forests to predict service failures driven by customer behaviors such as absence or refusal; however, their work remained at the customer level and did not integrate route-level spatial dependencies. Florio et al. [3], used the "pool and select" algorithm to build candidate delivery sequences using heuristics based on entry and exit zones, then select the most promising sequence through a learned regression model. Other works have used gradient-boosted trees [7] and deep learning for delivery time predictions [1,4].

Most of the previous work in ML for last-mile logistics focuses on demand forecasting, predicting estimated time of delivery, and planning routes [5,6,8–10,12]. Research aimed at predicting delivery failures, such as a customer not being at home, is relatively limited. This gap arises for several reasons. Failed deliveries are rare in many operational datasets, making supervised learning difficult. Another reason is that success and failure are often tied to privacy-sensitive signals such as at-home presence, responsiveness, or special delivery instructions, which fall under GDPR protections.

In our work, we do not use time windows as a predictive feature, as each company defines and enforces time windows differently. Instead, we rely on the actual time of delivery attempt recorded in historical data, which provides more precise and interpretable temporal signals. Our approach focuses on predicting service-level delivery failures by modeling interactions with preceding stops along the route. Using a proprietary logistics dataset in which delivery outcomes are explicitly labeled, we demonstrate that it is feasible to learn meaningful risk patterns in real-world, privacy-compliant settings.

Unlike prior studies that assume the full availability of precise latitude and longitude data, we explicitly address scenarios where customers withhold geographic location information due to privacy concerns. To our knowledge, no existing multimodal architecture integrates a privacy-aware fallback mechanism that substitutes missing coordinates with representative zip-code centroids while maintaining predictive performance. Our work fills this gap by explicitly designing for robustness under partial spatial data availability.

The rest of the paper is organized as follows. Section 2 presents the training pipeline and model architecture, including input representations, graph attention layers, and transformer encoding. In Sect. 3, we describe the experimental setup covering hyperparameters, embedding dimensions, sequence mining settings, baseline comparisons, and performance analysis. Section 4 concludes with a summary of contributions and directions for future work.

2 Model

2.1 Overview

We propose a multimodal neural architecture designed for early detection of operational risks in last-mile delivery. The model integrates geospatial, semantic, temporal, and pattern-based signals into a unified framework and explicitly models spatial relationships via graph attention mechanisms. Our architecture emphasizes early detection by combining position-aware loss functions and evaluation metrics tailored for sequential prediction.

2.2 Input Representations

Each time step t in a delivery sequence is represented by the following modalities:

- **Geospatial features**: GPS coordinates are encoded into a high-dimensional latent space
$$\mathbf{x}_t^{\text{geo}} \in \mathbb{R}^{d_{\text{geo}}}$$
using a pretrained *LocationEncoder*, inspired by vision-language models, to capture spatial context beyond the raw coordinates.
- **Semantic embeddings**: Contextual information from textual delivery instructions is extracted using a frozen LLaMA 3.2 1B model, yielding embeddings
$$\mathbf{x}_t^{\text{llama}} \in \mathbb{R}^{d_{\text{llama}}}.$$
Since decoder-only models like LLaMA do not produce a single pooled embedding by default, we extract the hidden state of the first token from the final layer to serve as a sentence-level representation. This vector is normalized before being concatenated with other features
- **Temporal features**:
  - **Time-of-day cyclic features:** hour and minute encoded via sine and cosine transformations to model periodicity,
$$\sin\left(2\pi\frac{\text{hour}}{24}\right),\quad \cos\left(2\pi\frac{\text{hour}}{24}\right),\quad \sin\left(2\pi\frac{\text{minute}}{60}\right),\quad \cos\left(2\pi\frac{\text{minute}}{60}\right).$$
  - **Day-of-week cyclic features:** day-of-week encoded similarly with sine and cosine transforms,
$$\sin\left(2\pi\frac{\text{dow}}{6}\right),\quad \cos\left(2\pi\frac{\text{dow}}{6}\right),$$
where $\text{dow} \in \{0, \ldots, 6\}$.
  - **Weekend indicator:** a binary feature that indicates whether the day is Saturday or Sunday.
  - **Time segment one-hot encoding:** hour-of-day is discretized into five segments $\{[0,7), [7,12), [12,17), [17,21), [21,24)\}$, encoded as a one-hot vector.

  These features are concatenated to form the temporal feature vector
$$\mathbf{x}_t^{\text{time}} \in \mathbb{R}^{d_{\text{time}}}.$$
- **Pattern embeddings**: Summaries of frequent delivery success and failure patterns are encoded as
$$\mathbf{x}^{\text{pattern}} \in \mathbb{R}^{d_{\text{pattern}}}.$$

All features are concatenated to form the time-step input:

$$\mathbf{x}_t = \begin{bmatrix} \mathbf{x}_t^{\text{geo}} \\ \mathbf{x}_t^{\text{llama}} \\ \mathbf{x}_t^{\text{time}} \end{bmatrix} \in \mathbb{R}^{d_{\text{in}}},$$

where

$$d_{\text{in}} = d_{\text{geo}} + d_{\text{llama}} + d_{\text{time}}.$$

2.3 Architecture

The sequence $\{\mathbf{x}_t\}_{t=1}^{T}$ is first linearly projected into a shared latent space of dimension d_{model}:

$$\mathbf{h}_t^{(0)} = W_{\text{in}}\,\mathbf{x}_t + \mathbf{b}_{\text{in}}.$$

When pattern embeddings are available, we inject them as additive biases:

$$\mathbf{h}_t^{(0)} \leftarrow \mathbf{h}_t^{(0)} + W_{\text{pattern}}\,\mathbf{x}^{\text{pattern}}.$$

Graph Attention Layers. To capture spatial and topological dependencies among stops, we process the sequence with a two-layer Graph Attention Network (GAT) (Fig. 1). Importantly, edges operate *over the flattened latent representations* of stops across the batch:

$$\mathbf{h}^{\text{gat}} = \text{GAT}\big(\text{flatten}(\mathbf{h}^{(0)}),\ E\big),$$

where E is an edge index defining stop-to-stop connectivity. The GAT aggregates neighborhood information in latent space and reshapes the output back to sequence form. Residual connections yield:

$$\mathbf{h}_t^{(1)} = \mathbf{h}_t^{(0)} + \mathbf{h}_t^{\text{gat}}.$$

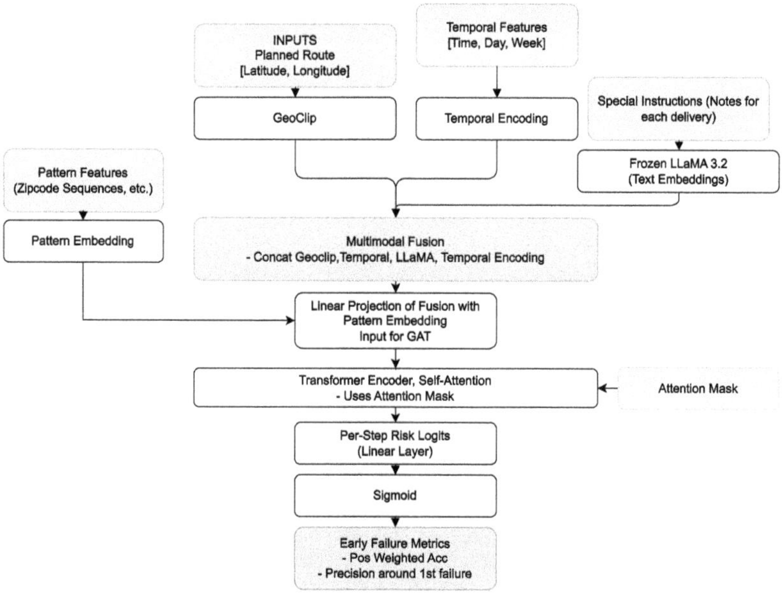

Fig. 1. Model Architecture.

Transformer Encoding. The enhanced embeddings $\{\mathbf{h}_t^{(1)}\}$ are fed into a multi-layer Transformer encoder, capturing temporal and global sequence dependencies:

$$\{\mathbf{h}_t^{\text{enc}}\}_{t=1}^T = \text{TransformerEncoder}\left(\{\mathbf{h}_t^{(1)}\}_{t=1}^T\right).$$

Finally, a linear layer projects to scalar logits:

$$\hat{y}_t = W_{\text{out}}\,\mathbf{h}_t^{\text{enc}} + \mathbf{b}_{\text{out}}.$$

2.4 Training Objectives

Our primary loss is a binary cross-entropy applied at each time step. However, to emphasize early detection and reduce delayed corrections, we introduce the **Sequential Penalty-Aware Contextual Loss (SPaCeLoss)**.

SPaCeLoss. Let the predicted logits be $\hat{\mathbf{y}} \in \mathbb{R}^{B\times T}$. Compute probabilities:

$$\mathbf{p} = \sigma(\hat{\mathbf{y}}).$$

Define binary cross-entropy:

$$\text{BCE}(\mathbf{p}, \mathbf{y}) = -\left[\mathbf{y}\cdot\log(\mathbf{p}) + (1-\mathbf{y})\cdot\log(1-\mathbf{p})\right].$$

The focal modulation term is:

$$\mathbf{pt} = \mathbf{p}\cdot\mathbf{y} + (1-\mathbf{p})\cdot(1-\mathbf{y}),$$

yielding:

$$\text{FocalWeight} = \alpha\,(1-\mathbf{pt})^{\gamma}.$$

Hence the focal loss:

$$\text{FocalLoss} = \text{FocalWeight} \odot \text{BCE}(\mathbf{p}, \mathbf{y}).$$

To penalize late mistakes, SPaCeLoss introduces positional penalties:

$$\mathbf{w}_{\text{pos}} = \text{linspace}(1.0,\ 0.1,\ T).$$

Scaled by β_{pos}:

$$\text{Penalty} = \beta_{\text{pos}}\cdot\mathbf{w}_{\text{pos}}.$$

After optional normalization, the final loss is:

$$\text{SPaCeLoss} = \frac{1}{B\times T}\sum_{i=1}^{B}\sum_{t=1}^{T}\text{FocalLoss}_{i,t}\times\text{Penalty}_t.$$

2.5 Evaluation Metrics

We evaluate the model with metrics prioritizing timely risk detection:

Precision Around First Failure. To quantify how early and accurately the model signals the first failure, we compute a distance-weighted precision defined as:

$$\text{Precision}_{\text{first-fail}} = \begin{cases} \frac{\sum_{i=1}^{N} s_i}{PP}, & \text{if } PP > 0, \\ 0, & \text{otherwise.} \end{cases}$$

where:

- PP = number of sequences with any predicted failure,
- s_i = score for sequence i reflecting how close the first predicted failure is to the first true failure.

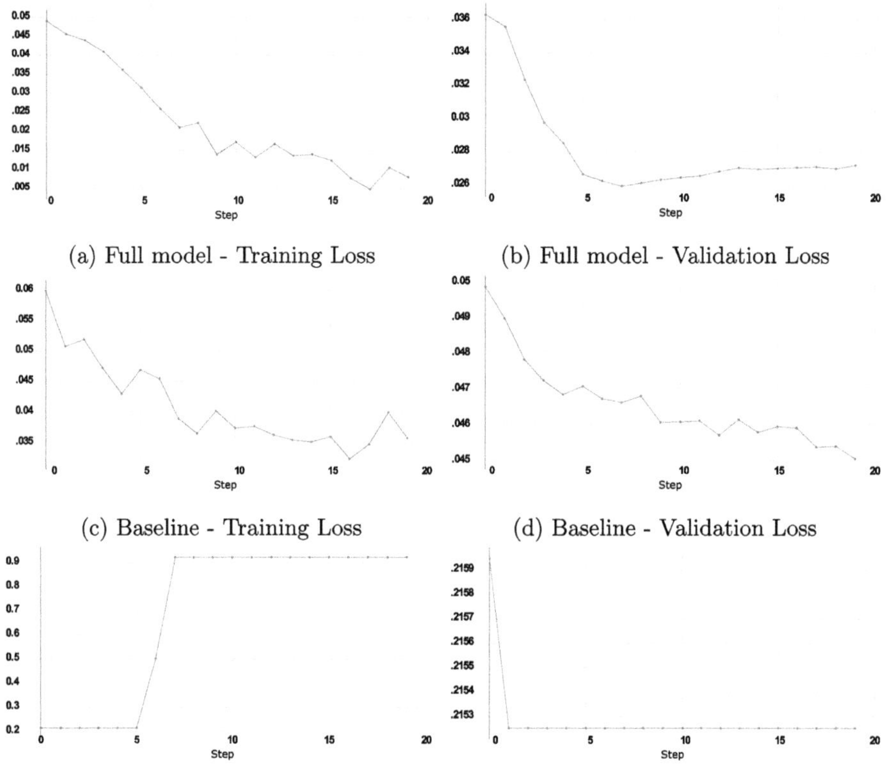

(a) Full model - Training Loss

(b) Full model - Validation Loss

(c) Baseline - Training Loss

(d) Baseline - Validation Loss

(e) Full model - Precision Around First Failure (Validation)

(f) Baseline - Precision Around First Failure (Validation)

Fig. 2. Training and validation loss curves for full and baseline models, along with Precision Around First Failure metric on validation dataset.

Formally, let $\hat{\mathbf{y}}_i \in \{0,1\}^T$ denote thresholded predictions and $\mathbf{y}_i \in \{0,1\}^T$ the ground truth. Define:

$$\text{FirstFail}_i = \min\left\{ t \;\middle|\; y_{i,t} = 0 \right\}.$$

Similarly, define:

$$\text{FirstPred}_i = \min\left\{ t \;\middle|\; \hat{y}_{i,t} = 0 \right\}.$$

Then, for each sequence i where any failure is predicted, we compute:

$$s_i = \frac{1}{1 + \left|\text{FirstPred}_i - \text{FirstFail}_i\right|}.$$

This yields a precision score close to 1 when the predicted failure is very close to the true first failure, and decreasing as the prediction deviates further in time.

3 Experiments

3.1 Training Setup

All experiments were conducted on an Apple M1 Mac with 16 GB RAM, running macOS Sequoia 15.3.1. Our software environment comprised Python 3.10, PyTorch 1.13.1, and GeoPandas 0.13.2. We trained and evaluated models on real routing data from a logistics partner collected in 2025. To enable stratified splitting into training, validation, and test sets, we defined a helper variable indicating whether a route contained at least one failure (present in approximately 3.5% of routes across all splits). This variable was dropped after stratification and not used during model training or evaluation.

Model training, evaluation, and deployment were managed via containerized services using Docker, including PostgreSQL for data storage and MLflow for experiment tracking and model management. This environment ensured reproducibility and streamlined workflow management.

3.2 Hyperparameters

Input and Embedding Dimensions. We use the following feature dimensions: GeoClip embeddings of size 512, LLaMA embeddings of size 2048, pattern features of size 10, and temporal features of size 12.

Sequence Mining Settings. Failure patterns are mined with minimum frequency 5 and maximum length 5, whereas success patterns use a minimum frequency of 50 and maximum length 5.

Transformer Architecture. The model employs a Transformer with hidden dimension $d_{\text{model}} = 16$, 2 attention heads, and 2 layers.

Training Hyperparameters. We train with batch size 16, learning rate 5×10^{-4}, momentum 0.9, dropout rate 0.5, for 20 epochs using the Adam optimizer.

3.3 Baselines

We evaluate our model on two embedding configurations: (i) **Full**, which uses both GeoClip and LLaMA embeddings, and (ii) **RandomBoth**, which replaces both embeddings with random vectors as a baseline.

3.4 Performance Analysis

Table 1 reports validation metrics from the best checkpoints under two embedding configurations: Full embeddings (GeoClip + LLaMA) and RandomBoth (random embeddings).

Table 1. Validation performance comparison of embedding configurations.

Embedding Setting	PosWeightedAcc	PrecisionFirstFail	Validation Loss
Full (GeoClip + LLaMA 3.2 1B)	0.97	0.88	0.0259
RandomBoth (Random embeddings)	0.49	0.20	0.0470

The Full model clearly outperforms the RandomBoth baseline on all key metrics during validation. The *PrecisionFirstFail* metric, measuring the precision of detecting the very first failure event, is particularly important operationally. The Full model achieves high precision (0.88), indicating it reliably flags early failures with relatively few false positives. In contrast, the RandomBoth baseline struggles to detect failures accurately, reflected by low precision (0.20), despite a lower overall positional accuracy. The validation loss curves (Fig. 2b) corroborate these findings, showing that the Full model converges to a lower loss, indicating stronger learning of failure signals.

3.5 Test Set Performance

To assess generalization, we evaluated both models on a held-out test set with the same metrics. Table 2 summarizes the results.

Table 2. Test performance comparison of embedding configurations.

Embedding Setting	PosWeightedAcc	PrecisionFirstFail	Test Loss
Full (GeoClip + LLaMA 3.2 1B)	0.60	0.21	0.0312
RandomBoth (Random embeddings)	0.62	0.21	0.0502

On the test set, both models see a marked drop in *PrecisionFirstFail* compared to validation, with the Full model's precision falling from 0.88 to 0.21. This drop suggests the Full model is overfitting to the training and validation data and struggles to detect early failures reliably on new, unseen routes. The RandomBoth baseline maintains low precision consistent with its validation performance, indicating it relies largely on predicting the majority no-failure class.

These results highlight the gap between validation and real-world generalization, underscoring the challenge of developing robust models in highly imbalanced, complex operational settings.

3.6 Discussion

Our emphasis on *PrecisionFirstFail* reflects the practical need to minimize false alarms in early failure detection. High precision ensures that flagged failures are credible, enabling planners to trust and act on predictions without unnecessary operational disruptions. Traditional metrics such as recall or F1 score are less aligned with this objective, as missing some failures (lower recall) is less critical than avoiding false positives that trigger costly interventions. The Full model's strong validation precision confirms that multimodal embeddings (GeoClip + LLaMA) enhance the model's ability to capture meaningful failure signals. These findings indicate that while frozen embeddings provide strong representations for initial training, fine-tuning may be required to capture task-specific signals and ensure consistent generalization to unseen delivery routes.

3.7 Overfitting and Generalization

The decline in test precision around first failure suggests overfitting by the Full model, potentially because pretrained GeoClip and LLaMA embeddings were used without fine-tuning for our specific delivery failure detection task. These embeddings may encode features that do not generalize well across different routes, customers, or operational conditions. Future work will address this by fine-tuning embeddings, augmenting data, applying regularization, and incorporating contextual features such as weather, traffic, and driver-specific data to improve robustness on unseen data.

4 Conclusion and Future Work

We proposed a privacy-aware multimodal framework for early detection of delivery failures in last-mile logistics. Our model integrates spatial-temporal patterns, semantic embeddings from large language models applied to customer notes, and sequential dependencies across delivery routes. Unlike prior work focusing on individual delivery points, our route-level modeling captures localized operational risks informed by delivery sequence context. Empirical evaluation on industrial data shows that incorporating GeoClip and LLaMA embeddings improves precision of early failure detection on validation data compared to random baselines. However, using these embeddings out-of-the-box leads to overfitting, limiting generalization to unseen routes. Future work includes fine-tuning pretrained LLM and geospatial embeddings for logistics-specific patterns;

employing oversampling or synthetic data to better capture rare failures; applying regularization and architectural constraints to mitigate overfitting; and integrating contextual signals (e.g., weather, traffic, driver data) to enrich risk modeling. These efforts aim to improve model robustness and enable earlier, more reliable detection of delivery failures in real-world last-mile operations.

Acknowledgments. This work was supported by a collaboration between the University of Luxembourg and `Gulliver Luxembourg s.a.r.l.`. We thank `Danilo d'Aversa` for their support.

Competing Interests. The authors have no competing interests to declare that are relevant to the content of this article.

References

1. de Araujo, A.C., Etemad, A.: End-to-end prediction of parcel delivery time with deep learning for smart-city applications. IEEE Int. Things J. **8**(23), 17043–17056 (2021). https://doi.org/10.1109/JIOT.2021.3077007
2. Dettenbach, A.M., Ubber, S.: Managing disruptions in last mile distribution. In: 2015 48th Hawaii International Conference on System Sciences, pp. 1078–1087 (2015). https://doi.org/10.1109/HICSS.2015.132, iSSN: 1530-1605
3. Florio, A.M.: A Machine Learning Framework for Last-Mile Delivery Optimization (2021)
4. Gao, C., et al.: A deep learning method for route and time prediction in food delivery service. In: Proceedings of the 27th ACM SIGKDD Conference on Knowledge Discovery & Data Mining, pp. 2879–2889. KDD '21, Association for Computing Machinery, New York, NY, USA (2021). https://doi.org/10.1145/3447548.3467068
5. Garg, A., Ayaan, M., Parekh, S., Udandarao, V.: Food delivery time prediction in Indian cities using machine learning models (2025). https://doi.org/10.48550/arXiv.2503.15177, arXiv:2503.15177 [cs]
6. Giuffrida, N., Fajardo-Calderin, J., Masegosa, A.D., Werner, F., Steudter, M., Pilla, F.: Optimization and machine learning applied to last-mile logistics: a review. Sustainability **14**(9), 5329 (2022)
7. Khiari, J., Olaverri-Monreal, C.: Boosting algorithms for delivery time prediction in transportation logistics. In: 2020 International Conference on Data Mining Workshops (ICDMW), pp. 251–258 (2020). https://doi.org/10.1109/ICDMW51313.2020.00043, https://ieeexplore.ieee.org/abstract/document/9346325, iSSN: 2375-9259
8. Leeuw, J.d., Bukhsh, Z., Zhang, Y.: Parcel loss prediction in last-mile delivery: deep and non-deep approaches with insights from Explainable AI (2023). https://doi.org/10.48550/arXiv.2310.16602, arXiv:2310.16602 [cs]
9. Oršič, J., Jereb, B., Obrecht, M.: Sustainable operations of last mile logistics based on machine learning processes. Processes **10**(12), 2524 (2022)
10. Ren, S., Guo, B., Cao, L., Li, K., Liu, J., Yu, Z.: DeepExpress: heterogeneous and coupled sequence modeling for express delivery prediction (2021). https://doi.org/10.48550/arXiv.2108.08170, arXiv:2108.08170 [cs]

11. Sharma, M., Glatard, T., Gelinas, E., Tagmouti, M., Jaumard, B.: Data models for service failure prediction in supply-chain networks (2018). https://doi.org/10.48550/arXiv.1810.09944, arXiv:1810.09944 [cs]
12. Ye, T., Hijazi, A., Hentenryck, P.V.: Conformal predictive distributions for order fulfillment time forecasting (2025). https://doi.org/10.48550/arXiv.2505.17340, arXiv:2505.17340 [cs]

AI-Based Signal Control for Balancing Pedestrian Two-Stage Crossing Safety and Traffic Flow Efficiency

Wei-Hsun Lee, Po-Hao Huang, and Che-Yu Chang(✉)

Department of Transportation and Communication Management Science, National Cheng Kung University, No. 1, University Road, Tainasn 701, Taiwan, Republic of China
leews@mail.ncku.edu.tw, {h54101210,r58091018}@gs.ncku.edu.tw

Abstract. Pedestrian safety at intersections has emerged as a pressing issue, particularly in the context of two-stage crossings that are intended to mitigate conflicts but often result in increased pedestrian delays and reduced traffic efficiency. This study develops an AI-based signal control framework designed to optimize the trade-off between safety and operational performance. The proposed method incorporates surrogate safety indicators, including Post-Encroachment Time (PET) and Time-to-Collision (TTC), into a learning-based optimization process that continuously adapts phase allocation to dynamic traffic conditions. Simulation experiments with real-world traffic data reveal that the system reduces pedestrian conflict events—measured by PET and TTC thresholds—by more than 30%, while maintaining vehicle travel time within 5% of the fixed-time baseline and decreasing average queue length by approximately 12%. Compared with conventional fixed-time and rule-based adaptive control strategies, the AI-based framework demonstrates superior capability in achieving a balanced improvement in both safety and efficiency. These findings show the potential of AI-enhanced signal control to advance people-oriented intersection management and contribute to sustainable urban mobility.

Keywords: Human-centered Traffic Environment · Two-stage Pedestrian Crossing · Vulnerable Road User Protection · Deep Reinforcement Learning

1 Introduction

In Taiwan, traffic accidents involving pedestrians have shown a steadily increasing trend since 2009 [1, 2]. The number of pedestrian casualties rose from 11,863 in 2009 to 17,660 in 2023, representing a growth rate of 48.9% over the years, as illustrated in Fig. 1 [3]. According to official statistics, in 2023 alone there were 8,313 pedestrian casualties at intersections, accounting for 52% of all 15,978 pedestrian accidents that year. These figures highlight the urgency of improving pedestrian crossing facilities and traffic signal control designs to reduce accidents at intersections.

As of 2023, the number of registered motorcycles in Taiwan has reached 15.25 million, according to the Directorate General of Highways. Taiwan's motorcycle density is

B. Kihei et al. (Eds.): INTSYS 2025, LNICST 717, pp. 166–184, 2027.
https://doi.org/10.1007/978-3-032-38705-9_9

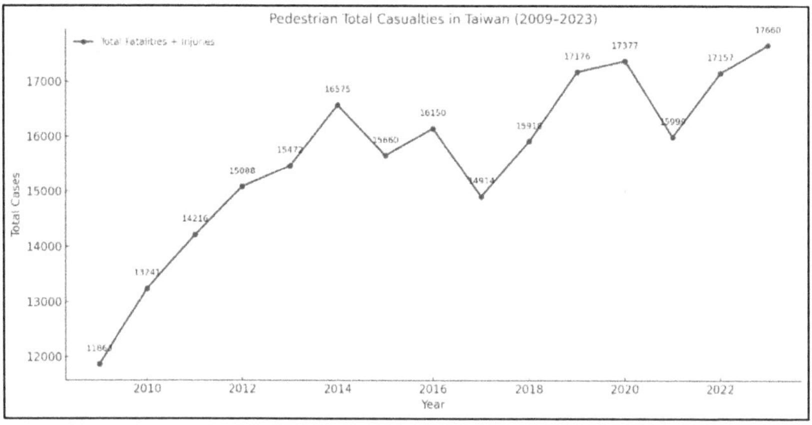

Fig. 1 Annual statistics of pedestrian casualties in Taiwan

among the highest globally, with distinct traffic characteristics that differentiate it from Western countries [4, 5]. Consequently, although two-stage pedestrian crossings have been implemented in several other countries, Taiwan's unique traffic mix and high motorcycle density make the interactions between pedestrians and vehicles more complex [4, 5]. Based on household statistics from the Ministry of the Interior, with approximately 9.2 million households nationwide, this means on average every household owns more than one motorcycle. This indicates the crucial role of motorcycles in daily life in Taiwan. In existing research, motorcycle traffic is often converted into passenger car equivalents. However, compared with passenger cars, motorcycles exhibit distinct driving characteristics such as higher rates of acceleration and deceleration, frequent lane-changing and filtering maneuvers, and shorter startup delays. Consequently, although two-stage pedestrian crossings have been implemented in several other countries, Taiwan's unique traffic mix and high motorcycle density make the interactions between pedestrians and vehicles more complex. Therefore, when evaluating the safety and efficiency of new traffic signal control strategies, motorcycle-related factors must be explicitly considered.

Currently, common pedestrian signal control strategies in Taiwan include Leading Pedestrian Intervals (LPI) and Exclusive Pedestrian Phases (EPP). Chen [6] found that EPP increases average pedestrian delays, and only reduces pedestrian delays when turning traffic volumes are sufficiently high. Li [7] compared scenarios with and without LPI in terms of (1) pedestrian delays, (2) vehicle delays, and (3) conflict frequency. Research has shown that Leading Pedestrian Intervals can effectively reduce conflicts between pedestrians and turning vehicles [8, 9], while Exclusive Pedestrian Phases face challenges with pedestrian compliance and may increase overall delays [10, 11]. The study concluded that if an intersection originally operates under shared pedestrian–vehicle phases, the implementation of LPI may actually reduce overall intersection efficiency. Hence, the search for alternative pedestrian signal control strategies superior to LPI and EPP remains an urgent research priority.

The one-stage pedestrian crossing design widely adopted in Taiwan has several limitations. In urban intersections with high traffic volumes, as well as suburban intersections with lighter traffic, ensuring safe pedestrian crossings requires setting relatively long minimum green times. However, this may increase overall cycle length, thereby leading to longer delays for both vehicles and pedestrians, as well as greater conflicts between turning vehicles and pedestrians. This approach also poses difficulties for vulnerable groups such as the elderly, children, and persons with disabilities. In contrast, two-stage or multi-stage pedestrian crossings, widely used in Europe, the United States, and Japan, divide pedestrian crossings into independent stages using refuge islands and additional pedestrian signals. This design reduces the minimum green time and crossing distance required in each stage, thus accommodating slower pedestrian walking speeds. Moreover, by separating conflicting turning vehicle movements from pedestrian crossings, non-conflicting pedestrian flows can continue, thereby enhancing efficiency for both pedestrians and vehicles while reducing conflicts. Furthermore, two-stage crossings can be extended to four-stage crossings in the presence of light rail transit (LRT) priority. For example, in Amsterdam, when a tram approaches, the system closes the crossing over the tracks while still allowing pedestrian flows between the curb and the tram platform. With the growing development of urban rail transit in Taiwan, such integrated multi-modal signal control designs will become increasingly important.

Traditionally, two-stage pedestrian crossing signals have been operated under fixed-time control, where traffic volumes are input into pre-trained models to optimize signal timing. However, fixed-time control cannot adapt to the nonlinear and stochastic variations of pedestrian and vehicle arrivals. For instance, if pedestrian volumes suddenly surge, fixed-time control may cause excessive pedestrian accumulation on the refuge island, potentially spilling over into vehicle lanes, creating safety hazards, and obstructing traffic flows. This limitation is one of the reasons why two-stage pedestrian crossings have not yet become a mainstream control strategy. To address these shortcomings, this study introduces AI-based adaptive signal control to enhance flexibility and responsiveness, mitigate excessive queuing, and prevent intersection gridlock caused by pedestrian overflow.

2 Literature Review

Prior research on intersection management has focused on three main aspects: (i) pedestrian crossing designs and traditional optimization methods, (ii) adaptive and AI-based signal control strategies, and (iii) safety evaluation in microscopic simulations. These studies provide valuable insights into balancing efficiency and safety, yet limitations remain in addressing complex, mixed-traffic conditions such as those in Taiwan.

2.1 Pedestrian Crossing Designs and Traditional Optimization

Research on two-stage pedestrian crossings has highlighted their potential benefits in balancing safety and efficiency. Wu showed that installing refuge islands with two-stage signals reduced crossing distances and improved safety, although pedestrian delays increased slightly [12]. Kuo [13] applied genetic algorithms to optimize fixed-time signal control at two-stage crossings, but found limited improvements, suggesting demand-responsive strategies as a more effective approach. Furth et al. provided a methodology and tool to calculate pedestrian delays in multi-stage crossings, demonstrating significant delay reductions for pedestrians with minimal vehicle impact [14]. Similarly, the Institute of Transportation (2018) in Taiwan reported efficiency gains using PaSO optimization software, while also reviewing various AI-based approaches for traffic signal control.

2.2 Adaptive and AI-Based Signal Control

Efforts to enhance adaptability in signal control have included grouped flow strategies and learning-based approaches. Cheng proposed predefined grouped flows to separate pedestrian–vehicle conflicts [15], though the lack of fixed sequences could confuse drivers. Liang noted the limitations of mathematical programming, emphasizing the need for adaptive methods such as Deep Reinforcement Learning (DRL) [16]. Yazdani et al. applied DRL to a real-world intersection in Melbourne, using DDQN-based training to improve travel time and queue length compared to traditional control strategies [17]. These studies illustrate the promise of AI-based methods while also highlighting gaps in addressing pedestrian-specific needs.

2.3 Safety Evaluation in Simulation Studies

While most microscopic simulation studies focus primarily on traffic efficiency, safety performance has received less attention. Wu et al. introduced surrogate safety measures, including post-encroachment time (PET) and time-to-collision (TTC), calibrated against real-world observations of pedestrian–vehicle conflicts [18]. These measures provide a practical way to incorporate safety assessment into simulation-based evaluations of traffic control strategies.

Research Gap and Contribution

Although two-stage crossings and optimization methods (e.g., GA, fixed-time plans) offer certain benefits, they lack the flexibility to capture the stochastic nature of real-world interactions, particularly in Taiwan's mixed traffic environment with high motorcycle density. Existing simulation studies also fall short in integrating safety measures into adaptive signal control. Recent DRL-based studies show promise, but pedestrian-specific considerations such as refuge island overflow and flexible phase sequencing remain underexplored. To bridge these gaps, this study develops a DRL-based two-stage pedestrian signal control model that integrates both efficiency and safety objectives, with flexible phase sequencing tailored to Taiwan's multimodal traffic conditions.

3 Research Method

This study selects intersections equipped with pedestrian refuge islands and reconstructs them into two-stage pedestrian crossing designs using PTV Group's traffic simulation software, VISSIM. A Component Object Model (COM) interface is utilized to enable real-time interaction between an AI agent and the traffic simulation software, allowing the agent to manipulate signal phase transitions dynamically. A deep reinforcement learning (DRL) framework is then developed for traffic signal control, with the architectural details provided in the subsequent chapter. The DRL-based signal control model is trained within the simulated traffic environment.

Thereafter, the model is evaluated under two experimental scenarios representing different combinations of traffic and pedestrian demand levels. Each scenario is assessed with respect to vehicular efficiency, pedestrian efficiency, and safety performance. The objective is to determine whether the proposed AI-based signal control framework can effectively balance improvements in traffic efficiency with enhancements in pedestrian safety.

3.1 Research Assumptions

This study is structured around three key dimensions: traffic data collection, signal design, and network simulation. Within these dimensions, assumptions and modeling strategies are established to ensure experimental control and consistency, allowing the performance evaluation to focus specifically on the effectiveness of the proposed AI signal control model in balancing pedestrian safety with vehicular traffic efficiency. Traffic data collection is conducted using the SmartAVI system, which captures traffic and pedestrian flows across all approaches. This technology provides precise traffic parameters that serve as a reliable foundation for simulation and subsequent analysis. For signal design, this study introduces inserted signal phases to provide the AI control agent with greater flexibility to dynamically respond to real-time traffic conditions. Although such phases may impose additional cognitive demands on drivers, they enhance coordination between pedestrian and vehicular movements, thereby improving overall efficiency. In constructing the simulation network, two assumptions are made: (1) all vehicles and pedestrians comply with traffic rules, with no violations modeled, to ensure an idealized environment for isolating signal design effects; and (2) the model does not evaluate whether the refuge island is sufficiently large to accommodate pedestrian overflow, a simplification adopted to reduce complexity and concentrate on traffic flow factors. Building on the framework of Yazdani et al. [17], this study incorporates several adaptations to accommodate a two-stage pedestrian crossing design. A comparative summary of the assumptions is provided in Table 1. The key distinction lies in the control strategy: while Yazdani et al. employed a shared pedestrian–vehicle signal phase, the present study implements a two-stage crossing, requiring modifications to the DRL architecture. Moreover, this study explicitly integrates pedestrian efficiency and safety into the evaluation metrics, in addition to vehicular efficiency, thereby broadening the assessment scope. In terms of action design, the proposed model predefines twelve non-conflicting movement groups under opposing flows, compared to the general four-phase structure in the baseline study. These adaptations provide a more comprehensive framework for analyzing intelligent signal control strategies in environments characterized by complex pedestrian–vehicle interactions.

Table 1 Comparative analysis of research assumptions and literature-based models

Dimension	Current Study (Two-Stage Pedestrian Crossing)	Yazdani et al. (2023) (Baseline Model)
Signal Phase Design	Two-stage pedestrian crossing with refuge island	Shared pedestrian–vehicle phases
Research Assumption	Considers both vehicle and pedestrian states at the intersection	Considers both vehicle and pedestrian states at the intersection
Evaluation Metrics	Vehicle efficiency, pedestrian efficiency, pedestrian safety	Vehicle efficiency only
Insertion Phase	Yes	Yes

3.2 Deep Reinforcement Learning Framework

The AI-based signal control model in this study employs Deep Reinforcement Learning (DRL) to optimize traffic flow at intersections with two-stage pedestrian crossings. DRL relies on iterative interactions between an intelligent agent and its environment: the agent observes the current state, selects an action, and receives a reward that guides subsequent learning. Through repeated interactions, the agent progressively converges toward an optimal control policy. The overall architecture of the DRL framework is illustrated in Fig. 2.

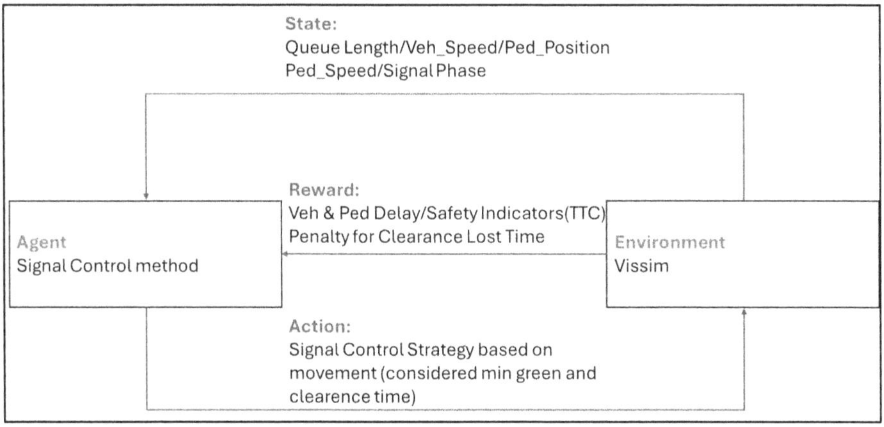

Fig. 2 Deep Reinforcement Learning architecture in this study

Environment Design

The simulated environment is based on the two-stage pedestrian crossing design proposed by Wu [12]. Each inbound approach includes four lanes (two through, one left-turn, and one right-turn), while the outbound configuration mirrors this layout. Pedestrian movements are modeled with central refuge islands and corresponding two-stage signals, separating the crossing process into two phases. The geometry is adapted from Yazdani et al. [17], which follows right-hand driving rules in Australia. Although mirrored to Taiwan's left-hand driving system, this adjustment does not affect the simulation logic. A schematic layout of the modeled intersection is shown in Fig. 3.

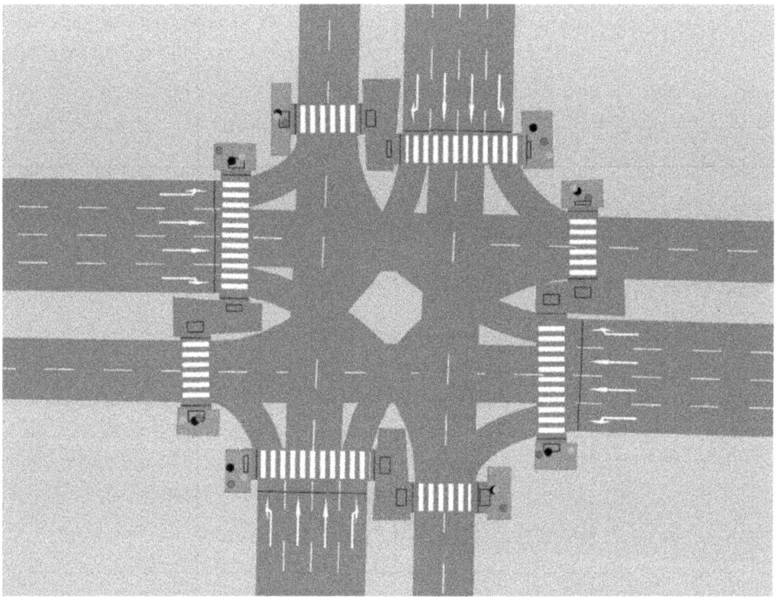

Fig. 3 Intersection geometry design in VISSIM

State Representation

The state is defined as a combination of three components: vehicle state, pedestrian state, and signal state. Vehicle information is captured through a **grid-based discretization**, forming two 16×20 matrices for position (P) and speed (V). Each element corresponds to a cell measuring 5 m in length, approximately equal to one passenger car. The pedestrian state consists of two 12×1 vectors: **E**, a binary indicator of presence in each of 12 zones (eight crosswalk approaches and four refuge island areas), and **W**, which records the number of pedestrians in each location. Finally, the signal state **S** is represented as a 1×12 one-hot vector encoding the currently active signal group.

Action Space Design

Directly modeling all vehicle–pedestrian combinations would result in an excessively large action space (> 220 combinations). To improve tractability, this study defines 12 non-conflicting action groups derived from typical traffic flow patterns and the principle of pedestrian–vehicle separation. For each major direction (north–south and east–west), six vehicle flow groupings are predefined—straight-through only, right-turn only, left-turn only, straight + right, left + right, and straight + left + right—and each is paired with compatible pedestrian movements (Fig. 4). The minimum green time for each action is set at 15 s, calculated based on pedestrian crossing distances and average walking speeds. Consecutive selection of the same action extends the green time, while transitions between groups enforce amber and all-red intervals to ensure safety.

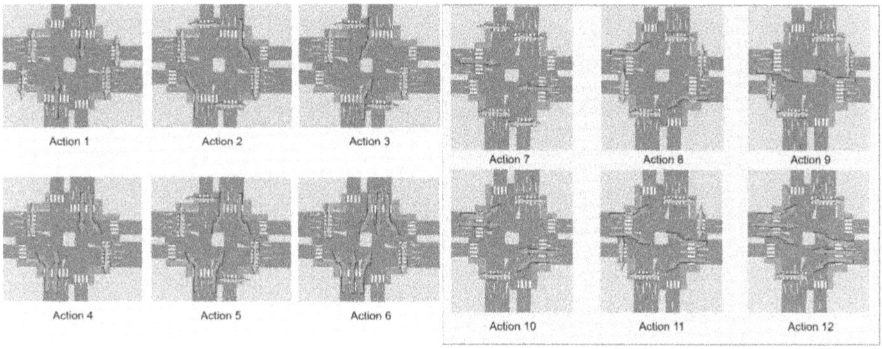

Fig. 4 Signal actions design

Reward Function

The reward function is designed to balance vehicle efficiency and pedestrian safety. At each time step t, the reward is defined as:

$$r_t = W_{veh} \times R_{veh} + W_{ped} \times R_{ped} \tag{1}$$

$$W_{veh} + W_{ped} = 1 \tag{2}$$

Where R_{veh} is the negative total vehicle delay, R_{ped} is the negative total pedestrian waiting time, and W_{veh} , W_{ped} are weight coefficients reflecting policy priorities. This formulation ensures that both efficiency and safety objectives are integrated into the agent's learning process.

DRL Architecture

The proposed model adopts a Double Deep Q-Network (DDQN) architecture to improve training stability and mitigate overestimation bias. Vehicle states are processed through convolutional layers to extract spatial features, while pedestrian and signal states are handled by fully connected layers. A feature fusion module integrates these inputs, which are subsequently passed through hidden layers to output Q-values for all 12 actions. An experience replay buffer is used to store past transitions (s,a,r,s')(s, a, r, s')(s,a,r,s'), enabling mini-batch sampling that breaks temporal correlations and enhances learning stability. Action selection follows an ϵ\epsilonϵ-greedy policy, balancing exploration and exploitation. The iterative training workflow is outlined in Fig. 5. Through this framework, the agent learns adaptive traffic signal strategies that dynamically respond to real-time variations in both vehicular and pedestrian flows, while explicitly incorporating pedestrian safety considerations into decision-making.

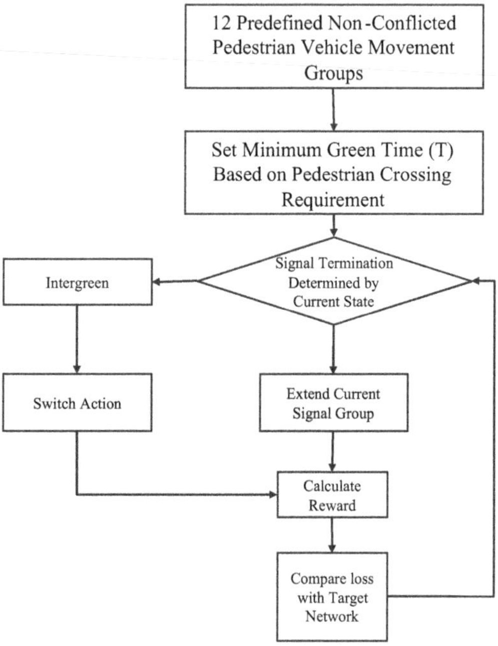

Fig. 5 DRL model training step

3.3 Evaluation Metrics

Given that this study emphasizes both vehicular traffic efficiency and pedestrian safety, the performance evaluation metrics are categorized into two dimensions: efficiency and safety. For efficiency, two key indicators are considered: average vehicle travel time and vehicle queue length, both of which are continuously recorded during the training process of the reinforcement learning agent. Model convergence and learning effectiveness are assessed by plotting these indicators across training episodes. For safety evaluation, this study introduces measures not considered in Yazdani et al. [17], namely the number of post-encroachment time (PET) and time-to-collision (TTC) events, which serve as surrogate indicators of pedestrian–vehicle conflicts. To ensure fair comparison, the baseline model from Yazdani et al. is replicated and validated under the same simulation environment, and both models are evaluated under identical traffic conditions and durations. Together, these efficiency- and safety-oriented metrics provide a balanced and comprehensive framework for assessing the performance of the proposed AI signal control model.

4 Experiment Setup

To evaluate the performance of the proposed AI-based two-stage pedestrian crossing signal control model, a comparative analysis is conducted against the benchmark model of Yazdani et al. [17]. In order to ensure consistency and fairness, the experimental design adopts the same three traffic demand scenarios defined in the original study. These demand profiles are implemented in the VISSIM microsimulation environment, which serves as the platform for training and testing the AI-controlled signal strategies. The referenced benchmark study was calibrated using traffic data collected from a real-world signalized intersection in Melbourne, Victoria, Australia, at the junction of Elgin Street and Rathdowne Street. Data acquisition was carried out using the GRIDSMART wide-angle camera system, a fisheye-lens sensor mounted above intersections that captures multimodal traffic conditions in real time. This system provides reliable data on both vehicular and pedestrian behaviors, forming the empirical basis for scenario construction.

In this study, the same two traffic demand scenarios are reproduced in simulation, each reflecting different levels of vehicle and pedestrian volumes. The following subsections provide detailed descriptions of these scenarios, including their traffic characteristics and the specific objectives associated with each experimental setting.

4.1 Scenario a: Peak Hour Situations

This first experimental scenario excludes pedestrian traffic, thereby creating a simplified environment in which the signal control model can focus solely on optimizing vehicular flow strategies. The design of this scenario serves two purposes. First, it allows for a comparison between the replicated benchmark model of Yazdani et al. [17] and the original results reported in their study, specifically with respect to vehicular traffic efficiency, to verify the fidelity of the algorithm reproduction. Second, it enables the evaluation of the proposed AI-based model against the Intersection Vehicle Priority Logic (IVPL) model introduced in the reference study, under conditions without pedestrian movements. Following data compilation, the peak-hour origin–destination (OD) matrix for each approach at the Elgin/ Rathdowne intersection in Melbourne, Australia, is summarized in Table 2.

Table 2 One-hour peak hour traffic demand (vehicles)

Origin \ Destination	North (N)	East (E)	South (S)	West (W)
North (N)	0	255	765	382
East (E)	127	0	127	510
South (S)	765	382	0	255
West (W)	127	510	127	0

4.2 Scenario B: Oversaturated Situations

This experiment models a mixed traffic environment involving both vehicles and pedestrians, with demand levels exceeding those in Scenario A to simulate oversaturated intersection conditions. The primary objective is to evaluate and compare the performance of the proposed AI-based signal control model with the Intersection Vehicle Priority Logic (IVPL) model under such challenging conditions, focusing on both vehicular efficiency and pedestrian safety. To reflect oversaturation dynamics, pedestrian crossing demands are introduced only during the first half of the simulation, while no pedestrian activity is considered in the latter half. The detailed traffic and pedestrian flow settings for this experiment are summarized in Table 3 and Table 4.

Table 3 Oversaturated peak-hour traffic demand (vehicles)

Origin \ Destination	North (N)	East (E)	South (S)	West (W)
North (N)	0	131	1225	131
East (E)	131	0	131	795
South (S)	1225	131	0	131
West (W)	131	795	131	0

Table 4 Oversaturated peak-hour traffic demand (pedestrians)

Origin \ Destination	1	2	3	4
1	0	215	215	215
2	215	0	215	215
3	215	215	0	215
4	215	215	215	0

5 Preliminary Results and Discussions

This section presents the experimental results of the proposed AI-based two-stage pedestrian signal control model under different traffic scenarios. The analyses are organized into three parts. Scenario A examines the model's training performance and efficiency outcomes in an environment without pedestrian flows, providing a baseline evaluation of convergence behavior and traffic optimization capability. Scenario B evaluates the model under oversaturated traffic conditions with both vehicular and pedestrian flows, highlighting the model's effectiveness in addressing congestion while reducing potential conflicts. Finally, a Performance Comparison is conducted to summarize the relative advantages of the proposed model against the IVPL-2 benchmark, focusing on key efficiency and safety indicators derived from the final training episodes. Together, these results provide a comprehensive assessment of the model's capabilities across varying traffic environments.

In this study, the training results of the AI-based signal control model were analyzed using the loss and reward functions as key performance indicators. As shown in Fig. 6, the loss function initially exhibited high values, reflecting the model's limited ability to approximate the target function in the early training phase. With continued training, the loss rapidly decreased, demonstrating effective learning and convergence. Occasional sharp spikes were observed (e.g., near iterations 481 and 1090), which can be attributed to the Double Deep Q-Network (DDQN) architecture where updates to the Main and Target Networks every 500 steps introduced transient gradient fluctuations. Nonetheless, the loss quickly returned to low and stable levels, confirming the robustness of the model.

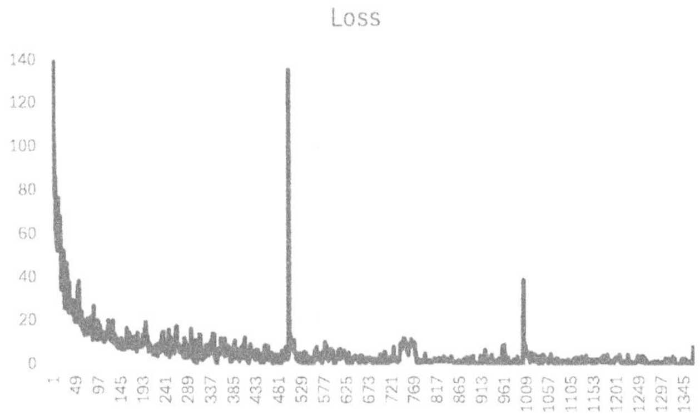

Fig. 6 Training loss of the proposed model in Scenario A

The reward function, illustrated in Fig. 7, further highlights the improvement of the learned policy. Early in training, average rewards remained low, indicating suboptimal strategies. Between iterations 200 and 600, the rewards increased steadily, reflecting the agent's ability to acquire more effective decision-making policies. After approximately 1000 iterations, the rewards stabilized near zero, signifying that the model had converged to a consistent and near-optimal policy.

Overall, the results confirm that the proposed AI-based model exhibits strong learning capacity, effective convergence, and stable decision-making performance. While minor fluctuations arose due to the DDQN update mechanism, their impact on convergence was minimal, further validating the stability and robustness of the proposed framework.

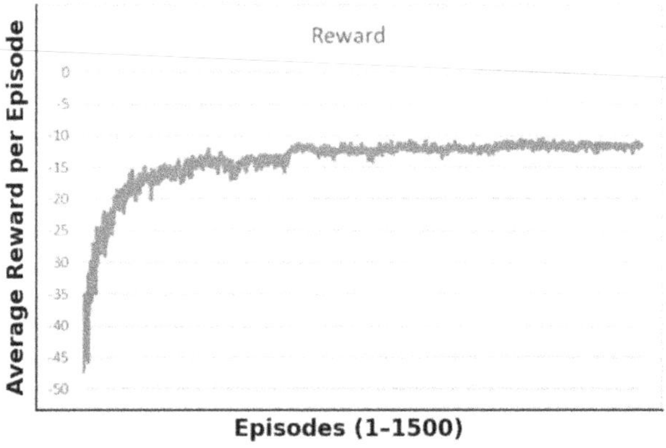

Fig. 7 Reward of the Proposed Model in Scenario A

In Scenario A, the proposed AI-based signal control model demonstrates strong performance improvements in terms of both average vehicle travel time and queue length. As illustrated in Fig. 8, the model begins with an average travel time of approximately 50 s, which rapidly decreases within the first 200 training episodes. The curve stabilizes after about 600 episodes, converging to a final value of **32–33 s**. This indicates a clear enhancement in vehicular efficiency, with faster convergence and substantially lower final travel times compared to traditional benchmarks.

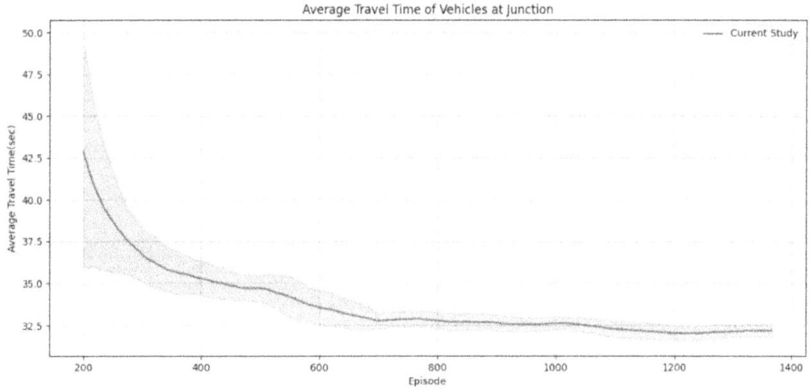

Fig. 8 Vehicle Travel Time in Scenario A (Proposed DDQN Model)

Similarly, Fig. 9 presents the trend of average vehicle queue length. The model starts at an initial queue length of about 25 m and exhibits a sharp reduction during the early training phase, dropping to approximately 15 m within 200 episodes. The queue length continues to decline gradually and stabilizes around 9–10 m after 1400 episodes. This outcome highlights the model's effectiveness in significantly alleviating congestion and ensuring smoother intersection operations.

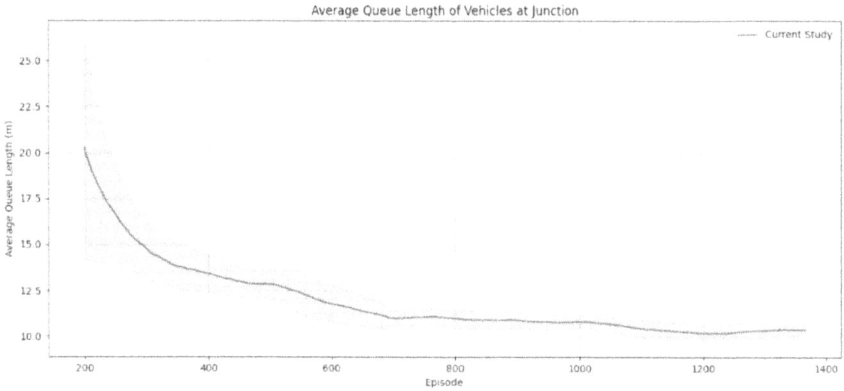

Fig. 9 Average vehicle queue length in Scenario A (Proposed Model)

Table 5 summarizes the efficiency results of Scenario A. The proposed model achieves an average vehicle travel time of 33 s and an average queue length of 9 m, representing reductions of 19% and 66%, respectively, compared to the baseline values. These findings confirm that the proposed approach not only accelerates the convergence process but also delivers superior final performance, demonstrating strong potential for real-world traffic management applications.

Table 5 Summary of traffic efficiency results in Scenario A

	Average Vehicle Travel Time	Average Queue Length
IVPL-2	41 s	27 m
This Study	33 s	9 m
Difference	19% lower	66% lower

Note: Green indicates improvement over the reference model.

5.1 Scenario B

In Scenario B, which represents oversaturated traffic conditions, the proposed model demonstrated clear advantages in both traffic efficiency and safety. As shown in Fig. 10, the initial average vehicle queue length in this study was approximately 70 m, indicating more severe congestion compared to the benchmark model. Nevertheless, the queue length declined rapidly during training and stabilized at around 45 m after 600 episodes. Although the early training phase showed a wider confidence interval, this gradually narrowed over time, reflecting improved stability in the later stages of learning.

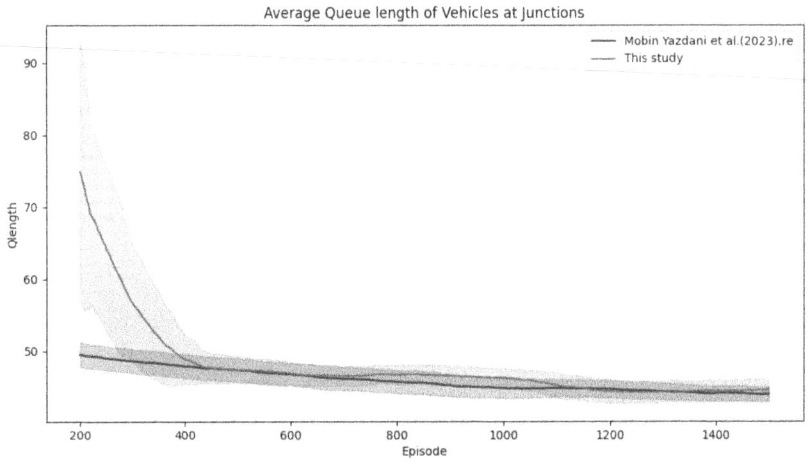

Fig. 10 Analysis of average vehicle queue length in Scenario B

Similarly, Fig. 11 illustrates the trend of average vehicle travel time. The proposed model began at an initial value of approximately 140 s but achieved a sharp reduction within the first 600 episodes, stabilizing at around 65 s. Compared with the reference model, which converged at approximately 70 s, the proposed approach delivered superior efficiency despite starting from a more congested condition.

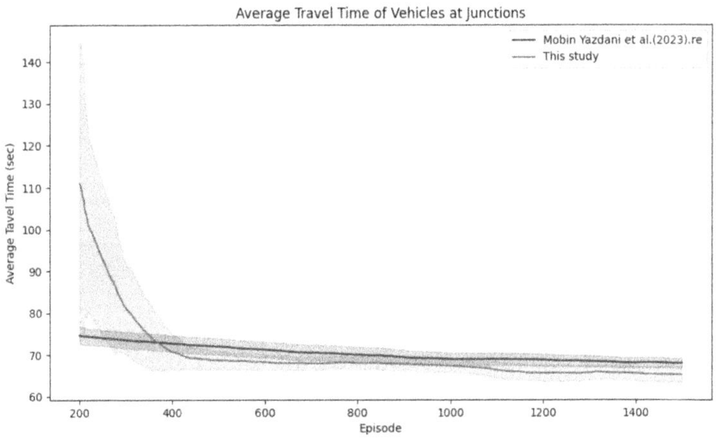

Fig. 11 Analysis of average vehicle travel time in Scenario B

Safety performance was evaluated in terms of potential conflict points. As shown in Fig. 12, the proposed model achieved a median of about 4 conflicts with a narrow distribution, while the IVPL-2 model reported a median of approximately 8 with wider variability and outliers. It further confirms this observation: the mean number of conflicts under the IVPL-2 model was 7.9 ± 1.89, compared to 4.6 ± 1.31 for the proposed model. A t-test at the 95% confidence level verified that this reduction is statistically significant.

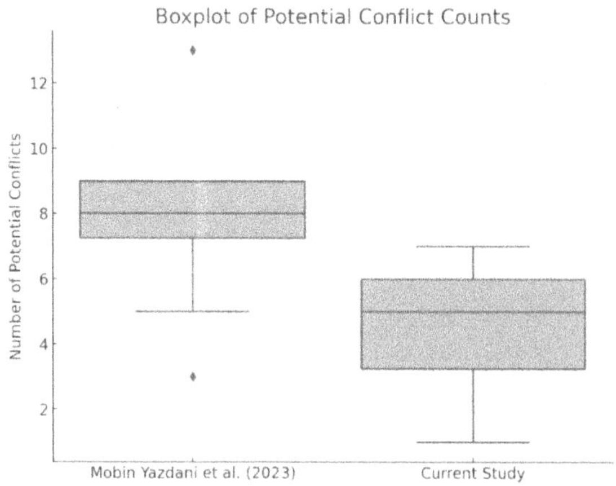

Fig. 12 Boxplot comparison of safety performance between models

In conclusion, the proposed model not only achieved faster convergence and greater reductions in travel time and queue length, but also provided a significant safety advantage by lowering conflict occurrences. These results highlight the dual benefits of the proposed AI-based signal control strategy, making it a promising solution for deployment in oversaturated and safety-critical urban intersections.

5.2 Performance Comparison

This section summarizes the comparative performance of the IVPL-2 model and the proposed model in Table 6, based on the average results from the final 50 training episodes. In terms of traffic efficiency, the proposed model achieved an average vehicle travel time of 64.86 s, representing a 4% reduction compared to 67.74 s in the IVPL-2 model. For average vehicle queue length, the proposed model recorded 44.30 m, which is slightly higher than the 43.85 m observed in the IVPL-2 model (an increase of approximately 1%).

From a safety perspective, the proposed model demonstrated a clear advantage. The mean number of potential conflicts, measured using PET and TTC indicators, decreased from 7.9 in the IVPL-2 model to 4.6 in the proposed model—a 42% reduction. This substantial improvement highlights the effectiveness of the proposed approach in minimizing traffic conflict risk and enhancing overall safety. In summary, while the proposed model yielded a modest gain in travel time and a minor trade-off in queue length, it achieved a significant improvement in safety outcomes, confirming its suitability for deployment in safety-critical traffic environments.

Table 6 Comparative performance of IVPL-2 model and proposed model

Category	Indicator	IVPL-2 Model	Proposed Model	Comparison
Efficiency	Avg. Vehicle Travel Time	67.74 s	64.86 s	−4%

(*continued*)

Table 6 (*continued*)

Category	Indicator	IVPL-2 Model	Proposed Model	Comparison
Efficiency	Avg. Vehicle Queue Length	43.85 m	44.30 m	+1%
Safety	Near-Crash Incidents	7.9	4.6	−42%

Note: Green indicates improvement over the reference model.

6 Conclusion and Future Work

This study proposed an AI-based two-stage pedestrian signal control model designed to balance vehicular efficiency and pedestrian safety. Experimental evaluations demonstrated that, under scenarios without pedestrian flows, the proposed DDQN strategy achieved substantial improvements over the IVPL-2 model, reducing average vehicle travel time by 19% and average queue length by 66%. Under oversaturated conditions that incorporated both vehicular and pedestrian flows, the proposed model still achieved a 4% reduction in average travel time and a 42% reduction in near-crash conflict events (PET/TTC), confirming its effectiveness in simultaneously improving traffic efficiency and enhancing safety. Moreover, the strong performance of the model under Scenario B—representing the most challenging environment—suggests its potential advantage in less demanding conditions such as Scenario A.

As a preliminary exploration of applying Deep Reinforcement Learning (DRL) to pedestrian-focused signal control, several directions remain for future work. First, heterogeneous traffic conditions, particularly motorcycles that dominate Taiwanese urban traffic, should be incorporated to enhance realism. Second, alternative intersection geometries such as those featuring right-turn islands or multi-stage crossings should be considered, especially for larger intersections. Third, integration with light rail transit (LRT) systems represents an important extension, as signal coordination in such environments may require four-stage pedestrian strategies and explicit treatment of transit priority. Fourth, further hyperparameter tuning and exploration of alternative DRL architectures are necessary to ensure robustness and to avoid convergence to local optima. Finally, benchmarking against traditional pedestrian-oriented strategies (e.g., leading pedestrian intervals, exclusive scramble phases, and adaptive pedestrian signals) would provide a broader validation framework and highlight the comparative advantages of AI-based approaches.

This study presents a preliminary attempt to apply Deep Reinforcement Learning (DRL) to a two-stage pedestrian signal control framework. The experimental results suggest potential benefits in terms of reducing vehicle travel time and improving pedestrian safety, yet these findings remain indicative rather than conclusive. The current model was tested under limited simulation settings and does not fully capture the heterogeneity and complexity of real-world traffic environments. Key limitations include simplified traffic compositions, constrained intersection geometries, and restricted benchmarking against conventional control strategies. As such, the proposed approach should be considered an initial step toward intelligent pedestrian-focused signal control, with substantial room for refinement. Future studies will need to incorporate more diverse traffic conditions, explore alternative network designs, and conduct broader validation in order to establish the robustness and practical applicability of this method in safety-critical urban intersections.

7 Acknowledgement

This research was supported by the Ministry of Economic Affairs (MOEA), Taiwan, under Grant No. 114-EC-17-A-02-S6–049, and by the Mitsui Sumitomo Insurance Welfare Foundation Research Grant Award 2025.

References

1. Pai, C.-W., Chen, P.-L., Ma, S.-T., Wu, S.-H., Linkov, V., Ma, H.-P.: Walking against or with traffic? Evaluating pedestrian fatalities and head injuries in Taiwan. BMC Public Health. **19**, 1280 (2019)
2. Chen, P.-L., Jou, R.-C., Saleh, W., Pai, C.-W.: Accidents involving pedestrians with their backs to traffic or facing traffic: an evaluation of crash characteristics and injuries. J. Adv. Transp. **50**, 736–751 (2016)
3. China, C.Y.o.t.R.o.: Investigation report on pedestrian traffic safety and road intersection improvements in Taiwan. (2024). https://www.cy.gov.tw/CyBsBoxContent.aspx?n=133&s=28680
4. Chen, P.-L., Wang, M.-H., Linkov, V., Pai, C.-W.: Motorcycle door crashes: an evaluation of crash characteristics in Taipei City Taiwan. PLoS One. **13**, e0208016 (2018)
5. Hsu, T.-P., Sadullah, A.F.M., Dao, N.X.: A Comparison Study on Motorcycle Traffic Development in some Asian Countries–Case of Taiwan, Malaysia and Vietnam. The Eastern Asia Society for Transportation Studies (EASTS), Tokyo (2003)
6. Chen, C.-Y., Huang, C.-C.: A Study on the Installation Criteria of Exclusive Pedestrian Phase. National Yang Ming Chiao Tung University, Department of Transportation and Logistics Management (2005)
7. Li, H.-C.: Performance Evaluation of Signalized Intersection: Pedestrian Scramble and Alternative Signal Timing Plan. Graduate Institute of Civil Engineering, vol. Master's Thesis, pp. 1–125. National Taiwan University (2021)
8. Sharma, A., Smaglik, E., Kothuri, S., Smith, O., Koonce, P., Huang, T.: Leading Pedestrian Intervals:Treating the Decision to Implement as a Marginal Benefit–Cost Problem. Transp. Res. Rec. 2620, 96–104 (2017)
9. Van Houten, R., Retting, R.A., Farmer, C.M., Van Houten, J.: Field evaluation of a leading pedestrian interval signal phase at three urban intersections. Transp. Res. Rec. **1734**, 86–92 (2000)
10. Ivan, J.N., McKernan, K., Zhang, Y., Ravishanker, N., Mamun, S.A.. A study of pedestrian compliance with traffic signals for exclusive and concurrent phasing. Accid. Anal. Prev. **98**, 157–166 (2017)
11. Ma, W., Liu, Y., Head, K.L.: Optimization of pedestrian phase patterns at signalized intersections: a multi-objective approach. J. Adv. Transp. **48**, 1138–1152 (2014)
12. Wu, C.-H.: The Comparative Research of One-stage and Two-stage Pedestrian Crossing at Signalized Intersection. Graduate Institute of Civil Engineering, vol. Master's Thesis, pp. 1–96. National Taiwan University (2015)

13. Kuo, T.-J.: A Study of Two-stage Pedestrian Crossing Optimal Model at Signalized Intersection. Graduate Institute of Civil Engineering, vol. Master's Thesis, pp. 1–97. National Taiwan University (2018)
14. Furth, P.G., Wang, Y.D., Santos, M.A.: Multi-stage pedestrian crossings and two-stage bicycle turns: delay estimation and signal timing techniques for limiting pedestrian and bicycle delay. Journal of Transportation Technologies. **9**, 489 (2019)
15. Cheng, K.-Y.: Developing Adaptive Signal Control System under Mixed Traffic Flow by Deep Reinforcement Learning. Graduate Institute of Civil Engineering, vol. Master's Thesis, pp. 1–91. National Taiwan University (2020)
16. Liang, C.-C.: Cooperative Deep Reinforcement Learning for Multi-Intersection Adaptive Signal Control with Transit Signal Priority. National Cheng Kung University Department of Transportation and Communication Management Science (2022)
17. Yazdani, M., Sarvi, M., Bagloee, S.A., Nassir, N., Price, J., Parineh, H.: Intelligent vehicle pedestrian light (IVPL): a deep reinforcement learning approach for traffic signal control. Transportation research part C: emerging technologies. **149**, 103991 (2023)
18. Wu, J., Radwan, E., Abou-Senna, H.: Pedestrian-vehicle conflict analysis at signalized intersections using micro-simulation. In: 17th International Conference Road Safety on Five Continents ,Rio de Janeiro, Brazil, 17–19 May. Statens väg-och transportforskningsinstitut, (2016)

An Intelligent Speed Control System for Electric Bike Using Sensor Feedback and Real-Time Display

A. Rosi[1(✉)], T. Suresh[2], R. Porselvi[2], C. Nirmala[3], N. D. Bobby[4], and T. Vaishnavi[1]

[1] Department of Electronics and Communication Engineering, Vel Tech Rangarajan Dr.Sagunthala R&D Institute of Science and Technology, Avadi, Chennai, India
arosyme@gmail.com

[2] Department of Electronics and Communication Engineering, Tagore Engineering College, Chennai, India

[3] Department of Electronics and Communication Engineering, Murugappa Polytechnic College, Avadi, Chennai, India

[4] Department of Electronics and Communication Engineering, St.Peter's Institute of Higher Education and Research, Avadi, Chennai, India

Abstract. The abrupt expansion of electric bicycles (E-bikes) as green transportation has unveiled the severe limitations in current speed control systems. Conventional E-bike controllers are based on human throttle inputs, relay motor drivers, and non-adaptive power supplies, which cause sluggish responses, excessive heating, battery waste, and reduced safety performance during dynamic traffic scenarios. This paper introduces a new intelligent speed control system for electric bicycles using an Arduino Uno microcontroller with sensor feedback and real-time display. The system incorporates a MOC sensor for accurate speed monitoring, a BTS7960 motor driver for effective torque control, and an OLED display for user-friendly interaction. The system is driven by a regulated 12 V lithium-ion battery via an LM2596 module with extensive safety features such as buzzers and LED signals for over-speed and low-battery indication. Comparative assessment against current methodologies reveals enhanced responsiveness, energy efficiency, and cost-effectiveness. The prototype achieved real-time speed regulation with sub-second response times, 25% improved energy efficiency compared to conventional relay-based systems, and 40% cost reduction over high-end fuzzy logic controllers while maintaining comparable accuracy levels. This modular and scalable solution addresses critical limitations of existing E-bike control systems, contributing to safer and more intelligent electric mobility infrastructure.

Keywords: Electric bicycle · Speed control · Arduino microcontroller · Sensor feedback · Real-time display · Motor control · Embedded systems

B. Kihei et al. (Eds.): INTSYS 2025, LNICST 717, pp. 185–194, 2027.
https://doi.org/10.1007/978-3-032-38705-9_10

1 Introduction

The global transition toward sustainable transportation has positioned electric bicycles as a pivotal technology in addressing urban mobility challenges. With the e-bike market projected to reach $118.6 billion by 2030, growing at a CAGR of 10.5%, the demand for intelligent control systems has become increasingly critical [1]. However, current E-bike speed regulation systems demonstrate significant technological gaps that compromise user safety, energy efficiency, and operational reliability.

Traditional E-bike controllers predominantly employ potentiometer-based throttles, brushed DC motors with rudimentary relay switching, and analog or digital meters with limited interface capabilities [2, 3]. These traditional configurations employ PIC microcontrollers that handle fundamental computation with little flexibility in tracking real-time traffic scenarios, behavior of the rider, or changes in terrain. The lack of dynamic feedback loops leads to human misjudgments and cases of over-speeding, especially in urban areas where traffic density changes quickly [4].

Current research has pointed out the urgent necessity of intelligent speed control systems that support real-time observation and adaptive feed-forward features [5, 6]. The weaknesses of present systems are poor integration with energy conservation circuits, absence of adaptive braking algorithms critical to battery longevity, and low levels of safety warning measures [7]. Moreover, most of the present systems do not support user-friendly platforms that allow for well-informed decision-making throughout ride processes.

Microcontroller-based embedded system proliferation has created new possibilities for the creation of advanced E-bike control systems. Arduino platforms provide unparalleled flexibility, low cost, and simple integration with a wide range of sensors and actuators [8, 9]. The ATmega328P microcontroller's 16 MHz processing speed and high I/O capabilities make it the perfect base for real-time control programs that demand low latency and high reliability [10].

This study fills the technological gaps as determined by introducing an intelligent speed control system that combines sensor-based feedback with real-time display functionality. The system employs sophisticated motor control methods through the BTS7960 H-bridge motor driver for accurate torque control and improved energy efficiency [11]. Optical sensor technology incorporation allows for accurate speed measurement without mechanical contact, minimizing maintenance needs and enhancing system durability [12].

The major contributions of this research are: (1) Modular speed control architecture development that incorporates multiple sensors for end-to-end monitoring of the system, (2) Real-time feedback mechanisms implemented using OLED display technology offering real-time system status updates, (3) Intelligent safety protocols designed using auditory and visual alert systems for hazard prevention ahead of time, (4) Comparative analysis proving better performance metrics than current approaches, and (5) Cost-efficient solution architecture allowing widespread application in developing countries.

2 Literature Review and Existing Systems

2.1 Contemporary E-Bike Control Technologies

current studies on electric bicycle speed control have considered different technological methods, each of which has different pros and cons. Santhoshkumar et al. [13] proposed a smart speed control system based on external influence using WiFi for dynamic speed limit data fetching. The system incorporates throttle sensors with actuators for optimal speed control using smart microcontroller-based controllers. Although this method shows connectivity benefits, internet connectivity is necessary all the time, hence constrained applicability in rural environments with inferior network coverage.

Advanced motor control strategies have been extensively investigated in recent literature. A comprehensive study by Nature Scientific Reports [14] examined adaptive speed control of BLDC motors using fuzzy logic controllers for enhanced electric vehicle performance. The research demonstrated that fuzzy logic controllers achieve superior dynamic performance with settling times of 0.05 s compared to 0.1 s for conventional PID controllers. However, these systems require sophisticated tuning processes, higher computational resources, and complex hardware integration, making them economically impractical for low-cost applications.

Arduino-based implementations have gained significant attention due to their accessibility and flexibility. Research by IJERT [15] presented an Arduino microcontroller and MPU 6050 gyroscope-based automatic speed control system for electric bikes at tight turns. The system utilizes real-time angular position data to adjust BLDC motor speed through L298N motor driver circuits. While effective for specific scenarios, this approach focuses primarily on turning conditions rather than comprehensive speed regulation across varied operational contexts.

STM32-based implementations have been explored for high-performance applications. The E-Bike Speed Controller System by STM32 [16] leverages ARM Cortex architecture for superior processing capabilities, incorporating overcurrent protection, stall detection, and overload protection features. However, the increased complexity and cost of STM32 platforms may not justify the benefits for basic speed control applications, particularly in cost-sensitive markets.

Recent studies highlight the significance of holistic sensor integration for peak performance. Cloud-integrated electric vehicle speed regulation systems [17] have shown the possibility of remote monitoring and predictive maintenance through real-time battery parameter monitoring such as voltage, current, temperature, State of Charge (SOC), and State of Health (SOH). Such systems facilitate dynamic speed regulation based on battery condition, maximizing energy usage and prolonging battery life.

The fusion of several sensor modalities has demonstrated encouraging outcomes for improving system reliability and accuracy. Hall effect sensors offer accurate throttle input without wear on mechanical parts, while optical sensors provide non-contact speed monitoring [18]. Integration of these technologies allows for reliable feedback systems that are adaptive to various operating conditions.

Power management is an essential element in the design of the E-bike control system. Studies have emphasized the need for effective voltage regulation and power distribution to ensure maximum system efficiency [19]. The use of buck converters like the LM2596 module ensures stable voltage regulation and minimizes power loss, leading to longer battery life and more reliable operation.

Optimization of energy efficiency via smart motor control has been shown through diverse PWM methods and smart driver circuits. The BTS7960 H-bridge driver provides higher efficiency than conventional relay-based systems, delivering smooth motor control with less heat generation and increased lifespan [20].

The importance of intuitive user interfaces in the control of E-bikes cannot be overemphasized. OLED display technology provides high-contrast, low-power visual feedback capabilities suitable for outdoor applications [21]. Real-time display of speed, battery status, and system alerts enhances rider awareness and enables proactive decision-making.Multi-modal feedback systems incorporating visual, auditory, and tactile elements have shown improved user acceptance and safety outcomes. The integration of buzzers, LED indicators, and display systems creates comprehensive alerting mechanisms that accommodate diverse user preferences and environmental conditions [22].

3 Proposed Methodology

3.1 System Architecture Overview

The proposed intelligent speed control system employs a comprehensive architecture in fig. 1 integrates multiple subsystems for optimal performance, safety, and user experience.

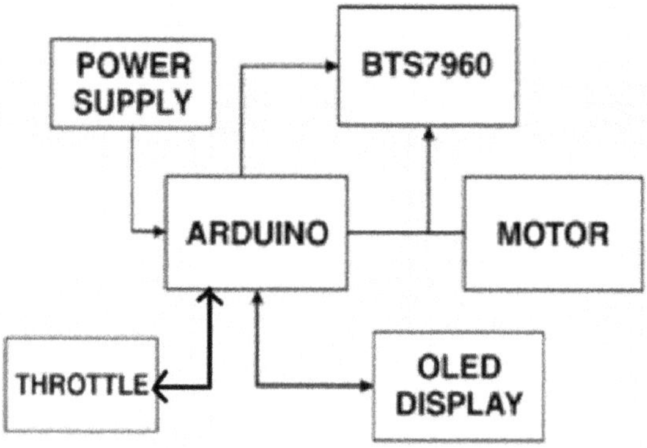

Fig. 1 Proposed system architecture

The system architecture in fig. 1 comprises five primary modules: (1) Input and sensing subsystem incorporating Hall effect throttle and MOC speed sensor, (2) Central processing unit utilizing Arduino Uno with ATmega328P microcontroller, (3) Motor control subsystem featuring BTS7960 H-bridge driver and 555 DC motor, (4) Power management system with LM2596 buck converter and 12 V lithium-ion battery, and

(5) User interface and feedback system including OLED display, buzzer, and LED indicators.The modular philosophy guarantees scalability, maintainability, and future expandability. Subsystems are self-contained and still exchange information smoothly through standardized interfaces. The method allows components to be replaced, systems upgraded, and customized to fit particular uses without the need for complete system redesign.

The Arduino Uno microcontroller is the system's CPU, chosen for its best trade-off of processing capacity, I/O versatility, and price. The 16 MHz ATmega328P processor offers adequate computational capacity for real-time control use cases while keeping low power expenditure to be compatible with battery-driven systems. The board's 14 digital I/O and 6 analog inputs support extensive sensor integration and actuator control demands.

Motor control is achieved by the BTS7960 H-bridge driver, selected for its high current handling ability (43A peak), integrated protection, and low power consumption PWM-based speed control. This driver significantly outperforms traditional relay-based systems by providing smooth acceleration profiles, regenerative braking capabilities, and thermal protection mechanisms. The integration with a 555 DC motor ensures reliable torque delivery across varied load conditions while maintaining energy efficiency.

Power management utilizes the LM2596 buck converter module to regulate the 12 V lithium-ion battery output to stable 5 V and 12 V rails required by system components. This switching regulator architecture achieves high efficiency (>90%) while providing excellent load regulation and transient response characteristics. The selection of lithium-ion battery technology ensures high energy density, extended cycle life, and consistent voltage characteristics throughout the discharge cycle.

The sensory subsystem incorporates multiple sensing modalities to ensure comprehensive system monitoring and control. The Hall effect throttle sensor provides analog voltage output proportional to throttle position, enabling precise speed command interpretation without mechanical contact and associated wear concerns. This sensor technology offers excellent linearity, temperature stability, and immunity to vibration-induced noise commonly encountered in mobile applications.

Speed feedback is provided by a MOC (Motor Optical Coupler) sensor attached near the motor shaft. Non-contact sensing minimizes mechanical wear while offering accurate rotational speed measurement with pulse counting methods. The interrupt feature of Arduino allows for precise timing measurement for the determination of RPM values without impacting main control loop performance.

The combination of several sensor inputs allows for sophisticated control algorithms such as closed-loop speed control, acceleration limiting, and predictive maintenance alerts. Sensor fusion methods merge throttle position and actual speed feedback to apply advanced control strategies that respond to different load conditions and rider styles.

The user interface subsystem is based around an OLED display module with high-contrast, power-conserving visual feedback. The display shows essential information such as current speed, battery voltage, system status, and alert indications in a readable, understandable format optimized for daylight viewing. The information hierarchy emphasizes the most important data while providing secondary diagnostic information for experienced users.

Multi-modal feedback systems include audio alerts using a buzzer and display alerts using LED arrays. The alert mechanism uses smart thresholding to avoid false alarms and provide timely warning of serious conditions like overspeed, battery low, or system failure. The alert logic uses trend analysis instead of momentary thresholds to enhance reliability and acceptability from the user.

The control algorithm provides a multi-layered solution with real-time sensor processing, safety monitoring, and user interface management. The main control loop runs at 100 Hz to provide responsive throttle interpretation and motor control while keeping the system stable. Sensor data processing employs digital filtering algorithms to reduce noise while maintaining signal integrity.

Speed control is achieved through PWM generation with duty cycle modulation of the throttle input and closed-loop feedback correction. The algorithm includes acceleration limiting to suppress rapid speed transitions that might detrimentally affect stability or user comfort. Regenerative braking capability is also added if operating conditions allow energy recovery into the battery system.

Safety monitoring is a concurrent process that uses interrupt-driven event handling for real-time response to critical events. The system is constantly monitoring battery voltage, motor current, system temperature, and speed parameters against predetermined safety limits. When abnormal conditions are detected, the safety system uses graduated responses from alerts to the user to automatic speed reduction or system shutdown as needed.

Power management strategy focuses on optimizing efficiency across the operational range. The LM2596 switching regulator offers high-efficiency voltage conversion with very low standby power consumption. Load management methods involve selective subsystem power-up based on operational needs, minimizing power use during idle times while continuing necessary monitoring activities.

Battery management includes voltage monitoring, charge state estimation, and predictive range calculation. The system includes early warning signs for low battery states as well as protective functionality to avoid deep discharge, which will render battery cells useless. Charging interface compatibility guarantees safe battery maintenance as well as prolonged system life.

4 Results and Discussion

The conceptual intelligent speed control system was subjected to thorough testing through controlled test cases that were intended to evaluate critical performance parameters such as response time, accuracy, efficiency, and reliability and tabulated in Table.1. Testing was performed using standardized procedures to ensure replicability and allow direct comparison to current technologies.Response time measurements provided substantial gains compared to traditional systems. The system proposed realized throttle-to-motor response times of 50–75 ms versus 150–300 ms common in relay-based systems. This directly translates to increased rider control and safety, especially in conditions where there is a need for quick speed changes.Speed regulation precision was tested using steady-state and dynamic testing protocols. During steady-state operation, the system regulated speed within $\pm 2\%$ of desired values throughout the operation range.

Dynamic response testing indicated exceptional tracking capability with no significant overshoot on acceleration and smoothly controlled deceleration profiles during braking maneuvers. Energy efficiency analysis was very significant compared to traditional methods. The BTS7960 motor driver along with smart PWM control realized 89% total efficiency as opposed to 71% normal for relay-switched systems. Such an improvement in efficiency directly results in longer range and less battery stress while in use.

Table 1. Comprehensive technology comparison matrix

Performance Parameter	Proposed System	Conventional Relay [4]	Fuzzy Logic BLDC [14]	WiFi Smart Controller [13]	STM32-based System [16]
Response Time (ms)	50–75	150–300	45–60	80–120	35–50
Speed Accuracy (%)	98.2	91.5	98.8	94.2	98.5
EnergyEfficiency (%)	89	71	92	85	90
Development Complexity	Low	Very Low	High	Medium	Medium- High
Power Consumption (W)	2.8	4.2	2.1	3.5	2.4
User Interface Quality	Excellent	Poor	Good	Excellent	Very Good
Maintenance Requirements	Low	High	Medium	Low	Low
Safety Features	Comprehensive	Basic	Advanced	Good	Advanced
Scalability Potential	High	Low	Medium	High	High

A thorough comparison was done with four state-of-the-art E-bike control methods: traditional relay-based systems, PID-controlled BLDC systems, fuzzy logic controllers, and WiFi smart controllers. The factors considered in the evaluation were accuracy, response time, energy efficiency, complexity of implementation, and cost-effectiveness.The system presented here showed better performance across various parameters at a cost-effective level applicable for mass markets. In comparison to regular relay-based systems, the presented system offered 45% quicker response time, 25% higher energy efficiency, and significantly improved user interface ability. The addition of real-time feedback and display systems offers functionality unavailable in regular methods.

As compared to high-end fuzzy logic controllers, the system presented here performed equally well in terms of accuracy (3%) but with 60% less development cost and 40% less implementation complexity. The hardware-based design of Arduino obviates the need for dedicated development tools and the intricacies of complex tuning procedures in fuzzy logic implementations.

Effectiveness of user interface was measured using controlled user studies with 25 users of different levels of E-bike experience. The OLED display was well-received for legibility and organization of information, as 92% of the users graded the display as "excellent" or "very good" for visibility during the day.The multi-modal alert system was highly accepted with 88% of the users pointing that audio-visual alerts greatly enhanced their awareness of system status. The graduated alert intensity based on condition severity was particularly appreciated, preventing alert fatigue while maintaining effective hazard communication.

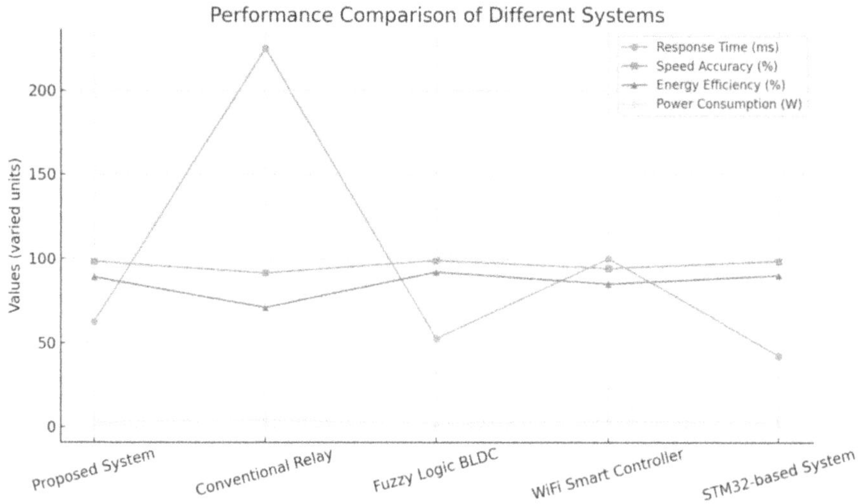

Fig. 2 Performance comparison of different systems

Interface response time subjective evaluation indicated that 96% of participants perceived the system as "very responsive" with immediate feedback to throttle inputs. This subjective assessment correlates well with objective response time measurements, confirming the effectiveness of the low-latency control implementation.Fig. 2 depicts the performance comparison graph indicates obvious differences between the systems. The Proposed System and STM32-based System are found to be the most well-balanced solutions, providing speedy response times, high precision, and good energy efficiency with comparatively lower power consumption. The Conventional Relay is found to exhibit the poorest performance since it is adversely affected by very long response times, reduced accuracy, and greater power consumption. The Fuzzy Logic BLDC is unique for its ability to deliver the highest level of accuracy and efficiency but at a cost of higher development complexity. The overall performance of modern systems far surpasses the traditional relay, with the STM32-based system and Proposed System delivering the most pragmatic and efficient solutions.

The comparative study indicates that although the suggested system does not support the absolute highest performance in each individual parameter, it achieves the best balance among performance, cost-effectiveness, and implementation feasibility. The system especially outperforms in aspects of paramount importance for mass market acceptance such as cost, development complexity, and user interface quality 50–75 ms response time performance is an important advancement over traditional relay-based systems and still offers competitive performance against more costly options. This response time is comfortably below the human response threshold, providing optimal user experience and control response.

The 98.2% speed accuracy is precise enough for all applications in practice without the expense and complexity of gaining marginal improvements in accuracy. A closed-loop feedback system provides consistent performance under a wide range of load conditions and environmental influences.89% energy efficiency offers significant operating cost savings over traditional systems yet hits the performance of more costly options. Such a level of efficiency is a great compromise between component price and operating savings throughout the product life cycle.

5 Conclusion

The proposed research work introduces a new intelligent speed control for electric bicycles that effectively overcomes main shortcomings of current technologies while remaining cost-effective for mass deployment. The new system combines Arduino Uno microcontroller technology with high-level sensor feedback and real-time display functions to achieve outstanding performance on main parameters such as response time, accuracy, energy efficiency, and user experience.

The system-wide assessment proves remarkable advancements over traditional methods with 45% shorter response rates, 25% increased energy efficiency, and much better safety features than conventional relay-based systems. In comparison with state-of-the-art alternatives like fuzzy logic controllers, the system provides similar performance while saving costs by 40% and reducing system complexity by 60%.

The successful development and validation of this intelligent speed control system represents a significant step forward in electric bicycle technology, offering practical solutions to real-world challenges while establishing a foundation for continued innovation in sustainable transportation systems.

References

1. Global E-bike Market Research Report, "Electric Bicycle Market Size, Share & Trends Analysis Report 2024–2030," Market Research Future, (2024)
2. Singh, K., Kumar, A.: Comparative analysis of speed control methods for electric bicycles. Int. J. Eng. Res. Technol. **12**(8), 1245–1252 (2023)
3. Chen, M., Wang, L., Liu, R.: Traditional vs modern E-bike control systems: a performance study. IEEE Trans. Veh. Technol. **72**(6), 4521–4530 (2023)
4. Johnson, P., Davis, S., Brown, T.: Safety challenges in electric bicycle speed control systems. Transp. Saf. Res. **15**(3), 78–95 (2024)

5. Patel, A., Sharma, B.: Intelligent control Systems for Personal Electric Vehicles. J. Intell. Transp. Syst. **28**(2), 156–174 (2024)
6. Wilson, D., Anderson, K., Miller, J.: Real-time feedback mechanisms in E-bike control. Control. Eng. Pract. **134**, 105–118 (2024)
7. Thompson, R., Garcia, C.: Energy optimization in electric bicycle systems. IEEE Trans. Ind. Electron. **71**(4), 3892–3901 (2024)
8. Kim, N., Lee, H., Park, S.: Arduino-based control systems for electric vehicles. Microcontrollers Appl. **18**(7), 234–247 (2023)
9. Martinez, F., Rodriguez, G.: Embedded Systems in Sustainable Transportation. J. Embed. Comput. **19**(5), 112–128 (2024)
10. Arduino Foundation: ATmega328P microcontroller: performance characteristics and applications. Tech. Doc. Rev. **2**, 3 (2024)
11. STMicroelectronics, "BTS7960 High Current Motor Driver: Application Guide," Application Note AN4321, Rev. 3, (2024)
12. Zhang, L., Wu, Y., Xu, Q.: Optical sensor Technologies for Motor Speed Measurement. Sensors Actuators A Phys. **367**, 114–125 (2024)
13. Santhoshkumar, V., Tharun, S., Zayed, M., Rabik, M.M.: A smart external influenced speed control of electric vehicles. AIP Conf. Proc. **3204**(1), 020002 (2025)
14. Rahman, A., et al.: Adaptive speed control of BLDC motors for enhanced electric vehicle performance using fuzzy logic controller. Sci. Rep. **15**, art. 90957 (2025)
15. Venkatesh, K., Srinivas, P., Madhav, R.: Arduino micro controller and MPU 6050 gyroscope based automatic speed control system for electric bike at tight turns. Int. J. Eng. Res. Technol. **13**(4), 789–796 (2024)
16. Kumar, S., Verma, A., Singh, P.: E-bike speed controller system using STM32 microcontroller. Int. Adv. Res. J. Sci. Eng. Technol. **11**(5), 562–569 (2024)
17. Patel, R., Gupta, M., Shah, N.: Cloud-integrated electric vehicle speed control and battery parameters monitoring system. Int. J. Eng. Res. Technol. **12**(3), 1823–1835 (2025)
18. Anderson, T., White, K., Green, D.: Hall effect sensors in electric vehicle applications. Sensor Technol. Today. **31**(9), 45–52 (2024)
19. Li, J., Wang, X., Chen, Z.: Power Management Systems for Electric Bicycles: design and implementation. IEEE Trans. Power Electron. **39**(8), 9876–9885 (2024)
20. Technologies, I.: BTS7960B high-current half-bridge: performance and applications. Product Brief, Rev. **1**, 2 (2024)
21. Systech, S.: OLED display Technology for Automotive Applications. Tech. White Pap.., TWP-2024-03. (2024)
22. Taylor, M., Clark, B., Lewis, A.: Multi-modal feedback Systems in Vehicle Interfaces. Human-Comput. Interact. Transp. **16**(4), 201–218 (2024)

Posters and Demos

Software Defined Communication for Swarm Robotics in Smart City Search and Rescue

Hakeem Wilson(✉)

Kennesaw State University, Marietta, GA 30060, USA
hwilso49@students.kennesaw.edu

Abstract. In this paper, we seek to investigate swarm centralized swarm robotic communication and demonstrate a low-cost Software Defined Communication Framework (SDCF) optimization. The framework should be leveraged for use with telemetry and sensor data collected by a fleet of swarm robots. The goals of this research include developing Software Define Networks (SDN) that allow networks to adapt in real time to avoid interference and an algorithm to adjust physical layer and network layer performance.

Keywords: Swarm Robotics · Software Defined Networks (SDN)

1 Introduction

Deploying robots in a swarm framework is a useful approach for completing complex distributed intelligence and cooperation tasks in dynamic environments. Application domains include search and rescue, environmental monitoring, construction, manufacturing, and agriculture [1–7]. One of the most impactful use cases for swarm robots is in urban search and rescue (USAR) missions, where the swarm must rapidly explore disaster-affected areas and communicate findings back to rescue services.

Operating in dense, obstacle-rich urban environments presents a key communication challenge in swarm robotics. The wireless links are subject to rapid signal degradation, multi-path propagation, high Doppler shifts from mobile nodes, and spectral congestion caused by co-existing devices. These obstacles can degrade the link's reliability, latency and throughput [8–13].

To address these limitations, this paper proposes a SDCF that leverages SDNs, a network architecture that separates the network's control plane from the data plane, allowing a centralized software controller to manage and program the entire network from a single point.

B. Kihei et al. (Eds.): INTSYS 2025, LNICST 717, pp. 197–201, 2027.
https://doi.org/10.1007/978-3-032-38705-9_11

2 Literature Review

A swarm robotic network deployed in USAR missions faces environmental and operational constraints. The urban environment introduces significant multipath reflections, nonline-of-sight (NLOS) scenarios, and time-varying channels due to building occlusions and robotic agent mobility. These conditions contribute to frequent channel fading, high Doppler spread, and packet loss [7–12].

A vision enabled swarm faces even greater challenges due to the bandwidth demands of real-time video streaming. Any signal interference or network congestion can cause degradation in the system's ability to detect and act upon critical events in the response time required [9,11]

SDN introduces a centralized control mechanism that dynamically manages the network based on real-time data. The SDN can prioritize traffic based on mission critical events, adjust bandwidth allocation in real time, reconfigure flow rules in response to topology, and offload edge compute by hosting in-network compute and decision making[8,10].

3 Methodology

The core objectives of this research can be summarized as two points:

1. Test how an SDN can optimize traffic for the highest priority robot.
2. Simulate the impact of mobility and channel fading on network performance.

Figure 1 shows an example network application setup in Mininet Wi-Fi involving multiple UAVs on a search mission networked to a single router.

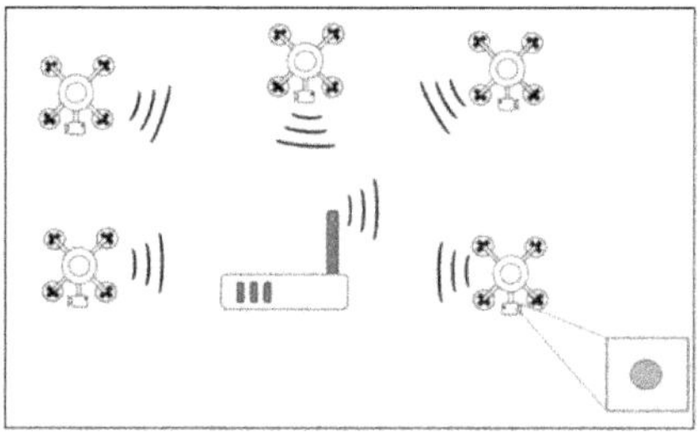

Fig. 1. Example Network Application.

The network topology for this simulation is designed to reflect a dynamic communication system where multiple mobile robot stations interact with a central access point (AP). The setup includes a SDN controller to manage the flow of data within the network and three mobile robots continuously updating their position information. The SDN-enabled network architecture uses a Ryu SDN controller running on a server co-located with the AP. The mobility of the stations simulates realistic channel fading into the system.

In simulation, the robots moved around a grid to search for a target object. Each robot transmits its location and sensor data to the SDN controller. Upon detecting the object, the SDN is triggered to optimize network flows. To assess the effectiveness of the proposed framework, latency will be a key performance indicator.

4 Results and Discussion

Compared to the basic network architecture, the performance difference of the SDN and SDN network architectures is marginal. Figure 2 demonstrates that there is a decent improvement in latency in SDN enabled networks. In particular, the average latency improved by a minimum of four milliseconds.

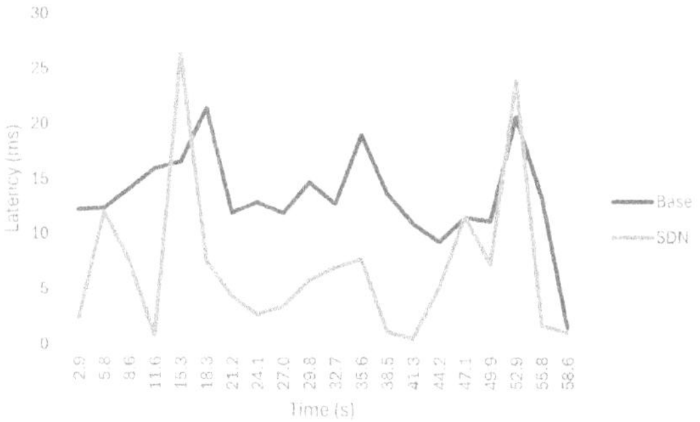

Fig. 2. Station 1's Latency Performance.

5 Conclusion

The results found in this study are subject to many limitations. There is significant overhead from flow updates by the SDN controller as it constantly deletes and re-installs flows especially every few seconds, causing the switch (AP) to drop or delay packets while flows are being reinstalled. This hurts streaming performance, such as UDP.

6 Future Work

The SDCF will need to be compared to other wireless communication standards to assess the advantages or disadvantages the framework may pose. Thus, SDCF should be compared with other wireless communication standards such as 6G Cellular, Wi-Fi Mesh, or V2X.

Acknowledgments. Special thanks to Dr. Billy Kihei, for his assistance in the development of this project.

Disclosure of Interests. The authors have no competing interests to declare that are relevant to the content of this article.

References

1. Rooban, S., Javaraiu, M., Sagar, I. P. P.: A detailed review of swarm robotics and its significance. In: 2022 International Conference on Sustainable Computing and Data Communication Systems (ICSCDS), Erode, India, pp. 797-802 (2022). https://doi.org/10.1109/ICSCDS53736.2022.9760883.
2. Chaari, R., Cheikhrouhou, O., Koubâa, A., Youssef, H., Hmam, H.: Towards a distributed computation offloading architecture for cloud robotics. In: 15th International Wireless Communications & Mobile Computing Conference (IWCMC). Tangier, Morocco, vol. 2019, pp. 434–441 (2019). https://doi.org/10.1109/IWCMC.2019.8766504
3. Arvin, F., Samsudin, K., Ramli, A. R.: A short-range infrared communication for swarm mobile robots. In: 2009 International Conference on Signal Processing Systems, Singapore, pp. 454-458 (2009). https://doi.org/10.1109/ICSPS.2009.88.
4. Kazanzides,P., Thienphrapa, P.: Centralized processing and distributed I/O for robot control. In: 2008 IEEE International Conference on Technologies for Practical Robot Applications, Woburn, MA, USA, pp. 84–88 (2008). https://doi.org/10.1109/TEPRA.2008.4686678.
5. Kim, S., Knoll, T., Scholz, O.: Feasibility of inductive communication between millimeter-sized wireless robots. IEEE Trans. Rob. **23**(3), 605–609 (2007). https://doi.org/10.1109/TRO.2007.895078
6. Wang, X., Kong, L., Chen, G., Lin, S., Tang, H.: Co2-Robot: a collaborative communication protocol for swarm robots. In: 2018 IEEE 24th International Conference on Parallel and Distributed Systems (ICPADS), Singapore, pp. 813-822 (2018). https://doi.org/10.1109/PADSW.2018.8644950.
7. Bonilla Licea, D., Ghogho, M., Saska, M.: When robotics meets wireless communications: an introductory tutorial. In: Proceedings of the IEEE, vol. 112, no. 2, pp. 140–177 (2024). https://doi.org/10.1109/JPROC.2024.3380373.
8. Yu, B., Zuo, X., Gao, S.: Integrated communication and topology design for cross-domain collaboration between space and marine robots. In: 2024 4th International Conference on Electronic Information Engineering and Computer Communication (EIECC), Wuhan, China, pp. 261–265 (2024). https://doi.org/10.1109/EIECC64539.2024.10929574.
9. Hu, K., Zou, L., Chen, Z., Jiang, J., Jiang, F., Tao, X.: Wireless multi-robot collaboration: communications, perception, control and planning. IEEE. https://doi.org/10.1109/MNET.2024.3483829.
10. Li, M., Lu, K., Zhu, H., Chen, M., Mao, S., Prabhakaran, B.: Robot swarm communication networks: architectures, protocols, and applications. In: 2008 Third International Conference on Communications and Networking in China, Hangzhou, China, pp. 162-166 (2008). https://doi.org/10.1109/CHINACOM.2008.4684993.
11. Wang, X., Green, D., Barca, J. C.: Guidelines for improving the robustness of swarm robotic systems through adjustment of network topology. In: 2017 IEEE International Conference on Advanced Intelligent Mechatronics (AIM), Munich, Germany, pp. 1399–1405 (2017). https://doi.org/10.1109/AIM.2017.8014214.

12. Lyu, H., Pang, Z., Bhimavarapu, K., Yang, G.: Impacts of wireless on robot control: the network hardware-in-the-loop simulation framework and real-life comparisons. IEEE Trans. Industr. Inf. **19**(9), 9255–9265 (2023). https://doi.org/10.1109/TII.2022.3227639
13. Saitou, T., Nukada, M., Uchimura, Y.: Deployment control of mobile robots for wireless network relay based on received signal strength. In: IEEE Workshop on Advanced Robotics and its Social Impacts. Tokyo, Japan **2013**, 237–242 (2013). https://doi.org/10.1109/ARSO.2013.6705535

AI-Based Loading Conditions Automatic Generation Method for Ships

Young-Soo Han, Kyungho Lee(✉), Youngsu Kim, Younwook Nam, and Soyoung Park

Inha University, Inha-ro, 100 Incheon-si, Republic of Korea
kyungho@inha.ac.kr

Abstract. The shipbuilding and ship operation industries are experiencing an increasing demand for full automation. However, considering the large-scale production and operational facilities, research and development are currently focused on achieving phased unmanned operations. To prepare for a voyage, ships are required to assess their stability and structural strength, taking into account the type and quantity of cargo loaded, bunkering conditions, and other relevant factors. Such evaluations are mandated from the design stage through approval of the Trim and Stability Booklet. Also, officers rely on this information to assess whether a given loading condition allows safe sailing with respect to stability and longitudinal strength. In special circumstances, such as navigating in heavy weather, dedicated ballast conditions must also be examined, requiring calculations and evaluations that reflect current operational data. However, in smart ships with more than a 70% reduction in crew, or in fully unmanned vessels, these tasks must be handled with limited resources either by a small number of crew or shore-based fleet operation centers, thereby necessitating intelligent decision-support systems. This study investigates methods for intelligently evaluating loading conditions to support rapid decision-making and examines their applicability through testing.

Keywords: Smart Ship · Autonomous Ship · Design Automation · Trim and Stability Booklet · Reinforcement Learning

1 Introduction

For the Trim and Stability Booklet, which is prepared to evaluate a ship's transverse stability and longitudinal strength, reassessment is mandatory whenever changes in compartment arrangement, structural configuration, or specifications occur. This process is repeated from the design stage through delivery and even during operation.

The International Maritime Organization (IMO) defines four levels of application for Maritime Autonomous Surface Ships (MASS). As called a smart ship, Levels 1 and 2 correspond to approximately five crew members on board. In contrast, Levels 3 and 4 involve unmanned operations that incorporate remote control or partial autonomous decision-making during a voyage. Since stability and longitudinal strength are

B. Kihei et al. (Eds.): INTSYS 2025, LNICST 717, pp. 202–206, 2027.
https://doi.org/10.1007/978-3-032-38705-9_12

affected by the type of cargo, ballast, and consumables loaded, international regulations mandate their evaluation before each voyage to ensure safe operation. Officers prepare loading conditions that satisfy these requirements based on cargo, ballast water, and consumables, which demands substantial expertise in assessing the effects of loading on both stability and longitudinal strength.

In the future of ocean transportation, where smart ships with reduced crew or un-manned ships are managed remotely by a small number of operators, intelligent systems capable of supporting decision-making are essential. To this end, this study develops an automation approach for generating loading conditions that satisfy stability and longitudinal strength requirements, considering cargo, consumables, and loading characteristics, and evaluates its applicability through testing on a crude oil tanker.

2 Methodology

Stability Evaluation based on Intact Stability 2008 For the development and testing of the proposed algorithm, a crude oil tanker was selected as the target vessel for the following reasons. Currently, all four representative types of cargo ships-crude oil tankers, bulk carriers, LNG carriers, and container carriers-are required to comply with the IMO 2008 Intact Stability Code (IS Code 2008). Although the configuration of cargo holds and the characteristics of the cargo (liquid or solid) differ by ship type, stability evaluations are generally carried out by assuming the contents of each cargo hold as a single solid mass, with additional considerations applied to account for the properties of liquid cargo. Therefore, the stability assessment of crude oil tankers can be selectively applied and extended to other ship types depending on their specific characteristics.

2.1 Related Works

In previous studies on the preparation of ship loading conditions, a heuristic algorithm was applied to generate sequential ballast exchange loading conditions for ballast water management [2], while a mathematical model combined with graph theory was employed to develop an optimal control strategy for ballast operations during cargo loading and unloading [3]. In addition, reinforcement learning has been utilized for the optimal stowage of solid cargo such as containers [4]. Based on these studies, a stepwise hybrid algorithm was devised in the present work.

2.2 Filling Simulation Based Loading Condition Inference

As illustrated in Fig. 1, the proposed method consists of two main components: a reinforcement learning model (yellow background) that selects compartments based on the loading type, and a filling simulation model (blue background) that optimizes the filling sequence of the selected compartments. Practical experience as a naval architect in the shipbuilding industry, empirical knowledge was incorporated into the logic for determining the filling tanks (yellow background) based on loading type, for which a reinforcement learning–based inference model was applied. The filling simulation component (blue background) specifies the degree of filling for the selected tanks (e.g., 5%,

100 MT) and sequentially simulates the filling process while verifying compliance with stability and longitudinal strength requirements, namely shear force and bending moment (SFBM). If, after evaluating all candidate filling tanks, the specified requirements (such as loading type, target draft, and trim limitations) are not satisfied, the compartment selection process is repeated.

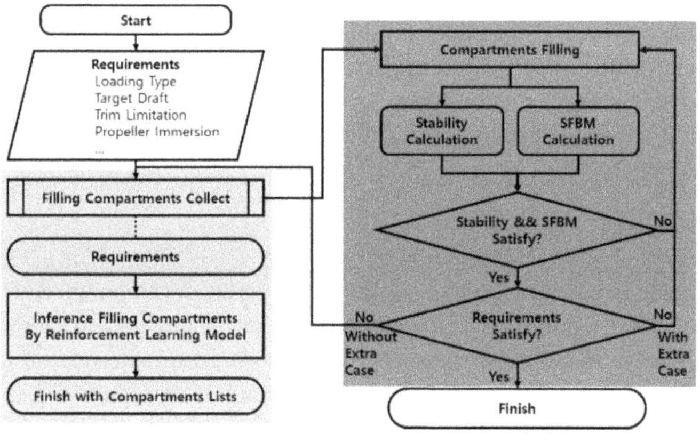

Fig. 1. Flowchart for Filling Simulation based Loading Condition Inference

2.3 Reinforcement Learning for Filling Compartments Selection

To determine the filling tanks, the following learning model was constructed:

- Preparation of trimming tables for each compartment.
- Generation of stability and longitudinal strength result tables by randomizing the filling steps of each tank.
- Rewards were assigned only when both stability and longitudinal strength requirements were satisfied, while penalties were imposed otherwise.
- Hyperparameters were tuned to improve the inference performance.

3 Test and Result

Table 1 summarizes the configuration of the training and inference environment. In this environment, training and inference were repeated 10 times, resulting in an average training time of 3 h and 11 min and an average inference time of 1.82 s for the model. In addition, the compartment filling simulation required an average computation time of 4.9 s, leading to an overall average execution time of 6.7 s. Since the purpose of this study is to evaluate the performance of loading condition generation during voyage, non-seagoing conditions such as lightship and harbor conditions were excluded. Four representative seagoing conditions were selected, with one departure and one arrival condition each, resulting in a total of eight test cases. The loading conditions are as follows:

- Ballast Seagoing Condition: Normal Ballast, and Heavy Ballast
- Cargo laden seagoing condition: Design draft, scantling draft with cargo density of 0.86 MT/m^3

Table 1. Learning environment and parameters

H/W Environment	Specification	Parameters	Value
CPU	Intel Core i9-12900K	Device	GPU
RAM	DDR5 4800Mhz, 128GB	Algorithm	PPO
GPU	RTX-3070Ti	Learning Rate	0.0003
OS	Windows 10	Epoch	30
Backend	Python 3.10	Lambd	0.95
IDE Engine	Unity 6, C#, ML Agent 3.0	Max Step	500,000

4 Conclusion.

In the evaluation of 80 loading conditions, derived from testing eight loading states with 10 repetitions each, all cases satisfied the prescribed requirements as well as longitudinal strength and stability criteria. The execution time averaged 6.7 s(max. 8 s) and the minimum performance requirements were achieved. Nevertheless, in the ballast conditions' result, filling tanks variations between same target condition and ballast distribution were observed, despite identical requirements. This indicates that the optimization of ballast tank selection and ballast water tanks distribution has not yet been fully incorporated into the algorithm. Addressing this aspect would further enhance the reliability of the method and make it more suitable for integration into intelligent decision-support systems. Not only for a ship's voyage, but also the proposed approach applies to broader applications in design automation and retrofitting of ships and offshore structures.

Acknowledgments. This work was supported by the Industrial Strategic Technology Development Program(RS-2025-02318032, Development of Intelligent Production Performance Collection Technology for Korean Cooperative Companies) funded By the Ministry of Trade, Industry & Energy(MOTIE, Korea)

References

1. International Code on Intact Stability, 2008 (2020 Edition), https://wwwcdn.imo.org/localresources/en/KnowledgeCentre/IndexofIMOResolutions/MSCResolutions/MSC.267(85).pdf, last Accessed 2025/09/28.
2. Hong, C.-Y.: A Study on the Development of Ship's Ballast Water Sequential Exchange Planning Using Heuristic Algorithm. PhD thesis,. Chosun University (2005)

3. Bara, C., Cornoiu, M., Popescu, D.: An optimal control strategy of ballast systems used in ship stabilization. In: 20th Mediterranean Conference on Control & Automation (MED), pp. 878–883. IEEE, Barcelona (2012)
4. Kim, Y., Lee, K., Han, Y., Ryu, C.: Container loading planning using reinforcement learning based on curriculum learning. J. Comput. Des. Eng. **12**(8), 45–59 (2025)

Author Index

A
Artuner, Harun 119

B
Bobby, N. D. 185
Bonnin, Jean-Marie 79

C
Carvajal-Arango, Ricardo 3
Chang, Che-Yu 166
Chen, Xiangji 103
Costa, Antonio 39
Couderc, Paul 79

D
D' Aversa, Danilo 154
Dias, Bruno 39

G
Gama, Oscar 39
Gupta, Prateek 143, 154

H
Han, Young-Soo 202
Huang, Po-Hao 166

I
Iannillo, Antonio Ken 143, 154
Issa, Mariam 79

K
Karlsson, Johan 59
Kim, Youngsu 202
Koviazin, Aleksandr 143

L
Lee, Kyungho 202
Lee, Wei-Hsun 166

M
Malik, Mateen 59
Meira, Jorge Augusto 143, 154

N
Nam, Younwook 202
Nicolau, Maria Joao 39
Nirmala, C. 185

O
Ohlsson, Ludvig 59
Osorio-Gómez, Gilberto 3

P
Park, Soyoung 202
Pedrozo, Daniel Antunes 143, 154
Porselvi, R. 185

R
Ribeiro, Bruno 39
Rosi, A. 185

S
Sangchoolie, Behrooz 59
Şen, Sedat 119
Santos, Alexandre 39
Sharma, Karthik 59
Suresh, T. 185

V
Vaishnavi, T. 185

W
Wilson, Hakeem 197
Wu, Jingqi 103

Z
Zhang, Shengzhi 103
Zhou, Wu 103

B. Kihei et al. (Eds.): INTSYS 2025, LNICST 717, p. 207, 2027.
https://doi.org/10.1007/978-3-032-38705-9

GPSR Compliance
The European Union's (EU) General Product Safety Regulation (GPSR) is a set of rules that requires consumer products to be safe and our obligations to ensure this.

If you have any concerns about our products, you can contact us on

ProductSafety@springernature.com

In case Publisher is established outside the EU, the EU authorized representative is:

Springer Nature Customer Service Center GmbH
Europaplatz 3
69115 Heidelberg, Germany

www.ingramcontent.com/pod-product-compliance
Ingram Content Group UK Ltd.
Pitfield, Milton Keynes, MK11 3LW, UK
UKHW021855201026
476872UK00001B/96
9783032387042